COMMON MAN'S GUIDE TO COMPUTERS

BOOKS BY THE SAME AUTHOR

- *Dynamics of Formulating Policy in the Government of India* (co-author)
- *Operational Analysis and Indian Defence*
- *Information Management in Government*
- *Management Perspectives*
- *Computer Applications for Techno-Economic Development* (Ed.)
- *Computer Management and Planning*
- *Computer, compiler!*
- *Computer Applications for Rural Development* (Ed.)
- *Management Information System: A Framework* (co-author)
- *Information Technology for Common Man* (Ed.)

COMMON MAN'S GUIDE TO COMPUTERS

Concepts, Applications, Issues

UTPAL K. BANERJEE

CONCEPT PUBLISHING COMPANY, NEW DELHI 110059

ISBN 81-7022-441-1

First Published 1992

Published and Printed by
Ashok Kumar Mittal
Concept Publishing Company
A/15-16, Commercial Block, Mohan Garden
NEW DELHI-110059 (India)

Lasertypeset by
Microtech Advance Printing Systems (P) Ltd.
H-13, Bali Nagar
NEW DELHI-110015

DEDICATED

TO

Major General A. Balasubramaniam

for bringing me into India's mainstream
computer community, after return from England

Professor S. Sampath

for using my services for Union Public Service Commission,
Indian Institute of Technology
Defence R&D Organisation and Computer Society of India

and

Professor H.N. Mahabala

for asking me to write this book, responding to the
suggestion from the enlightened readers of the "Hindu"

CONTENTS

PART THREE
RELATED ISSUES

INTRODUCTION

Common man in India including all echelons of management – which would comprise managers, administrators and executives in industrial enterprises, government departments, public utilities and business organisations — have now been caught up with the avalanche of computers and "information revolution". Learned journals, popular magazines, financial papers and even the daily press have been dinning out, day in and day out, the miracles of the new machine and their manifold applications, apart from the problems and prospects raised by the upsurge of the new revolution. What has been conspicuous is a comparative dearth of reading material that would grapple with the concepts, applications and issues related to computers in their severely national context. It is this lack of India-based knowledge and awareness that this book is set about to rectify.

For the sake of reading convenience, the book has been divided into four parts. *Part One* deals with the fundamental concepts, although not in a too elementary fashion. Today's common man has sufficient acquaintance with the rudiments of the new discipline, thanks to the constant inundation of general literature. What they need to be acquainted is a fairly clear and ambiguity-free discussion on such basic concepts as microprocessing, personal computing, industrial control, quality regulation, selection process, – graduating into mini-computers and large systems and their capability from both the hardware and software points of view, their selection and evaluation mechanisms, their import restrictions, and linking them all into distributed processing, networks, overview of information management, prevalent MIS and their emerging trends.

Equipped with the above knowledge, it would be easy to understand the myriad applications that computers have helped in all walks of life. *Part Two* takes up a few selected sectors and provides broad information as to what has been happening in the chosen areas in the Indian environment. Agriculture, education, health, banking, railways and industry are all vital economic sectors whose well-being today is inextricably linked up with more and more efficient use of the incoming computing power. Equally important are the areas of law and order, bureaucratic practice and public utility systems. Two relatively little known areas are the computer aids for the handicapped and the liberal arts.

With the above illustrative ideas, the common man will get a broad mental picture of the nature and utility of computers coming up in India. What is desirable at the final stage is also to get familiar with the germane issues that keep cropping up in the conducting of socio-economic activities. *Part Three* is concerned with these issues, namely, desirability and scope of moving into computer usage; assessment as to how meaningful the usage is going to be; evaluation of computer services widely marketed today; impact of the new technology on labour and automation; involvement necessary (or crucial) for the general management with computers; provenness to accept whatever is being publicised as good; and some concern with user-training and education.

The two *appendices* are to check how the confrere discipline of operational research stand to gain from computer usage and the scope of a new approach, such as, Computer-Aided Optimisation (CAO).

A large volume of the material included saw the first light of the day in the pages of *The Hindu* and partly in *The Economic Times* and *The Business World.* The enthusiastic response that those earlier pieces received from the reading public emboldened the author to undertake this integrative venture which was, in fact, suggested by several readers. The entire material has been completely updated, using only the skeleton of the original.

In conclusion, it is to be suggested that an excellent companion volume for first principles of computers and their applications would be *Computers and Common Sense*, by Roger Hunt and John Shelly (Prentice-Hall, Delhi, 1987). Common man who encouraged by the present reading – may like to venture into getting involved with computers, would probably find this author's work *Computer Management and Planning* (Tata-McGraw Hill, Delhi, 1988) rewarding reading from a practical guidance viewpoint. For the common man, on the other hand, the best reading material in the Indian sub-continent would be *Information Technology for Common Man* (Concept, Delhi, 1992) explaining information technology in practice for day-to-day life.

July, 1992 — UTPAL K. BANERJEE
New Delhi

PART ONE

BASIC CONCEPTS

1

MEANING OF COMPUTING POWER

Introduction

To quote figures given out by M.G.K. Menon in the last decade, India registered an eight-fold increase in computing power between 1971 and 1979 alone and the growth has continued unabated ever since. This would mean that computing power had a compound growth-rate of 56 per cent between those years, thus doubling itself every fifteen months. It is no mean achievement for a developing country and the growth-pattern has shown no signs of abatement in the years to follow.

The Computer Brain

In order to understand the meaning of computing power (which can be defined as the measure of a few hundred thousand or more calculations done per second), one has to look into the computer as a device which carried out such computations in a sequence determined by human commands, without external intervention. All computations are carried out in the Central Processing Unit (CPU) resembling human brain, which comprises the arithmetic/logic unit and the control unit, for doing the actual "number crunching" and data manipulations, and directing their performance respectively. The set of instructions or commands (software), along with data, are stored into the memory from where CPU fetches them for execution. This improvement came only in the post-ENIAC computers, thanks to the mathematical genius of he Hungarian-born scientist John Von Neumann. The instructions as well as data are entered into the memory through the peripheral input/output (I/O) devices which are connected to the memory through channels for dataflow. While channels take commands from the CPU for carrying out and I/O operation, they have enough electronics built into them to carry out the commands independent of the CPU.

For nearly two decades since the mid-fifties, the most popular memory of modern computers had been the magnetic core, comprising thousands of tiny soft-iron rings within a precisely designed grid. Any specific location can be "addressed" almost instantly for retaining or retrieving a "bit" (for "binary digit") of information is magnetised (I) or demagnetised (O) form. The expensive core memory has long been replaced by far cheaper semiconductor memory on chips. While cost per bit has been higher in small core memories than in the big memories, semiconductor memories provide "random access" with a steady cost per bit, since the supporting electronic circuits are built in solid-state components.

Input and Output Devices

Semiconductor technology has not entered much in the field of storage (or auxiliary) memories in the form of magnetic tapes, discs and drums. These I/O devices have the advantage of large capacity and low cost, for storing information in bulk and having high speed of operation. Magnetic "bubble" memory has now entered the field as an improved technology, with the problem of "volatile" operation getting gradually solved. Optical technology is another contender giving risk to compact discs.

Input devices translate information from a variety of sources into a code that is understood by the computer. Key-boards are useful for data input of varying volume, although one can prepare an intermediate output on a faster medium (tape reel, floppy disc) for recurrent use. Other devices are touch-tone telephones, data-entry terminals (with keyboards and display units), optical scanners ("reading" characters at high speeds), electronics ears (recognising a limited number of spoken words), etc., all for specific applications. Processed data are translated into electrical impulses that can control a variety of output devices, such as, high-speed printers (using drum of chain), visual-display terminals, artificial voice or laser-operated printers.

Progress in Technology

It is salutary to comprehend at what rate improvements have taken place in the computer technology starting from the fifties. According to James Martin, the increase in number of logic circuits that can be packed into a given volume, has shown an expotential increase. At the same time, there has been a steady increase in the cost of logic circuitry in terms of millions of instructions per dollar, thus illustrating the gain in computer power per unit of cost over a very limited time-period. The increase in speeds of high-speed computers in terms of memory-cycles per second has been accompanied by the tremendous growth of the capacity of on-line data-files directly accessible by the computer. The dramatic rise in the computer capabilities over time is too evident to need elaboration.

Considering all factors, the computing power depends on the available hardware facilities. If the CPU is micro-programmed, the word-length (a group of bits which determines the characteristics of the micro-programming) is an indication of its power. Microprocessor-based systems come in 8-bit or 16-bit or 32-bit machines, with limited direct-address capability as well. In a large computer, instructions can be fetched from memory in a single reference, while in microprocessor-based systems several references to memory are required. Micro-computers including personal computers are thus small and slow with memory size between 640 Kilo Bytes (KB) and 8 Mega Bytes (MB) and suited ideally for simple business functions or a limited number applications at a low cost, where the hardware can be even pre-coded as per the user requirement. Mini-computers (32-bit) have memory-sizes varying between 4 MB and 16 MB, with the speed around a few million operations per second. Mainframe computers (64-bit and above) have a range of memory between 16 MB and 64 MB while super computers can go from 64 MB to a few hundred Mega Bytes — with increase in operating speeds, and more sophisticated and faster peripherals — having a wide range of applications.

Computer Operation

Each computer operation can be broken down into a series of sequential steps. If the hardware facilities are more, several steps can be converged to form a single step, thus reducing the time to execute an operation. Further, the speed and capacity of the CPU accessing memory also contribute to the computing power. If the memory is slow (like the earlier core-memory), it may introduce a waiting stage in the CPU. Instruction execution time depends, in turn, on the CPU cycle time and varies from low, medium to high for mainframe mini to microcomputers respectively.

When I/O devices are resorted to for auxiliary memory, they reduce the power of the machine, since access to these devices is comparatively slow. I/O devices play a major role in the overall performance of the computer. Their speed should conform to the bus speed in a bus-oriented microcomputer or to the channel speed in larger machines. Electro-mechanical components of the I/O devices are the main hindering factors and have often an attachment of *cache* memory in order to appear fast to the CPU. In the cost hierarchy, cost per bit is the highest for I/O parts (for exchange of information between user and machine), followed by the main memory and mass storage memory.

Throughout, measured in terms of number of jobs processed per unit time, depends on the computer environment and the type of jobs. Some instructions take a longer time to be executed and some shorter. A particular mix of instructions, known as Gibson Mix, gives a specific number of thousand operations in terms of frequency of usage. In order to have a high throughout, multiple programming (or multi-tasking) is used by running a mix of CPU-bound and I/O-bound jobs, resulting in better utilisation of all the resources. Thus, maximum computing power available with the machine gets utilised for useful work in a balanced fashion. Another way of increasing throughout is by multi-processing where more than one CPU is used either for specialised job (e.g., array/matrix processor), or in a master-slave mode (e.g., remote processor), or in independent mode with shared resources (e.g., front-end processor).

Conclusion

With the advancement of integration technology, the actual size of the machine is too deceptive for guessing its computing power. The latter depends entirely on the computer architecture and not on the size solely determined by technology. While a pure micro-processor (without peripheral devices) can remain embedded in a modern machine (like car engine helping its operations), a mainframe computer can come in a couple of cabinets running an entire factory through remote terminals!

2

UTILITY OF SOFTWARE TOOLS

Introduction

In the world today, there is a growing lag between computer *hardware* (machine with the peripherals) and *software* (set of instructions to operate the machine) technology. The cost of computing power has come down by several orders of magnitude in the last one generation, and the unit cost of memory and storage decreased at a compound annual rate of 40 per cent during this period. On the other hand, the cost of producing software necessary to exploit the growing computing power has risen steadily, and the increasing complexing of systems and application software has been truly overwhelming. Boehm's diagram at Fig. 2.1 on hardware/software cost trends brings out vividly the concept of spending more on software than hardware today.

Software, as a sequence of commands (programme) used to achieve the desired output, is not limited to one particular job or application. Advanced categories of software tools include operating systems, language compilers, application packages and user-written programmes.

Operating Systems

It is a distinguishing characteristic of third-generation computer systems that the hardware is designed to operate under control of rather sophisticated software. Especially in a multi-programming and/or multi-processing computer, *operating system* allocates system resources and sorts out problems of conflict, blocking and interference among simultaneous users of the computer. In particular, scheduling of operations, functions of the input/output devices and management of main and auxiliary storage are software activities that are centralised and carefully controlled by operating system.

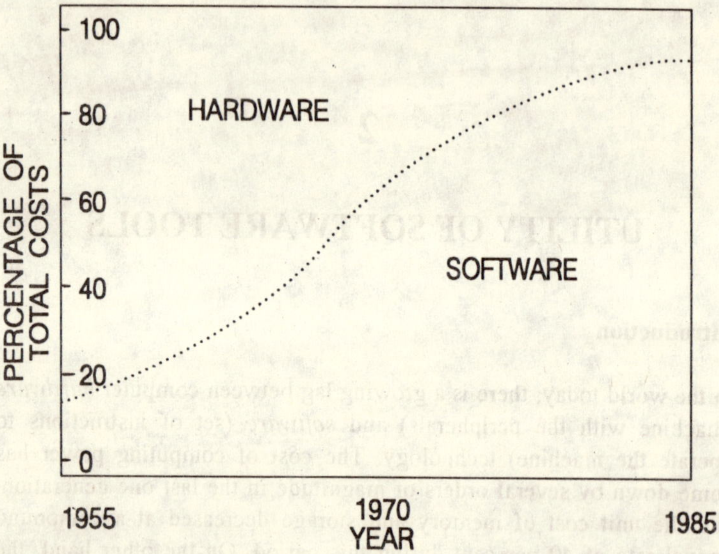

FIG. 2.1: Hardware/Software Cost Trends

Operating system aims at optimising the overall operations and achieving a comprehensive effectiveness, by supporting different modes of the user operation. For example, in *batch* mode, operating system supports running of a batch of programmes at a time. In *multi-programming* mode, many jobs are run concurrently, with one programme carrying out the input/output operation while the other programme makes use of the CPU for computation. In *remote batch* mode, programmes are run from a remote site where the actual processing is done. A communication link connects the central computer with the remote site having intelligent or non-intelligent terminals. In *time-sharing* mode, operating system allocates computer resources to the users in a shared fashion so that a particular user gets time-slices for specific intervals without bothering about other users. In *real-time* mode, data are entered and enquiries made from remote sites as processing is going on.

Compilers

Language compilers are types of basic software with which a computer system translates programmes written in high-level language into that cf machine language. Now, machine language is the sequence of bits for which the machine is designed architecturally to operate. Assembly language is a step removed from machine language, using a set of mnemonics and translating them through assembler into machine code. Among high-level languages, FORTRAN (Formula-Translation Language) has been evolving since 1954 and is very suitable for complex calculations of scientific kind with little data. COBOL (Common Business-Oriented Language) came from US Departments of Defence in 1961 and has been found useful for simple calculations of commercial kind with large-volume data. PL/1 (Programming Language 1) came in 1965 and combines the features of FORTRAN and COBOL for being used in both business and scientific applications. ALGOL (Algorithmic-Oriented Language) came in 1960 and is quite good in solving mathematical problems while RPG (Report Generator) is a powerful language for generating tabular reports. BASIC (Beginners All-Purpose Symbolic Instruction Code) is quite simple to use and fit for on-line interactive processing. The most recent powerful languages are PASCAL, C and ADA. Programmes written in the above languages are compatible with most available computer systems.

Other Software

A complete software system for a computer contains, besides operating system, a set of compilers for various languages as above, one or more system loaders, a filing system, a set of utility routines (for various input/output functions), special and general debugging systems, and generalised software for application, such as, sorting and merging, mathematical programming, engineering design, report generation, simulation, graphics, and so on. All these interface smoothly with operating system and its input/output conventions.

Until 1969, users were provided with all the general-purpose software by the manufacturer along with the purchased (or hired) machine at no extra cost. Since then, all manufacturers have followed IBM in "unbundling" of software: with the exception of operating system. All software products are now priced separately. Techniques of software development are also no longer *ad hoc* but use sets of modules that can be used as "off the shelf" components for developing new software products or modifying the old ones. Structured programming use prior verification methods to eliminate much of the programme-testing activity.

Application Packages

Application packages are ready-made and well-documented programmes for performing specific functions. These software packages are available on certain computer systems or for a certain class of users. They are often made flexible enough to be portable to other machines or adaptable to other users. Examples of common application packages in India, for scientific as well as business applications, cover Project Management System (PMS) for determining critical activities through project network and keeping up schedules of cost and resource allocation; Mathematical Programming System (MPS) for using linear programming to optimise given objectives subject to the constraints; General-Purpose Systems Simulation (GPSS) for discrete simulation of events; Vehicle Scheduling Package (VSP) for operating a fleet of vehicles with referent to route allocation and load distribution; Production Planning and Control System (PPCS) for planning production along with manpower and material allocation; Financial Accounting and Analysis Package (FAAP) for all financial functions of ledger-keeping, reconciliation and analysis, — apart from sales analysis, market research and survey analysis, electronic circuit analysis and numerical control programmes. Another package, called Statistical Package for Social Sciences (SPSS) has, in fact, been of very wide use.

In the conventional processing, the user accumulates data in computer files in his own format and utilises them for a specific application. In the case of data-base approach, prevalent now over two decades, data are organised in such a fashion that they can be used for many users for a variety of applications. This approach has considerable data independence and reduction in data redundancy. Two applications of data-base management like Customer Information Control System (CICS) and Information Management System (IMS) are well-known IBM packages and similar versions are available with compatible machines, such as, Reyad, Hitac, etc.

User-written programmes are generated in many applications where either application packages are too general-purpose to suit the specific user environment or just not available. Such programmes, having the advantage of being tailor-made for the purpose, can be easily altered to changed user-requirements, adapted to different machine organisations or made to satisfy different system constraints — although at a cost.

Conclusion

All software tools need good documentation for correct usage, wide dissemination and independence from the original creator. At least three manuals are needed: for the user, for the operator and for the maintenance programmer. Also, because of the complexity of large software systems, there are often errors (bugs)and inadequacies in running them. Maintenance groups are needed to keep track of all needs for correction. In some cases, extensive changes require major revision in documentation, thus needing release of a new version of the software product.

3

SELECTION OF COMPUTERS

Introduction

Computer is a highly complex device and a great deal can be made of the technical attributes of the individual machines in their actual usage. For instance, commercial data processing comprises reading data, printing out data, storing data and retrieving data from magnetic media. Computer performance for such work would be mainly determined by the speed and capability of input/output (I/O) and storage peripherals. Most jobs in government departments, industry, business houses and public utility systems are heavily I/O-bound. On the other hand, scientific, engineering and operations research problems require good computational facilities, such as, available core store and instruction speeds. Such jobs would be mostly found in academic institutions and R&D organisations.

The important factors to be considered for selection of computer for an organisation are: cost of equipment; availability of a suitable configuration; feasibility of upgrading the configuration to obtain more computer power; software availability and suitability; and quality of manufacturer's support-services, e.g., maintenance, training and systems support.

Alternative Approaches

After a proper configuration has been worked out in advance, appropriate computers should be looked for. Computers are not all alike in the market and the pricing structure varies from manufacturer to manufacturer. Some computers are rented out by manufacturers on a one-time installation charge and monthly rental thereafter. The rental covers a certain number of hours (prime shift) for which the maintenance is included. IBM in India used to follow this practice for their second-generation computer systems, all charges being extra beyond prime shift.

Alternatively, computer time can be hired from a service bureau. For this purpose, suitable service bureaus have to be explored in the neighbourhood and logistics worked out. One approach is to employ a few programmers and systems analysts for developing application programmes and purchase only computer-time from the service bureau for running the programmes. Typically, a regional computer service centre with a mainframe system would earlier charge Rs. 600 per hour for I/O-bound jobs and Rs. 2500 or Rs. 3000 or Rs. 3500 per hour of CPU time from academic community or business organisations or other consultants. The charges have considerably come down now. The other approach is to contract the entire job of designing, developing and implementing the application programmes to the service bureau on a turn-key basis. Once the job is ready, it can also be run on the service-bureau computer under a separate contract. Both these approaches permit shift of the job to an in-house computer whenever feasible.

Design Workstation Computer

The final alternative is to buy a computer system for in-house usage. This is the most difficult choice including heavy investment of capital (with a substantial amount of foreign currency, if the system is to be imported), employment of skilled people on a permanent basis and tying up with an available technology for considerable time especially when computer hardware is continually undergoing improvement.

Available Variety

Availability of a suitable configuration can be from a variety of manufacturers. Indian government was earlier following a policy of letting medium to large computers to be procured from abroad against import licence or open general licence, with all large manufacturers from the West (and Japan) competing for the Indian market. The leading world manufacturers included IBM, AMDAHL, REYAD, CDC, ITEL, CDC, DEC, HONEYWELL, NCR, BURROUGHS (now UNISYS), HP, UNIVAC, ICL, SIEMENS, DG, CRAY RESEARCH, PHILIPS, INTERDATA, FUJITSU, HITACHI, NIPPON, TOSHIBA and many others. Many computer models follow IBM architecture, with the first five manufacturers above being even plug-compatible with IBM systems.

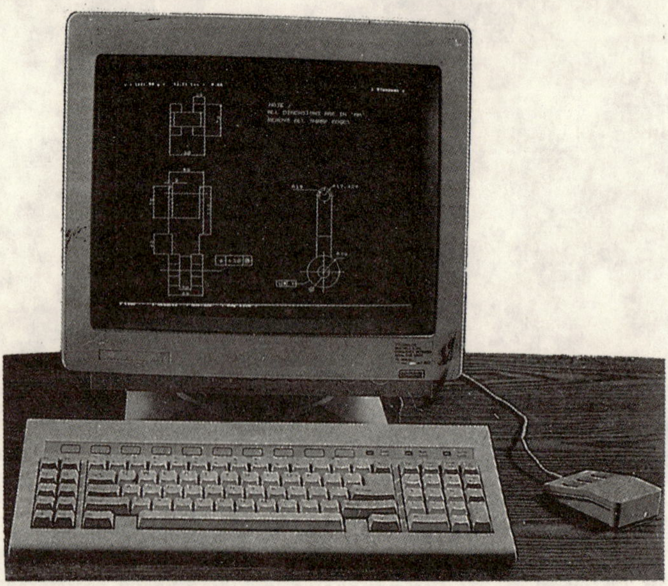

Draftman's Dream : Electronic Drafting

Micro, mini and mainframe systems are allowed now to be produced in India with gradually more liberal approach. Some of the manufacturers are ECIL, Hyderabad; BEL, Bangalore; HCL, Delhi; ICIM, Bombay; DCM Data Products, Delhi; ORG, Baroda; NELCO, Bombay; PSI, Bangalore; and several others. While microprocessor-based systems cost today around Rs. 15,000–5 lakhs, mini system can cost anywhere between 5–20 lakhs, mainframe system Rs. 20 lakhs–1 crore, and super system above Rs. 1 crore. Incidentally, REYAD computers (EC and SM series) available earlier against rupee payment from USSR and Eastern Europe, have fallen into disuse now. Even its costs are coming down everyday!

Expansion of Capacity

As computer load starts building up, the culture of date processing spreads within the organisation, leading to the need of expanding computer capacity by 3-4 years. The possibilities are either replacing the old computer by new machine or augmenting the computing power by adding more CPU and memory. The experience of wholesale replacement can be both traumatic and very expensive. For example, many Indian users have passed from second-generation and third-generation to fourth-generation computers, with a new concept of organising files and generating reports by using direct-access files, database management and sophisticated operating-system environment. The simple expedient of converting all programmes from second and third to fourth generation machines can prove to be the least cost-effective.

Augmentation of computing power can also be difficult, as most micro-computers are virtually non-expandable in terms of CPU and memory. Even peripherals cannot be increased beyond a limit due to limited plugging capabilities. Mini and mainframe systems have, on the other hand, specified scope for expansion both for CPU and memory, and peripherals. Future augmentation needs have to be kept in view at the time of procurement itself. While the cost of I/O devices remain still high without the benefit of micro-electronics having much reached them, the cost of CPU and memory is going down everyday. A well-tried device is to configure the current computer around high CPU and memory, with only limited I/O capability, and to add I/O devices gradually as work-load goes up without drastically changing the CPU and memory.

Application Packages

Computer manufacturers supply hardware today supported by only basic utilities and systems software, while the remaining application packages (which used to come free with the computer before 1968) are supplied at a price. It is important to consider which of these packages can meet the user organisation's requirements and to what extent. Application packages usually include engineering packages (civil engineering design calculations, space-frame analysis, stress-strain calculations, load-flow analysis, traffic-lighting system); operations research packages (linear programming, network analysis, vehicle scheduling); management packages (inventory control, production planning and control, bill of material, employee services); specialised packages suited to broad patterns of industry and machinery (process control, numerical control) and so on.

There is a cost-advantage in buying the above kind of packages since they are general-purpose in nature. On the other hand, the user organisation may develop application programmes by its own team of analysts and programmers, in which case the cost would be high but the in-house programmes may turn out to be more specifically suited to the user and prove ultimately to be more cost-effective than the general-purpose package. There is the additional option available to the user organisation to engage an outside consultant or service bureau for developing application programmes rather than deploy an in-house software team. While acquiring a computer, it is advisable to work out the economics of firming out contracts for application packages against generating on one's own.

Support Services

Support services available from the manufacturer are often difficult to unwrap from the attractive package presented by him. Maintenance of the computer, after its installation and the initial testing, is the responsibility of the manufacturer during the warranty period of one year or so. Thereafter the Computer Maintenance Corporation (now the CMC Ltd.) is encouraged by the Indian government to take over the maintenance responsibility, with the other alternatives being: continued maintenance under a new contract by the manufacturer (usually accepted by the latter); employment of in-house systems engineers to do the maintenance; or entrusting maintenance to a third party. The last two solutions may be a little costly due to the stocking of essential spares and timely procurement of the rest of spares. Training is looked after normally by the manufacturer for a specific number of personnel from the user organisation. Both scope and quality of training should be carefully watched to ensure comprehensiveness. It is always salutary to look for an all-India presence of the manufacturer's representative for being able to do the critical trouble-shooting.

Conclusion

Since a large number of organisations are going for the purchase of single or multiple PCs (in the range of PCs, PC/XTs and PC/ATs), it is worthwhile to summarise the selection criteria they should look for. These include: (a) knowledge of performance (through comparative statements or bench-marks); (b) possibility of upgradation in future in the CPU and I/O devices; (c) feed-back on other users' experience; (d) availability of support services (for hardware, system software and application software); (e) provision of documentation in the form of manuals; (f) arrangement for practical training by the vendor/manufacturer; (g) feasible alternatives for future maintenance; and (h) arrangement for securing computer-time from the vendor/manufacturer in the event of computer up-time being less than what is stipulated during purchase.

4

EVALUATION OF COMPUTERS

Introduction

The tremendous spurt in the growth of computer and calculation industry is reflected in its value of Rs. 18.50 crore in 1975 going up only to Rs. 30.00 crore in 1980 and reaching around a few thousand crore by 1990. It is estimated that the computer industry growth today far outstrips the growth of electronic industry as a whole. The microprocessor revolution has made the computer easily available to small industry and business houses. The large market competition that has ensued is due to the high rate of growth in a virtually limitless market, along with the simplicity of hardware design based on imported microprocessor chips and other peripherals.

Initial Survey and Feasibility Study

While the computer manufacturers are so many and so eager to sell their products which are often deceptively similar looking to each other, it becomes an important task for the likely user organisation to make a good job at the selection and evaluation of the best computer suited to its needs. The first step is a simple survey to explore if computerisation is at all worthwhile. It is surprising how many times a preliminary study of this nature would diagnose whether a computer would be useful at all, depending upon the nature and turnover of the organisation, its general work-load and information environment. Following the *diagnosis* if in favour of computer, it is advisable to launch a detailed *feasibility* study to assess what the likely application areas are; what the information needs would be in each area; and how an information flow could be best organised based on computer. Users who are as yet unfamiliar with computers or are about to step up considerably their computing activities can certainly seek external expert assistance in this evaluation process. Existing base of systems analysts and programmers may be all right for data processing management, but it seldom covers the experience of computer selection or of the scale and technology being investigated.

Feasibility study should lead on to determination of data-processing load and frequency, which should form the basis for assessing the likely configuration of CPU and memory, and the supporting I/O peripherals. It is at this stage that the user should start looking at the available computer systems and ask manufacturers to quote against a defined equipment specification. While saving some evaluation time in this process, the user may get some useful new ideas from one manufacturer that are still relevant if another is selected. The reaction from manufacturers to the specification also provides some idea as to his support capability. Further, timing the performance of the system by the manufacturer indicates his view of software overheads, simultaneous activity and so on.

Computer's Workstation : Thinking in Colour, Dimension and Motion

Evaluation Points

The user should insist from manufacturer the total cost estimate associated with his equipment, including space and air-conditioning.

Computer's Workstation

Besides, a number of specific questions can be asked on such factors as: availability and cost of support services (up to post-warranty maintenance, if needed); precise performance figures including reliability; maintenance terms with all shift-variations; variety of purchase and leasing terms; projected performance of the system against the specifications; upgradability without incurring upgradation or conversion costs; hardware and software compatibility across the entire series-range and with other systems; and versatility in operation due to a choice of high-level languages, a wide variety of "user friendly" utilities and application packages.

The obvious purpose of evaluation is to select the "best" computer for the user organisation. Definite costs should include such items as central computing equipment and later enhancements; communication equipment if needed; computer room and service; conversion cost from current systems; training cost for the user staff (less free services); user software cost (against manufacturers packages); un-bundled software cost; and programming cost (if language-dependent). While measurement of cost and performance (based on calculations, simulation, standard work-units like Gibson's mix or benchmarks) need not be precise, minor differences are best dissolved by holding discussions with manufacturers and taking reasonably pragmatic decision. Before the final selection, there should be a balance sheet of the short-listed systems drawn up over a period of years to get a true comparison of different machines.

An ingenious way of selecting a cost-effective computer is to go for an *integrated* system where a mix is obtained from Original Equipment Manufacturers (OEM) for the cheapest devices made by each. While this sounds simple and is also done by some manufacturers already (e.g., DEC series CPU and memory with memorex discs), the important criterion is to obtain full plug-compatibility in the OEM mix of devices. Otherwise, the integrated system can land the user in no end of troubles, as it is difficult to establish fool-proof hardware and software interfaces in the integrated system, even if it is cheap in cost. CMC in India has some useful experience in it, but not the full infrastructure yet nor any manufacturing facility for a proven integrated system.

For the very large variety of micro-computers (like personal computers), a few specific considerations arise in the matter of selection. First of all, there is inadequate knowledge of technology behind the hardware. While the hardware designs are simple (based on the manuals provided by the suppliers of the chips), the users are hardly ready with professional expertise to understand and evaluate the hardware impartially. As a result, there is the recurrent theme of buying hardware having either over-capacity or under-capacity *vis-a-vis* the needs of the user. Secondly, there from the beginning an inadequate involvement of the user who alone can understand their requirements in full and advise suitably the manufacturer while designing the software. Thirdly, there is inadequate understanding of the cost implications of hardware and software, with the latter going up to more than half the hardware cost with actual usage. Fourthly, there is often no proper definition of the user needs and what aspects of these needs would be precisely met by the microcomputer. Fifthly, there is no clear-cut provision of a minimum time-frame of, say, 3-4 months when the system should function without significant errors. Sixthly, there is often less than adequate after-sales service-support from the manufacturer due to either lack of precise knowledge of the new technology or sheer inability to sustain such services in the teeth of severe price-competition. Seventhly, the microcomputer is unable to add on future capability with change in technology. Finally, there is the "buy or hire" dilemma when the relatively low-cost microcomputer seems a suitable investment proposition straightway, although the volume of computer-load could easily be met by hiring that much computer-time.

Conclusion

Life of a microcomputer can be safely taken as 3-5 years, if proper maintenance is provided. The latter is satisfactory in the metropolitan cities but not so elsewhere. There is also the nagging question of reliability, particularly for peripherals like floppy discs. All in all, the total cost of setting up a microcomputer centre and its expansion needs later on, in keeping with the business-growth, remain matters of detailed analysis, on which time in the earlier stages must be spent and performance of various types of microcomputers evaluated, — rather than going for a machine on an imporomtu basis or, worse still, as a status symbol.

5

IMPORT OF COMPUTERS

Introduction

The world computer scene showed up at least a dozen giants whose worldwide revenue in the fiscal year 1980 had been above $ one billion. The related survey, whose results came out in late 1981, included such product areas as mainframes, minicomputers, microprocessors, small business systems and personal computers, terminals and peripherals, software and services, data-communication equipment, but excluded word processors, electronic registers and switching equipment. Table 5.1 lists the 12 largest computer concerns in the order of their world revenue, and does not include the Japanese giants like Fujitsu, Hitachi and Toshiba which have all been going overseas outside their huge and highly protected home market.

TABLE 5.1: World's top 12 computer concerns

Rank	Name	Country	World Revenue (Base=1980)
1.	International Business Machines	USA	$ 26,213 mill.
2.	Burroughs (Now UNISYS)	USA	$ 2,902 mill.
3.	Sperry Univac	USA	$ 2,800 mill.
4.	Control Data Corporation	USA	$ 2,791 mill.
5.	National Cash Register	USA	$ 2,525 mill.
6.	Digital Equipment Corporation	USA	$ 2,368 mill.
7.	Siemens	West Germany	$ 2,047 mill.
8.	Honeywell	USA	$ 1,634 mill.
9.	Howlett-Packard	USA	$ 1,546 mill.
10.	International Computers Ltd.	UK	$ 1,494 mill.
11.	Cii-Honeywell Bull	France	$ 1,489 mill.
12.	Olivetti	Italy	$ 1,221 mill.

It is heartening to note that while some 120 third and fourth generation computer systems from the overseas computer concerns were imported to India and made operational over the half decade between 1976-81 and the total number of computer systems increased from 120 in 1970 to around 600 in 1980, the figure went up to several thousand by 1990. The current computer scene in the country is marked by vastly greater number of wider range of computer-types, and higher overall computing capacity after 1990 than ever available in the 1970s and 1980s.

Import Parameters

Import of a computer system, irrespective of its value, requires the prior clearance of the Department of Electronics (DOE) in our government before issue of an import licence by Ministry of Commerce. This also applies to computer systems proposed for import by all R & D organisations. For clearance of import of computer systems up to Rs. 5 lakhs, a liberal procedure is followed. This includes determination of essentiality of the computer proposed for import, assessing whether needed computer can be procured from indigenous suppliers, drawing up — if otherwise — of specifications for the optimal system, floating of tenders, evaluation of bids and final approval for import.

Import of a computer system is allowed to only a few categories. First of all, an actual user who requires an imported computer for his own use, and not for business or trade in its given such a licence. Thus, in the case of an industrial undertaking (large-scale, small-scale or cottage-industries sector), the imported computer should be utilised for the manufacturing processes or operations conducted within its own promises. In the non-industrial category, such as, hospitals, R&D organisations, academic institutions, commercial establishments and individuals, the imported computer should be utilised for the specific purpose for which it was sought for import.

For importing a computer system over a value of Rs. 5 lakhs, the actual user draws up functional specifications, based on his current and anticipated applications. Help of outside consulting agencies used to be sought, if necessary, in earlier days. For instance, Central Government offices in Delhi (e.g., Customs, Income-tax, Audit, Insurance, etc.) could consult Department of Statistics whose computer centre they might be using. DOE then would scrutinises the given specifications in terms of national priorities laid down from time-to-time and would approve, in principle, the need for import with a specific configuration.

The user was associated in deciding upon the functional configuration for the import of a computer, with changes wherever necessary. DOE thereafter called for competitive sealed tenders from various manufacturers and agents on a global basis. After the user had provided to DOE a ranking of his preferences for computer-types, along with reasons, DOE appointed a committee of experts (comprising hardware, software and systems specialists) to evaluate the tenders and make technical recommendations. The latter were put up to an approval committee comprising senior government representatives from DOE, Ministry of Finance (Economic Affairs) and the administrative ministry for the user organisation. The approval committees decision was deemed to be final, for placing contract by the user organisation for the computer finally selected. It is to be noted that clearance from indigenous angle for imported computers was handled by DOE and not the normal channel of DGTD. The system stand fairly liberalised now, with the stringency gone.

Labour Angle

For procurement of imported computers, clearance from labour angle is generally necessary from Ministry of Labour. The latter needs, *inter alia*, certificate from the concerned State Government that labour union for the actual user organisation has no objection to the computer system being installed; reasons why the work cannot be done through existing computer facilities; types of applications, with their periodicity, which are proposed to be handled by the new computer; benefits to be expected as regards improvement in efficiency, quality, cost reduction and economy, likely effects on the employment in the establishment, especially in relevant departments; likely effects on conditions of employment, promotion prospects, working conditions and wages of the concerned workers; methods of adjusting any employees rendered surplus; and safeguards to protect the workers, interests including the method of sharing possible benefits.

Import Against Export

Besides actual users, import of a computer system may be allowed for : (a) an Indian organisation intending to export software and requiring foreign exchange (FE) for importing a computer for software development; (b) an Indian national, settled abroad, setting up an export-oriented software firm and wishing to import a computer with his own FE earned abroad; and (c) an Indian organisation wishing to import a computer with a view to enhancing or modifying hardware and software against specific export orders and then to re-export the computer.

The applicant for undertaking export of computer software presents a detailed project proposal to DOE, covering background of the applicant organisation technical capability and nature of export proposal. A standing committee of computer specialists set up by DOE examines, in depth, the capability as well as credibility of the applicant to undertake software generation for export, whether the applicant could use a locally manufactured computer for this purpose and, if not, whether he could use imported computers already in the country. If the standing committee finds the project acceptable from technical and economic angles, the applicant is permitted import of a computer (and related data processing equipment) through the special import procedure administered by DOE. After clearing a proposal, DOE monitors the progress of the project based on six-monthly performance reports from the party and periodic site-reviews carried out by DOE. Progress on a project is evaluated by a monitoring committee comprising representatives of DOE, CCI&E, Ministry of Commerce and Ministry of Law.

It is important that the applicants for categories (a) and (b) above have on hand guaranteed software export orders covering at least 20 per cent of the CIF value of the computer proposed for import. While imported computer price does not exceed 50 per cent of the project export commitment over 5 years for category (a), the import price can be 100 per cent of the export commitment for category (b). For category (c), import is allowed without any extra obligation, except that the imported computer should not be used for any domestic purpose. Legal bonds are executed for software export commitment involving import of a computer system, stipulating 20 per cent of the total export commitment by the end of second year, 40 per cent by the third year, 60 per cent by the fourth year and full by the fifth year. This apart, at least one-third of the time of the imported computer has to be solely used for software generation for export.

Special Considerations

The above are fairly stringent procedures, trying to cover some loopholes discovered in the recent past. Default in meeting the minimum export performance level could earlier lead to government instituting legal action for confiscation of the imported computer system. It is now possible that applicants from 100 per cent export-oriented software firms may be cleared directly by Ministry of Commerce within the above guidelines without reference to DOE, and all other cases of import of computer systems under export obligation will be cleared by DOE in any case.

The recent import policy seems not to favour import of computers except against software export, — the accent being heavily on use of indigenous systems. Another feature is the planning by DOE to put together the computer requirements of a group of similar users and then import systems that can serve them all. For education sector, for instance, it is possible to think of a few computers from the same vendor, — thus ensuring exchange of programmes among the educational users. It is a good idea which needs watching in application.

Conclusion

The CMC Limited has been normally recommended for maintenance of all imported systems, unless in-house maintenance is preferred by the user. CMC is often the designated procurement agency for spares, tools and test equipment for their maintenance. Others can import spares up to 3 per cent of CIF value of the imported system. The import duty on computers have undergone many changes from 40 per cent till 1978-79 to 178 per cent in 1982-83 and reduced again thereafter. Government thinking towards liberalisation of computer import or reduction in the import duty has always been welcome by the computer users and appears to have finally gained ground today.

6

THE WORLD OF MICROPROCESSOR

Introduction

Microprocessor has been hailed, since the advent of transistor in 1948, as the mst significant technological development. This device first came into being for applications in calculators in 1971 when Intel Corporation of USA announced a new processor Intel 4004 at a very low price. The device is a simple monolithic Integrated Circuit (IC), employing Large-Scale Integration (LSI) in a Metal-Oxide Semiconductor (MOS) technology. LSI involves multiplying the number of electronic circuits squeezed on to a silicon chip from the 10,000 or more of 1980s to a million or more in the 1990s.

Application-wise, innovations have gone far ahead from the mere calculation kind. Within a decade, designs are in hand for systems that can understand instructions issued in ordinary speech to be used for controlling robots, that can automatically translate languages, or can automatically diagnose and correct their own faults, and for a myriad other purposes. All these fall into the genre of very large-scale integration (VLSI) finding applications in the factory, office, hospital or home with equal facility.

Structure and Function, Microprocessor to Microcomputer

A microprocessor needs some additional circuits to be capable of arithmetic and logical manipulation of data. It thus functions as a complete central-processing unit (CPU),—consisting of an arithmetic/logic unit (ALU) and a control unit. When the microprocessor is combined with memory and input/output (I/O) devices, a microcomputer is formed.

In a microcomputer, the ALU performs the arithmetic and logic operations on data received from memory or input devices. The control unit controls the flow of data and instructions within the microcomputer, — by fetching instructions from the memory, by decoding and executing instructions, and by properly sequencing events performed by the ALU and I/O devices. While the memory is used to store data and instructions, the I/O devices provide a mechanism for transferring data to and from the outside world.

Microcomputers, like larger computers, manipulate information represented by binary digits, called *bits*. Groups of bits are called *words* and word-sizes vary from microprocessor to microprocessor as 4, 8, 12, 16 and 32 bits (64 bits and 128 bits being still at the planning stage). The word-length determines the characteristics of different microprocessors. Binary information is manipulated in an organised sequence of steps (programme) where each step is termed on *instruction.*

Design Aspects

A microcomputer design is based on four building blocks: input devices, memory, a microprocessor (with a calculating section and a decision capability for selecting alternate courses of action), and output devices. The building blocks are interconnected by a group of lines (one for each bit to be transferred) called a *bus*. Figure 6.1 illustrates a microcomputer block diagram where the I/O devices share the same bus. It also shows various data registers for temporary storage and manipulation of data and instructions.

Quite often the memory and I/O devices share the same bus in a microcomputer. In this case, the microprocessor may treat an I/O device as a memory element and gains the facility to add new memory blocks as and when needed. This is illustrated in Fig. 6.2.

ROM and RAM

A microcomputer needs to store programme steps and data, and recall them at the appropriate time, in order to perform its function. In situations where the memory values do not change, e.g., in dedicated systems, read-only memory (ROM) is used to store programme-steps and data-values. Read-write memory (RWM), also called random-access memory (RAM), is used to store data which changes during the operation of the system, e.g., results of calculations, or programmes which change frequently. In either case, the memory function is to store and provide on command a data-value or a programme-step.

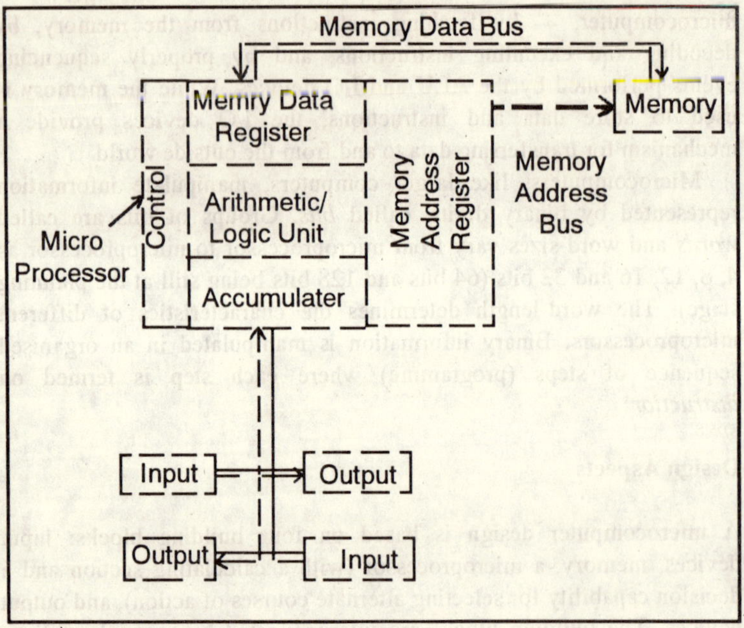

FIG. 6.1: Block Diagram of a Microcomputer

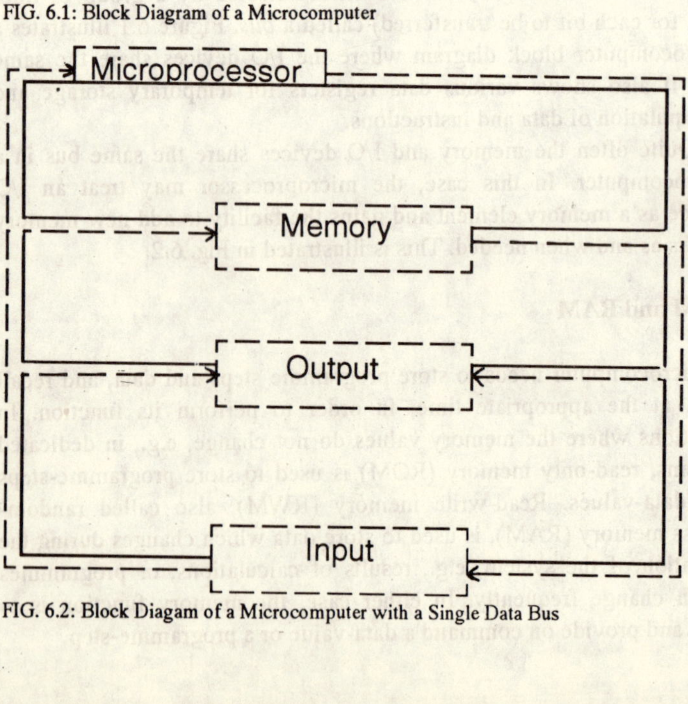

FIG. 6.2: Block Diagam of a Microcomputer with a Single Data Bus

Microprocessors are making an impact on the design of virtually all digital systems. They are increasingly finding applications in systems which formerly used random logic. In complex systems, a microprocessor is preferred to hard-wired random logic, because of the flexibility in programming simplified design, reduced cost and higher reliability. The microprocessor cost continues to diminish as integration moves up from a single LSI chip with 8,000 to 10,000 transistors to a single VLSI chip capable of incorporating 100,000 transistors or more.

Application Range

Typical range of applications, categorised by machine-size, can be as follows:

1. *4-bit devices*: Accounting systems, appliances, calculators, game machines, intelligent instrumentation, simple terminals;
2. *8-bit devices*: Control systems, intelligent terminals and instruments, point-of-sale terminals, traffic controllers, communication preprocessors (data concentrators), process control systems;
3. *16-bit and 32-bit devices*: Data acquisition systems, numerical control, process control, intelligent terminals, supervisory control (gas, power, water distribution), automatic testing systems.

Many microprocessor manufacturers provide prototyping systems for development purposes. These systems usually have microcomputers with extensive memory and I/O capabilities. They are particularly useful for designing microcomputers tailored to specific applications.

Types of microcomputers available fall under the categories of single-chip microprocessors, single-chip analogue-signal micro-processors, and microprocessors with a family of co-processors and I/O processors to form a high-throughput computer. The last-mentioned can be multi-microprocessors with fibre optics support for distributed processing and network.

Applications in electronics are legion today, with a few mentioned below:

(a) *Domestic electronics*: Appliances such as automated cooking ranges, sophisticated audio-video equipment in cars, home do-it-yourself microcomputer hobby kits;

(b) *Entertainment electronics*: Television and video games, home microcomputers for many purposes using multi-channel television sets as output display;

(c) *Industrial electronics*: Front-panel control with oscilloscopes and other measuring instruments for displaying readings and time-based concessions, interface control for generating complicated protocols to match different interface requirements, machine-tool control with numerically controlled machines (using ready-made boards), real-time data-logging conversion and storing for later analysis or process control.

Manufacture and Import

The computer section of Bhaba Atomic Research Centre (BARC) had developed LSI chip in the 1980 and manufacturing units like semi-computer complex at Chandigarh have already started functioning. Still a large number of microprocessors in India are imported from abroad and are based on popular components available from the US industries as follows:

1. *Intel series*: 4004 (4-bit), 8080/8085 (8-bit), 8088, 8086 (16-bit); 80386 (32-bit);
2. *Zilog series*: Z80 (8-bit), , Z8000 (16-bit);
3. *Motorolla series*: 6800 (8-bit); 68010 (16-bit); 68020 (32-bit);
4. *Texas Instruments series*: TI990 (8-bit); TI9900 (16-bit) onwards.

Out of 150-180 Indian firms licensed in the past few years to produce microcomputers about 40-50 firms have gone on stream. The total turnover of Indian microcomputers is nearly Rs. 750 crore per annum, in 1989-90 out of which nearly 30 per cent is exported.

To give an idea of speed and capabilities, Intel 8080 microprocessor has a set of 78 instructions, instruction execution speed of 2-9 microseconds, RAM speed of 500 nanoseconds, and ROM speed of 600 nanoseconds. As regards cost, while a microprocessor chip was priced at $ 160 in 1974, chips with new and improved performance are available in the $ 5-10 range all over the world.

Manufacturers of microprocessors have been trying to make their components suitable to a broad spectrum of usage by making, on the one hand, microprocessors specialising in low component count and useful for small applications and, on the other hand, microprocessor boards offering minicomputer capabilities.

Conclusion

Microprocessors can help in converting most hardware overheads into software (programmable) routines. Interface protocol controllers can be easily implemented using pre-assembled boards. Real-time data acquisition is made possible by these microprocessors for later test and analysis. A surprising amount of power is packed into an area as small as a thumb-nail!

Performance limitations (e.g., speed, shorter word-length, limited addressing modes, fewer internal registers) reduce the competitiveness of first and second-generation microcomputers where minicomputers are now used. These limitations are fast receding as more sophisticated technologies appear on the horizon.

7

MICROPROCESSORS AND INDUSTRIAL PROCESS CONTROL

Introduction

When any industrial process control system is looked at from closed quarters, its essential tasks appear to be monitoring of control variables, analysis of present values by processing these inputs and exercise of control using a pre-defined procedure. A spin-off product may be a reporting function which provides normal statistics and highlights alarm conditions.

Basic Characteristics

The industrial process control system should have the following characteristics:

(i) *Real-time response* — the control system should apply corrective action in a very short time, often within seconds;

(ii) *Normal and abnormal control* — the variables should be kept within a pre-defined range through finer control. In addition, the variables should be monitored for detecting unusually high or low values;

(iii) *Statistical report* — the data collected should be translated into management reports, for being analysed to improve the overall performances;

(iv) *Reliability* — the system should be as highly reliable as possible;

(v) *Ruggedness* — the system should be rugged enough to withstand dust, electrical motor noise, high temperature or high magnetic field;

(vi) *Fail-safe operations* — the system should be able to operate in such a manner that it has a safe operating mode (through self-diagnostic provision) in the event of failure;

(vii) *Low down-time* — the system should be capable of quick and on-site repair, with the hardware and packaging of the system made in a modular fashion.

Application Potential

The above characteristics make out a strong case for application of microcomputers in industrial process control for the following plus points:

(a) *Real-time response* — the high speed of microcomputer enables it to provide response in real time while monitoring or controlling the number of variables;

(b) *Memory* — a large amount of historical information can be collected by using memory. The table look-up procedure can also be considered as an alternative to storing data in memory;

(c) *Processing power* — the microcomputer can carry out elaborate control calculations by correlations and analysis of the inputs;

(d) *Decision-making* — the microcomputer can identify existing situations and alter the course of action accordingly through its dynamic logic capability;

(e) *Stored programme control* — the microcomputer can be programmed to follow independent procedure in each case. This availability permits use of standard hardware in varied applications and achievement of complete control function through "customised" control programmes;

(f) *Flexibility* — since the control function is a part of software, changes in control calculations or refinements (as a result of analysis of calculated statistics) can be easily accomplished;

(g) *Command driven modes* — the microcomputer can be operated for different modes through manual commands passed via keyboard.

Other Considerations

It is a logical choice to use microcomputers for real-time control application due to their minimum logic hardware, system flexibility, low cost per function and minimum system development time and cost, apart from the ease in updating the systems, low maintenance cost and built-in protection of system know-how.

Minimisation of logic hardware is achieved by using the integral concept of system architecture with the four functions: data, address, control and supervision.

System flexibility is achieved through software-orientation. For example, temperature control in a furnace can be achieved by calculations passed on input parameters. With a little experience gained on the furnace, it should be possible to carry out better calculations for controlling the temperature to finer limits.

Low cost per function is feasible by increasing the number of functions in the logic of software for the same cost of the microprocessor. For instance, more input terminals can be added to the microcomputer with hardly any cost.

Minimum system development time and cost is a very important advantage for a microcomputer. The microprocessor-based controller can be initially designed by carrying out a simulation of the chosen microprocessor on an universal microprocessor development system. Emulation (run on the actual microprocessor type) has some advantage over simulation (run on some other processor). The programme errors can be corrected and the programme then re-assembled and tested. Such development systems make possible an orderly section-by-section check-out of the complete system when the hardware and software are eventually brought together. In India, ECIL's Micro-78 can be well used as a microcomputer development system.

Real Time Control Applications

There exist a large potential for applying microprocessors in cases where it is difficult to implement hardwired logic or where a computer is likely to be underutilised. The following real-time control applications with microcomputer are worth our attention:

(a) Programmable Logic Controller (PLC) — industrial process control by PLCs can include conveying systems, packing operations, palletising gauging and testing, transfer lines, machine tools, sorting mechanisms, pumping stations, material handling, filter cycling, batch sequencing and food processing. The stored programme concept of the PLCs permits to design virtually any control system by simply creating the stored programme in the standard PLC. The business potential in India has already reached Rs. 10 crores per year;

(b) Supervisory Control And Data Acquisition (SCADA) — this has enormous potential in power generation equipment. It replaces hardware dedicated logic devices by connecting each remote SCADA to a master SCADA under the control of a mainframe computer. This is illustrated in Fig. 7.1 with serial telephone communication lines.

Other control applications using microprocessors are scanners and data loggers, real-time co-ordinate mapping and conversion, power-plant reheat temperature control, torque measurement and control, billet mill control, and weight compensation for the moisture present.

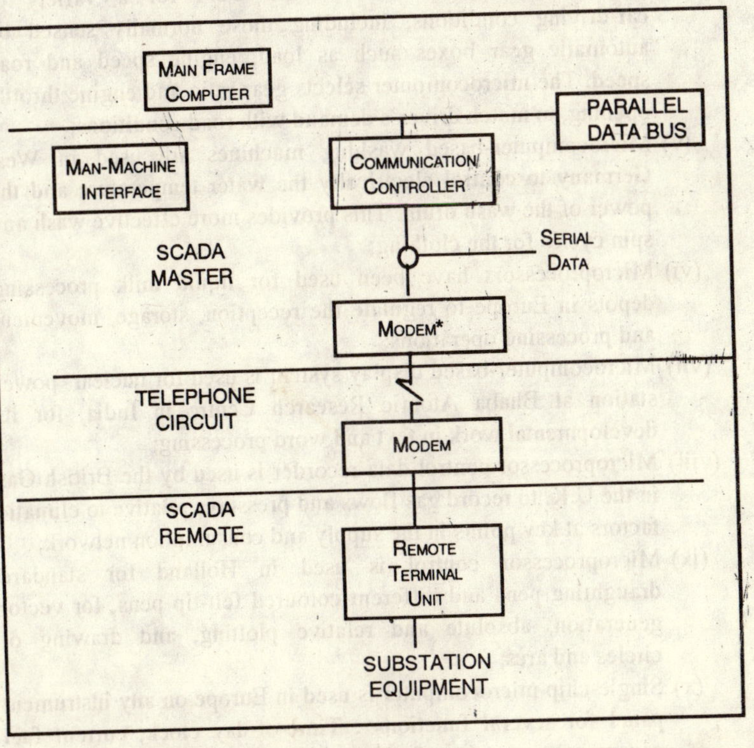

FIG. 7.1: SCADA System (Modulator — Demodulator)

Further Illustrations

A few such control applications are mentioned below:

(i) Modular microcomputer expansion power system has been used in Europe to control rolling mills, transfer lines for automobile engines and cigarette-packing and bottling machines;
(ii) Microprocessor-based calibrator and thermometers are used in the USA to calibrate temperature of thermocouples with laboratory accuracy;
(iii) A microprocessor-based locking system has been used for safe deposit lockers in West Germany where each locker is scanned electronically every two seconds and any fault (by attempt to open the locker) starts an alarm on the control panel;
(iv) Microcomputers are used in the USA for a variety of car-driving conditions, including those normally sensed by automatic gear boxes such as load, engine speed and road speed. The microcomputer selects gear ratio and engine throttle opening, to match driver's demand with road conditions;
(v) Microcomputer-based washing machines are used in West Germany to control electrically the water temperature and the power of the wash drum. This provides more effective wash and spin cycles for the clothing;
(vi) Microprocessors have been used for liquid milk processing depots in Europe to regulate the reception, storage, movement and processing operations;
(vii) Microcomputer-based display system is used for nuclear power station at Bhaba Atomic Research Centre in India, for its developmental work in text and word processing;
(viii) Microprocessor control data recorder is used by the British Gas in the U.K. to record gas flows and pressures relative to climatic factors at key points in the supply and consumption network;
(ix) Microprocessor control is used in Holland for standard draughting pens and different coloured felt-tip pens, for vector generation, absolute and relative plotting, and drawing of circles and arcs;
(x) Single-chip microcomputer is used in Europe on any instrument panel for several functions : Time-of-day clock, current fuel consumption, average fuel consumption, average speed, range on fuel available, timer and outside temperature monitoring.

Essential Steps

In order to develop a microcomputer-based industrial process control system, the following steps are required to be followed:

(a) The process to be controlled should be studied for identifying all important variables;
(b) Desired relationships among the variables should be worked out for control;
(c) Control calculations should be clearly defined for each set of conditions, including condition and alerting schemes;
(d) The control system should be designed to translate the requirements into firmware package;
(e) Interaction between firmware designer and end-user should be carried out for identifying the system extensions and modifying system response where necessary;
(f) The control calculations should be fully tested by simulating the control conditions;
(g) Field trial should be carefully planned with cooperation from end-user.

Conclusion

The microcomputer-based industrial process control system is a cost-effective solution for Indian industries. The system, when used properly, can result in higher production with improved quality, reduced wastage and finer precision. A significant fact is that besides applications in new plants, the microprocessor-based solutions are easily adaptable to existing processors or machines.

8

QUALITY CONTROL BY MICROS

Introduction

Imagine a large proscenium stage, on which a musical drama or a dance ballet is being performed, being lit up by 100 or so spot lights. Each "spot" is to be individually balanced against its neighbouring lights even during frequent changes. In a way, changes of lighting replace one stage picture with another. This is "cross-fading" often barely discovered by the audience, although a complete change has taken place in the lighting control.

Now imagine balancing of "spots" and control of "cross-fading" with complete accuracy night after night, when a play is being performed for many nights, — so that the "cues" are in full conformity with the altering emphasis and mood on the stage. The situation can be extraordinarily complex and the only answer is to use control systems based on a digital approach. Now the microprocessor technology has given rise to the "galaxy" console from where a lighting director programmes and controls the entire lighting sequence of the performance, — with his movements monitored and warnings given in the event of mistakes. "Galaxy" is already immensely popular in Europe and Australia, and has already appeared in the Middle East.

Closed and Open Loop Control Tasks

In the above application, the microprocessor continuously monitors the quality and intensity of light as two process variables, performs suitable calculations on these to generate control values and outputs these to the electro-mechanical units, which in turn control the process variables. This is known as *closed loop control.* If the microprocessor outputs the control values to the lighting director via video display units (VDUs being a given option), which in turn apply the necessary control values, then the control strategy is termed *open loop control.*

From simple-level controls to sophisticated instruments for quality control and process analysis, the trend is to incorporate the microprocessor into the instrumentation system. The tasks to be performed are four-fold: (i) closed loop or open loop control of selected critical loops; (ii) monitoring process variables for alarm conditions; (iii) calculating critical parameters like steam/gas ratio; and (iv) preparation of logs and management reports through printing attachments. For this purpose, basic data logging is done by sampling inputs at regular intervals and then storing each data in specified Random-Access Memory (RAM) locations temporarily, to be transferred later on to an external bulk-storage device, such as, magnetic tape or disc.

Advantages for Microprocessors

The advantages of the use of microprocessor for quality control applications are consistent and smooth operation, response to unusual conditions, avoidance of human errors and better utilisation of human skill. More sophisticated alarm techniques can be employed aiming at the prevention of upset condition in quality by predicting the alarm conditions.

Many vendors today have come up with "support chips" which add to the power of the microprocessor and hasten its entry to the "hybrid" environment of instrumentation. This is a welcome sign since such instrumentation systems are flexible (or, technically speaking, "programmable") because they are based on microprocessors "driven" by software. Very scanty changes in hardware are required even if the systems were to be used for different quality control purposes.

An important feature of microprocessor architecture is the "bus" concept. This feature makes it all the more easy to add on "support peripherals" as need arises. A few examples of such peripheral chips available easily in the market are : (1) keyboard controller; (2) floppy disc controller; (3) printer controller; (4) standard parallel/serial interface; (5) instrumentation standard interface controller; (6) digital-to-analog (DAC) and analog-to-digital (ADC) converters to which microprocessor bus is compatible; (7) VDU controller.

Typically for quality control, the controller can be used as a fixed set-point controller, sequential controller or ratio controller and for relative-speed controllers. It is also possible to provide controllers for special applications using optional devices, e.g., an external comparator. The controller consists of three modules: a comparator assembly, a controller assembly and an operator communication and display assembly. The comparator forms a standardised signal for the control deviation from the signal for the controlled variable — supplied by a current or voltage sensor, a thermo-couple or a resistance thermometer and from the signal for the set-point. The input signal formed by the comparator is processed in the controller assembly and indicated within ±5 per cent of the setpoint. The output signal of the control amplifier can be switched to one of three operating modes (automatic, follow-up or manual). The light-emitting diodes (LEDs) indicate the control deviation according to magnitude and direction.

Serial Procedure

By way of an example, we can consider the application of a microprocessor-based system as a front-end test instrument used in quality control of a direct current (DC) servo motor. Characteristically, such a motor should have a steady rotation (rpm), should produce little vibration and should have very low inertia. Furthermore, its temperature rise should be within specific limits and the change in its rpm should have a slope as required by specific standards. The first test can be devised as the rpm test, where a microprocessor can be used in conjunction with a DAC and other power-electronic circuits. Changes in the input power can be hooked on through a tachometer to an ADC, which in turn can monitor the resulting changes in rpm through the microprocessor bus.

The above results can be stored in a floppy disc connected in the microprocessor bus through a floppy disc controller. Results so stored can be compared to the standard data for acceptance or rejection signals displayed on the VDUs. The second test for inertial requirements can use the same hardware, with the entire instrumentation now "oriented" by freshly loaded software programme for the new test. The motor can be operated in start-stop mode and the resulting inertia effect can be observed through the same rpm monitor (by virtue of the changed software). The third test is to check for temperature rise and can be performed by attaching a thermometer probe to another ADC. Such a switch-over is very simple with a microprocessor-based system because both the monitors are connected to the "address space" of the same microprocessor but at different locations. The address switch-over is done using only one macro-instruction. The final test is for check on vibrations. This time a pressure transducer is connected to the ADC hooked up to the microprocessor, with the address switch-over being similar to the previous case.

After all the above tests are performed, a final O.K. signal is displayed on the VDU. If any test fails, the test data is recorded on the floppy disc and its contents printed for subsequent re-checking. The entire quality control system as mentioned above is elegant for its compactness and reduced down-time, the contrast to a conventional quality control system. The compactness is achieved by making software changes as the only variable and by keeping the total hardware unchanged throughout. The reduced down-time is due to the fact that only floppy discs have to be changed in between if separate test programmes are required.

Microprocessor-based instruments such as digital temperature scanners, dataloggers, etc., are in the process of manufacture, mainly by the small-scale sector. These equipments are being manufactured at Bombay, Baroda, Pune, Bangalore and Lucknow, etc. These sophisticated instruments are getting evaluated as regards their performance and accuracy, particularly in the chemical industries where the environment is not always favourable for the use of electronic instruments.

Conclusion

In selecting the proper type of microprocessor-based controller for an application, the prime factors to be considered are what precision of control is necessary and how difficult the process is to control. The desired result in some cases is precise adherence to the control point. In other cases, maintaining the temperature within a comparatively wide range is all that is necessary. For easier controller tuning and lowest initial cost, the simplest controller which will produce the desired result should be selected. A good method often used is to try a simple controller, e.g., proportional plus manual reset, and note the results compared to the desired system response. This will suggest what additional features are required or some that may be deleted.

9

SELECTION OF MICROPROCESSORS

Introduction

Microprocessor industry in India, in common with the rest of the world, is one of the fastest growing one. New microcomputers, based on the microprocessor, appear in the market almost every week and the increasingly large displays of such equipment in metropolitan cities during the national computer conventions in recent years have been an instance in point.

Microcomputers can be made "flexible" or "programmable" to do a bewildering variety of jobs in industry—beginning from entertainment electronics up to sophisticated instrumentation. It is interesting that the engineers are involved in the programming of the equipment in as much as the programmers are involved in the electronics which they have to programme.

Choice Considerations

It is perfectly possible for a buyer to select a wrong microcomputer because it is a 32-bit device, because it is fabricated using a new technology or because it has topped in a benchmark test. On a further probe, it may appear that the 32-bit device is really unnecessary for the particular usage, the new technology is perhaps not fully tested out in the market, or the benchmark is relevant only to the context of performance for a particular repertoire of instructions.

The selection process involves the following topics of importance:

1. Functions to be performed;
2. Hardware and software requirement;
3. Speed limitations;
4. Systems design aids including hardware and software.

Quite often it is the functions to be performed which determine the applicability of microcomputers to the task. First, microcomputers are economically more advantageous than the erstwhile minicomputers which were often underutilised. Secondly, microcomputers can apply to systems which formerly used random logic (combination and sequential networks). The resulting systems are relatively flexible, cheap and can often "customise" the system via software changes. Thirdly, the inexpensive computing power of microcomputer has led to many applications not covered before, such as, games, kitchen appliances and "smart" measuring instruments.

A Computer Environment

Hardware and Software Considerations

Hardware and software requirements include architecture, namely, word-length and speed, and programming flexibility. Word-length considerations include analogue resolution, computational accuracy, character length and width of parallel inputs or outputs. The larger the word-length, the better is the microprocessor in cases of calculation-oriented applications. The number of bits in address is important because the greater the number of bits the large is the "address space" of the microprocessor. This means more main storage space or larger accommodation for I/O in a memory-mapped I/O environment. The number of general or special purpose registers is also important because they provide easier and faster data handling. In cases of jump or call type of instructions, it is sometimes necessary to preserve programme parameter before the execution of such instructions. Such preservation can be done using stack-push type of operation. Another feature worth noting is the availability of hardware and software interrupts. Use of interrupts may be made to increase the throughout of system in that the CPU can wait for an interrupt from one source while it continues servicing an earlier one from another source. Most microprocessors have vectored interrupts and incorporate built-in priority among them.

Computer-to-Computer Networking

The speed of the microprocessor is also an important criterion. The speed is measured by cycle time, state time, minimum instruction time, register-to-register addition time and interrupt response time. Register-to-register addition time is a popular estimate of the computing speed because nearly every processor has an add instruction. These measures should not be the only criteria used in timing estimation since they do not measure the power of the instruction set.

The degree of programming flexibility can be assessed by an examination of the processor instruction set. Multiple addressing modes conserve memory, simplify programming and increase speed by using one-word memory reference instructions. Other important capabilities include arithmetic instructions, and logical and I/O control instructions.

Another important consideration is the ease with which the microprocessor can support the peripheral chip which the designer may want to use. There are some very powerful peripheral chips which can unfortunately be used with a few specific microprocessors. In some fields of application, other considerations like temperature range of working come into picture. The availability of a good range of support peripheral chips is also important in many applications.

Manufacturer's Support

Hardware and software support from the manufacturer are both important considerations. Software support includes documented manuals and applications literature. Both of these are an important measure of the manufacturer's commitment to servicing the needs of the user. Another system design consideration is the availability of a prototyping system which is essential to develop and debug hardware and software for a given application. Such a system usually includes a microcomputer system with extended memory capability and interface for an I/O device, such as, teletypewriter, a control console, ROM programming capability and software support. The software support should include, as a minimum, a monitor, an editor and an assembler.

Most of the systems from the semiconductor vendors are, despite individual claims of superiority for certain features, quite similar. All generally have resident software — monitor, assembler, editor and debugger — and the latest models are appearing with an in-circuit emulation capability, so that users can debug programmes using their actual prototype hardware. The software resident in the development systems — monitor assembler and editor — may not be an absolute necessity to the design of microprocessor-based systems, but the debugging features would be difficult to do without. The software tool sophistication has become similar to that of minicomputer software. The basic software tools are executive programmes (also called operating systems), text editors, assemblers, compilers and interpreters for programmes, linkers and debuggers. High-level language is an increasingly fundamental consideration. In general, a high-level language for microprocessor applications should have several characteristics. Foremost of these is block structuring which allows several design layers to work independently on programme modules of a large project.

Taking into account all the above requirements, the following microprocessor checklist (prepared by *Electronic Products Journal*) could be found very useful in the evaluation of the minicomputer:

A. Cost Considerations

Normally chip cost is not the largest factor, but it could be in a simple system. The major cost is usually in the circuitry needed to support the microprocessor. The engineering cost to put your system together, however, can be greatly influenced by the amount of quality of support the chip supplier has available.

1. *Support Circuitry*
   Clock circuitry and clock drivers — how many phases? Power supplies — common or special? Memory — standard or special? Power of instruction set (a good instruction set can reduce memory requirements by 40%); Support requirements (the larger these are, the more expensive the printed-circuit board (PCB) or the greater the number of PCB's required); Base of checkout (test *vs* purchased card); Processor card availability (small production and preproduction will use off-the-shelf cards).

2. *Support from Supplier*
   Hardware Support — prototyping systems; mechanical hardware; processor cards; memory cards; interface cards and cables.
   Software Support — high level languages; assemblers; utility programmes — debug and edit; loaders — absolute and relocatable; peripheral drivers (teletypewriters, card reader, line printer, floppy disc, etc.); special sub-routines.

3. *Literature*
   How well written the hardware and software manuals are determines how much time is spent in learning the system — Technical manuals; Software manuals; Application notes; Special interfaces — D/A, A/D peripherals.

4. *Technical Support*
   This can reduce the engineering time and cost required to get

the new product designed and into production — Area system specialist; Field application engineer; Plant applications and engineering groups.

B. Performance

1. *Speed*
   Efficiency of the instruction set — how many instructions are needed to solve a particular problem (a mathematical problem, a process control problem, data handling, etc.)? Execution time of each instruction; Microprogrammability — can the instruction set be changed?

2. *Interface*
   Input/output flexibility and capability — How many peripherals can be handled? How many commands to each peripheral? How large is the subroutine to handle any of the peripherals? How much logic is required?

Interrupt flexibility and capability — Can vectored interrupts and/or polled interrupts be handled by the processor? How many interrupts can be handled by the processor?

Special control features — Enable signals (single line control where fast response or ease of interface is important); Sense inputs (test a single input and respond accordingly).

Conclusion

Selection of microprocessors for specific types of jobs can be based on criteria which are divergent from the general selection criteria of computers discussed in Chapters 4 and 5. The feature brought out above have special relevance to the burgeoning use of microprocessors in our country.

10

ADVENT OF PERSONAL COMPUTER

Introduction

A personal computer is a microcomputer designed and installed exclusively for use by an individual. As a desk-top computer, it appears to be a typewriter-type keyboard with a television monitor sitting on top of it. Responding to the programmed instructions and executing the desired jobs, it has become an electronic consumer durable product in the West and is vastly popular already in the Indian metropolitan cities.

Genesis and Structure

1975 saw the first use of hobby computers, thus ushering in a personal computer industry. The dramatic growth began in 1977 when Apple II was introduced by Apple Computers, Pet by Commodore and TRS-80 by Radio Shack. Others to join the ranks soon were Exidy, Bally, Video Brain, Processor Technology, Cromemco, Ohio Scientific and Southwest Technical Products. Table 10.1 indicates some of the current personal computer types.

A personal computer, like any microcomputer, has three sub-systems of *hardware, software* and *firmware. Hardware* comprises the electronic circuitry, power supplies, memory, central processing unit (CPU) and peripheral devices, such as, video-display unit (VDU), audio-tape cassette, alpha-numerical keyboard, etc. *Software* is a set of instructions (programme) written in a language acceptable to the personal computer by an individual who can instruct the computer to execute his assigned job. Often manufacturers, too, supply pre-programmed software (in the media of floppy discs or magnetic or paper tapes) for executing specific jobs. *Firmware* is a system programme in read-only memory (ROM) which comes in hardware occupying some space in the personal computer memory and is supplied by manufacturers. The remaining portion of memory can be used by an individual for storing of his programme.

TABLE 10.1: Current Personal Computer Types

Microprocessor	Personal Computer	Manufacturer
Intel's 8080 or 8080A	MMD-1	E & L Instruments
	BYT-8	Byte Inc.
	8080	IMSAI
	Altair 8800B	MITS
	Poly 88	Poly Morphic System
	H-8	Heathkit
Zilog's Z-80 or Z-80A	Alpha Z-80	Alpha Digital Systems
	Various	Cromemco
	Horizon	North Star
	TRS-80	Radio Shack
Motorola's M-6800	Altair 680B	MITS
Rockwell's R-6502	Apple II	Apple Computer
	KIM-I	MOS Technology
	PET 2001	Commodore

Printouts Coming Out of a Body of Computers

Personal computers can run programmes written in machine language using strings of binary codes. Some operate in assembly language which uses specially defined characters to assemble instructions and converts the latter to machine language with one-to-one correspondence. A few popular ones use English-like languages, such as, beginners all-purpose symbolic instruction code (BASIC), common business-oriented languages (COBOL), formula translation language (FORTRAN) and 'C' language, in that order.

Computer''s Building Blocks : the Pointed Circuit Boards

Personal computers have grown in the USA alone at a spectacular rate of 200 per cent and more between 1977 and 1991, and constituted 40 per cent–50 per cent of the total computing power against a mere 8 per cent in the earlier year. Business-wise, it has crossed the multi-billion mark, i.e. much above Rs. 1,000 crores. Priced between $500 and $12,000, a personal computer can cater to any of the seven market segments: hobbyist, consumer, very small business, technical or professional, business, executive, educational and industrial. Table 10.2 given an idea of these market segments.

TABLE 10.2: Market Segments of Personal Computer

Segment	Application	Current Price ($)
Consumer		500 – 1,000
Adults	Education, Personal	
Children	Management Entertainment	
Technology-based user		1,000 – 4,000
Hobbyist	Hobbies, experimentation, creation	
Technical or Professional	Professional solution of individual application	
Business executive	Profession problems	
Very small business	Business Management Operation	4,000 –12,000
Educational		600 – 1,500
Schools	Programming	
University	Computer-aided instruction	
Industrial		600 – 2,000
Plant engineers	Process control; monitoring	
Electronic equipment supplier	Quality control	

Variety of Usage

In brief, hobbyist was the first customer of personal computer to use it for creating, learning and experimental purposes. Mass consumer and very small business user, on the other hand, need it for personal enjoyment (entertainment games), learning (educational games), personal management (record-keeping, cataloguing or computation), and monitoring and control of other equipment (appliances, security devices, lights, furnace or water-heater). For business executives, available application programmes include payroll, inventory accounting, project costing, cash management, hire-sales and income-tax calculations. Technical or professional user is primarily an engineer or scientist who uses the personal computer as a professional tool to help in design analysis (computer-aided design (CAD)) or to monitor and control experiments. Business executives may include such users as business analyst, operations and market researchers, and accountants. In educational sector, personal computers are used both to teach programming and to aid in other kinds of instruction. Industrial sector comprises primarily manufacturing organisations who use personal computers for process control, data logging or production monitoring.

The most important sector of applications is for the business computation, rightly termed *executive computing* or *managerial computing*, which has brought a revolution in the end-use of personal computers. This has been possible for the availability of a few software packages which are based on the 'C' language and have been made very friendly to the users.

The electronic spread-sheet is the first facility that provides visible tabulations on the computer screen and can change the rows or columns many times more in the table in order to assess the significance of the changes. LOTUS 1-2-3, VISICALC, SOFTCALC, etc., are the commercial packages for this purpose.

The second facility is that of graphics which can be combined in the form of graphs, bar-charts, pie-charts, block diagrams, venn diagrams, etc., along with the tables of the spread-sheet.

The third facility is that of word processing which provides total secretarial help in composing, modifying, deleting, adding, editing, spell-checking, right-hand or left-hand "justifying" (margin adjustment), etc., for all letters, reports, memos and other correspondence: in full or in parts. WORDSTAR, WORDPERFECT, SOFTWORD, etc., are the relevant packages.

The fourth facility is of data-base management for engendering queries and getting responses. This is an apposite facility for eliciting data and information for business purposes and is widely used through such packages as dBASE III+, dBASE IV, FOXBASE, SYBASE, SOFTBASE, etc.

Overseas Use

Combining the latest technological advances with economic pricing and aggressive marketing, personal computers are catering today to many specialised users, such as, doctors, automobile-dealers, hospitals, real-estate brokers, construction companies, insurance agencies and small factories. In Indonesia, for instance, personal computers are being marketed with VDUs and operator-oriented language, where computer "talks" to an individual in English or Bahasa Indonesian. Even people with no previous computer experience learn the fundamentals of computer operation literally within a few days.

Personal computer is a cost-effective, professional, productivity-improving tool which a manager — operating alone — can use to create, manipulate and analyse information. Computer-aided analysis has always been considered worthwhile for better decision-making, with benefits justifying the investment. Now analysts, line supervisors and middle managers are taking to personal computers for being more productive with own facilities, — 100,000 of them in the USA by early 1981.

Conclusion

It is remarkable how personal computers have invaded the Indian market. To realise its potential, it is understandable that personal computers have moved from a luxury market to a utility one, from entertaining to functional uses, and from high-cost, limited-application products to low-cost, broad-application products. In order to be really useful in India, there must be a few universal applications, the price must come done to Rs. 5,000 or less, and marketing must fit the existing distribution outlets. At the embryonic stage, the primary users for personal computers were hobbyists for whom a high operating performance for a low dollar-value was essential. With users like business executives and scientists, availability of application software and service has become increasingly able to consider today providing total system solutions — hardware and application software — for mass consumers and business users both of whom provide large markets. Such systems solutions can be developed internally or in partnership with indigenous or overseas hardware or software producers, — for business consultants, issue-house managers, educationists, architects, civil engineers or electronic design engineers, to name only a few.

11

DISTRIBUTED DATA PROCESSING

Introduction

Data Processing (DP) has come into being to provide accurate and timely information to assist the operation of a business. Data Processing as a function can and does exist in a manual fashion with the same objective. Usage of computer can help to achieve the objective at a fast pace and using a large volume of data. If one considers how DP can be made more effective, the idea of distributing this resource and managing the data being processed is a natural direction to take.

Basic Definition

The term *distributed data processing* is used to describe computer systems with multiple processors either at the same computer centre or in geographically separate locations. Rarely, the term is applied to the use of multiple minicomputers which are not connected at all. The degrees of dispersion for the distributed components can include interconnection to form a single computer complex; interconnection by cables in a computer room; interconnection by in-plant wiring; interconnection by permanent carrier telecommunication (e.g., a dedicated telephone line); interconnection by intermittent common carrier telecommunication (e.g., a dialled-up telephone connection); or some physical connection in one form or the other.

If telecommunication lines were fast enough, there would be no difference in function between a distributed computer system in one room and a geographically scattered system. Today, the telecommunication links used for data transmission are much slower than the channels which interconnect the devices within a computer room. Consequently the functions distributed geographically are different from those distributed within one machine room.

Aspects of Distribution

There are generally three aspects of systems that may be distributed: *processing, data* and *control.* Where interlinked processors are geographically scattered, the data they use may be scattered as well. In many systems, it is the structure and usage of the *data* that determines what is practical in the distribution of processors. Again, a system may have much of its *processing* geographically scattered and yet the overall management and *control* functions may reside separately at a central location.

Data can be stored either as straightforward data-files or as data-bases. A file is designed for data to serve a particular application or related group of applications. A data-base is an application-independent collection of data from which multiple records can be derived by software. There are major advantages in employing data-base software, but the software is complex and usually operates on data stored at one location. Distributed data are, therefore, organised often in the form of *data-files* (usually on-line) rather than as a data-base, although multiple data-base systems may also be interconnected.

Nature of Data

Different forms of data distribution involve central data with single host computer; central data with multiple host computers; dependent hierarchical data (data in the lower-level machines often a sub-set of the higher-level data); independent hierarchical data (all the processors being self-sufficient DP systems); split data (the same data-structure at different locations); separate data (different data-structure at different locations forming an integrated system); replicated data (multiple copies of data stored at different locations); and heterogeneous data systems (independent computer systems). Figure 11.1 shows a typical corporate configuration containing most of the above, as visualised by Martin.

DP exists to provide accurate and timely information to assist the operation of a business. If management places its emphasis on DP with all its attendant complexities, the concept of distributing this capability becomes one step in an overall plan for supporting a business through information system. A major US financial institution went ahead in eighties for a complete distribution of the DP function, resulting in a significant decrease in the DP effectiveness. This could be attributed to three factors: endorsement to distributed DP without careful technical analysis and design; placement of DP and responsibility for it in areas that were not prepared for either; and the lack of an overall plan for DP that magnified the first two issues.

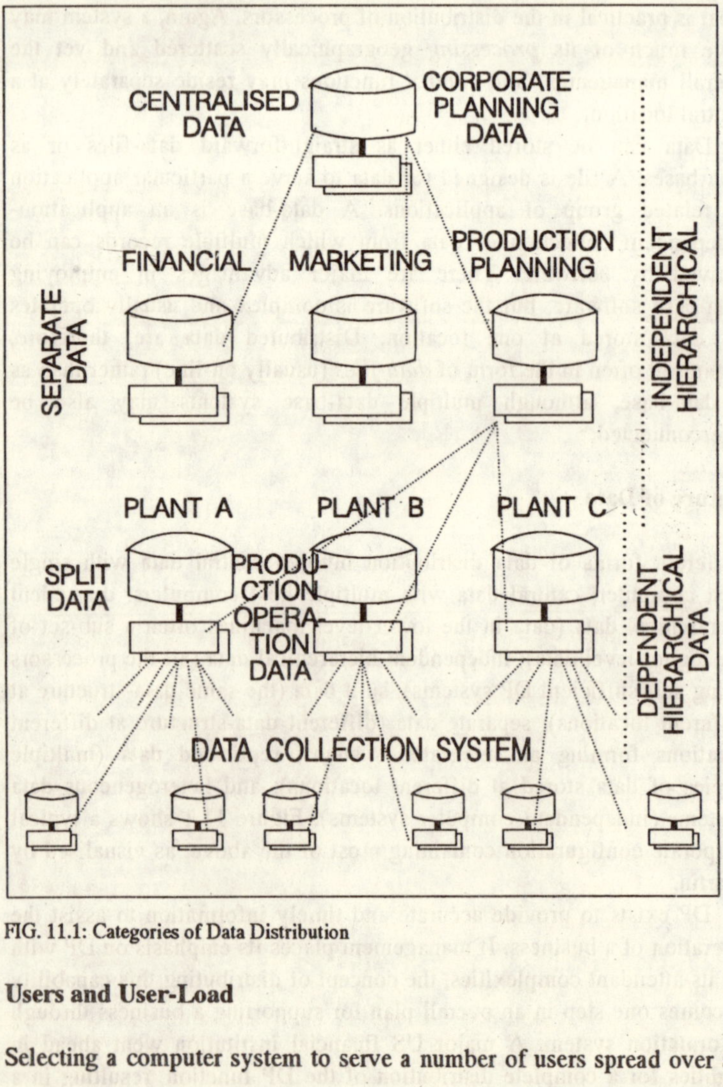

FIG. 11.1: Categories of Data Distribution

Users and User-Load

Selecting a computer system to serve a number of users spread over a wide area is a tricky problem, involving identification of user-groups (varying from inquiry-response systems to batch operations and even including real-time operations); assessment and merging together the different needs of each user-group (for instance, most inquiry-response system users would have common needs); and summarisation of responses into a form suitable for system specification.

Before drawing up a realistic profile of expected user-load, certain standard terms to describe users is necessary to be explained. Among the *interactive* applications (which "interact" with the computer with each transaction), *conversational* users come first with varying applications, but with the common characteristic of input-output being single line each (with less than 100 characters) and being balanced as well, and the expected response-time being 2-5 seconds. Then come the *inquiry-response* customers characterised by short input-messages and long responses (dependent on design, size and access-time for large data-bases), and expected response time rising to 20 seconds or so (for extensive querying). The third category is the *remote job-entry* (RJE) users who enter jobs for subsequent processing, and response-time can be quite long. The last category is the *data-entry* users with long inputs and short response-time (say, for generating database). Data entry may be done in conversational mode, with response-time less than 2 seconds. Among non-interactive applications come *batch-users*, with large volume of data-input and large amount of output, who may need large processing power and can be conveniently scheduled, often in off-shift hours.

The above standard terms can be illustrated from the distributed DP concept made operational at TISCO and TELCO. These two giant private-sector enterprises had each gone in for Burroughs 6806 computer as the host system at the plant, connected through high-speed line to Burroughs 1955 minicomputers as RJEs with 20 video-terminals each. 4 RJE minicomputers for TISCO and 3 for TELCO satisfied 70 to 80 per cent inquiries on the spot regarding production and inventory, with long-term production records and the historical data going to the central computer once in every shift (i.e., thrice daily). *Conversational* usage was for program development through command and editing languages, debugging, logic-flow: in short, for improving productivity of programmes. *Inquiry-response* usage was partly on 1955 and partly on 6806 systems on the extended data-base. *RJE* usage for starting such jobs as stock-movements and daily stock-status on 1955 systems. Lastly, *data-entry* usage was for updating store-stocks, entering part-numbers, etc., with some peripheral capability, adequate character-display and a few hard-copy attachments (or dot-matrix printers). The above description does not include such real-time applications as process control, where local interaction is often within microseconds. Interactions with other components in such a system may require a response-time in milliseconds.

Check-list for Users

The following check-list has been compiled in order to draw up a user-profile:

Interactive General

How many times per day does one log? When in the day and how does one log? What are average and maximum sizes of input? What are average and maximum sizes of output? What are average number of inputs in a 10-minute period?

Conversation

What applications are used and each how many times a day? Does one use specific applications at specific times? What are storage requirements (in characters) for each application?

Inquiry-Response

What applications are used and each how many times a day? Does one have specific applications at specific times? What data-bases are accessed and for which applications? What are percentage-uses of video-terminals?

Data-Entry

What databases are accessed and for which applications?

Batch

How many jobs (with descriptions) are submitted daily — types, formats, number of records, typical form and amount of output, run-time of jobs, required resources (memory, storage devices, slow peripherals), required turn-around time, modification of data-bases, best run-times?

Management Questions

What is the impact of the system not being available? Do expansion plans exist? Can access to the system be scheduled? What is the impact of undetected errors on users? Can the number of simultaneous users be limited?

Conclusion

Answers to the above questions need careful integration and balancing to arrive at a proper user-profile. In assessing available systems and letting the vendors interpret the user-needs, emphasis should be laid on capacity, performance, availability, reliability, flexibility, security and accountability, — each an important parameter in its own right.

12

DATA COMMUNICATION

Introduction

Data communication involves flow of digital signals with the help of telecommunication devices, mainly between computers or terminals or both. Its impact extend to the fields of education, industry, banking, government and business, involving such applications as on-line reservation by the airlines, buses and hotels; freight loading and wagon movement; checking of bills in industry; on-line transactions in banks; order-processing and inventory control in manufacturing industry, and so on.

Need for providing data communication in India emerged a few years ago and a beginning was made to introduce it in telephone-type circuits in the seventies. The speeds realised were up to around 2400 bits per second (BPS) for intra-city and inter-city links without resorting to any special conditioning. The number of computers in India has been increasing rapidly and quite a few are capable of supporting remote terminals. Concepts of new services, such as, digital fascimile, teletex, videotex and possibility of providing a variety of tele-processing applications make it necessary to have a close look at the data communication methods to meet both the short-term and long-term needs of the users.

Transmission Parameters

Communication lines provide a single signal path from transmitter to receiver, information being sent serially bit by bit. Due to the serial nature of the path, message control information has to be sent along the same path as the message. The direction characteristics of the line are described by such terms as simplex (one way only), half-duplex (both ways alternately) and full-duplex (both ways simultaneously). While information can be transferred in a simplex path only in one direction, half-and full-duplex lines transmit information in both directions. Care has to be taken with the half-duplex lines to avoid *contention*, i.e., both ends transmitting simultaneously and *lock-up*, i.e., both ends expecting each other to send the next message.

Asynchronous and synchronous are two main types of data transmission. In asynchronous communication, the data are sent with one character (composed of a fixed number of bits) at a time, preceded and terminated by start-bits and stop-bits for control. Such communication is commonly used with slow-speed manually operated terminals, such as, MECON terminal at Ranchi connected earlier for remote job-entry (RJE) to Regional Computer Centre, Calcutta. In synchronous communication, the message is sent as a continuous string of fixed-length characters and is started with a string of synchronisation characters used by the receiver to synchronise his clock with that of the sender. Synchronous transmission is normally done in inter-computer communication. The advantage of synchronous over asynchronous communication consists in sending more useful data-bits in a given time

The parameters of the message transmission are the direction characteristics (half- or full-duplex), the line-speed, the transmission type (synchronous or asynchronous), and the message control and code conventions expected by the receiver. These conventions are dependent on applications and manufacturers. The unit for measuring line-speed is "baud" which is the number of information-units transferred in one second. For binary information units, the baud rate is equal to the number of bits transmitted per second and can range from 110 to 50,000.

Message Switching

The 'receive' function is generally more difficult than the 'transmit' function, since the receiver decodes and interprets the bits and characters (which may have errors) received, whereas the transmitter knows the precise character-sequence sent. The ability to detect and correct errors is determined by the code-set and the transmission-discipline. The simplest error-detection available at the character level is *parity checking*, obtained by including an additional bit in each character. *Message switching* logic is used if the source and destination points are not physically connected by a communication path. The message is first transmitted to an intermediate point (usually a communication computer), and then re-transmitted to another intermediate point or the final destination.

Computers are used in communications either as switches or to control switches. In the first case, each switching computer accepts messages from data terminals and holds the records until a communication channel is available to the computer serving the message destination. In the second case, the computer controls the equipment which physically connects the origin with the destination. The subscriber then uses the end-to-end communication-channel capacity to transmit his information: voice or data.

Stored Program-Control

Switching systems, used in the exchanges, provide the user with the facility of connecting telephone, teleprinter or any communication device, to that of another user, as and when necessary. Message-switching minicomputers perform as the core of efficient communication systems and are an important in the Indian context. According to Ramani, while earlier telephone exchanges were entirely electro-mechanical, today's stored programme-control (SPC) exchanges incorporate a computer and the exchange-functions are largely determined by instructions given to the computer. An SPC exchange, for instance, has been installed at Prabhadevi in Bombay. In this exchange, a computer performs the control function, but continues to make and break ("analog") electrical paths for making connections, using relays. On the other hand, fully digital SPC exchanges convert signals to digital form and use digital circuits to set up calls between pairs of subscribers. The digital SPC exchanges have several advantages, including easy connection to digital transmission media, such as, satellite links or high-speed microwave links. An example is the SPC telex exchange in the Overseas Communication Service in Bombay in full operation for a long time.

SPC exchanges hold out many promises to Indian subscribers, such as, accurate and detailed recording and billing of calls: "tele-conferencing" (i.e., three or more people sharing a group-discussion over a distance via telephones); telephones in cars; coded control of STD calls; automatic testing of telephone equipment; abbreviated dialling for frequently used numbers; and so on.

Similar to the switching side, integrated circuits (ICs) have helped the transmission side as well. Major strides have been made in transmission by the communication satellite which can provide as many as 10,000 telephone transmission channels. A satellite can receive and re-transmit "broad-band" signals, i.e., signals carrying a large amount of information, say, for 1,000 voices. Ground equipment can combine ("multiplex") 10,000 voice signals into a broad-band signal for transmission and again separate them out ("demultiplex") on receipt. Among other advances in transmission with broad-band communication are microwave system between Bombay and Trivandrum carrying thousands of simultaneous telephone conversations, and co-axial system between Bombay and Pune for hundreds of such conversations.

User Benefits

For the common user, improved data communication means low cost, easy availability and high reliability of long-distance communication. The 'space segment' itself costs less than Rs. 10,000 per year for voice channel between two places visible to the communication satellite, that is, about eighty paise for three minutes for places separated by a few thousand miles.

In data transmission, a user's objective is to transfer and access data which are error-free, almost instantaneous and at the lowest possible cost. An optimal approach demands that incompatibilities in computer architecture, communication protocol (i.e., hardware and software linkages), peripherals and devices are to be kept to a minimum. At the same time, unplanned duplication of data-banks, uncoordinated demands for data-terminals, and circuit-terminating equipment and computers should be controlled as well. Aspects concerning reliability, availability and acceptable error-rates have also to be carefully balanced and defined within the available financial resources. All such parameters can be broadly classified as follows (according to the size of message and response time):

(a) Conversational applications, such as, airlines, bus and hotel reservation;
(b) Information retrieval, such as, bank accounts, insurance policy status and hospital information;
(c) RJE or batch processing, such as, remote card reading and access to computer at a distant end;
(d) Message switching, such as, "electronic mail" (transmission of

text, office-letters using own computer terminals and data-communication channels to a computer at the destination);

(e) Process control, such as, numerical control of machines and remote meter-readings;

(f) Inter-processor working, such as, communication between computers, programme and file sharing;

(g) Source data-entry, such as, inventory and payroll data preparation.

Conclusion

Looking into the future of tele-processing demands, Department of Electronics estimated that the data-link requirements would rise to 1600 around 1200 BPS, 325 around 2400 BPS, and 60 around 4800/9600 BPS, in 1983 from 200, 90 and 40 respectively in 1980. The actual demand has gone up much more since. The above data-channel demands do not include need of infrequently used data-links, with dialled data services. With the basic infrastructure available, the need for realising much more improved data communication services through Department of Telecommunications public-data networks is of paramount importance today. Their packet-switched public data network (PSPDN), under the name of VIKRAM Project, is gaining popularity in a large number of metropolitan cities and townships and fulfills a positive need of data transmission in the public domain.

13

COMPUTER NETWORK

Introduction

The purpose of most computer networks is to allow a fairly distributed community of users to share computer resources. The technology of distributed processing and computer networks has made it possible for computer to cease to be isolated machines, and use programmes and data stored by computers in other locations. There are quite a few types of computer networks, — caused by different types of distributed processing, different needs of users, different kinds of organisations operating the networks, and so on.

Categories of Networks

Nature of distributed processing makes for four categories of computer networks. First, geographically remote terminals and remote job-entry (RJE) stations can be connected to a central computer. Secondly, geographically remote small computers can be used for minor pre-processing tasks and input data are transferred through magnetic tapes off-line (by post or by hand) to a central computer for main processing. Thirdly, a central computer can perform major computing tasks and can have connections to smaller computers with specialised functions, such as, communication facilities and graphics. Finally, independent large computers (as "hosts") can communicate with one another, and share programmes or data. The last category of resource-sharing network of similar-computers is today the most prevalent one. Such a network was initially demonstrated in Bombay in 1980 with host systems at the Indian Institute of Science in Bangalore and the National Centre for Software Development and Computing Techniques (NCSDCT) in Bombay, among others; a number of users at these two centres utilised each other's computer with great ease for remote access and electronic messaging. The system has now caught on.

Different organisations create computer networks for meeting different needs. Some networks are built in a single corporation for a single need, such as, airlines reservations. Some corporate networks are designed for multiple applications which can share a common data-base for being cost-effective. Some large corporate networks may be designed as a general-purpose network, integrating separate networks used by the member-groups for purposes of economy and better-service. Some networks are constructed to serve groups of similar organisations, such as, banks airlines, universities, etc. These may be either general-purpose like ARPANET (connecting around 50 American universities and research institutions having dissimilar computers) or special-purpose like SWIFT electronic fund transfer network (connecting around 15 American and European banks having similar computers from UNISYS) or SITA airlines passenger reservation networks connecting all the major airlines of the world. A value-added computer provides a commercial network with leased lines to serve many customers in selected geographical areas. TYMNET and TELENET are examples of private corporations offering competitive service in the USA. Common carriers, such as, telephone companies, can provide nation-wide data-networks of different types, designed to move packets of data between subscribers in a fraction of a second. For instance, digital PCM trunks operate at speeds of millions of bits per second in North America. Multiple common carriers can also interconnect their data-networks. Finally, networks capable of carrying high band-width (i.e., a group of consecutive frequencies constituting a band) traffic are coming into existence for copying machines transmitting to copying machines, tele-conferencing, etc.

Proliferation of Networks

Computer networks are proliferating at a high rate throughout the world and becoming a powerful force in both private and public sectors, nationally as well as internationally. This recent upsurge of activity is due to three main technological trends: greatly increased reliability of computers; availability of low-priced minicomputers suitable for carrying out most functions needed to operate a network; and major cost-saving improvements in communications technology.

Many specialised computer networks have come up, operating more economically than the general-purpose networks described above. This is due to the fact that the variety of large computers, minicomputers, microcomputers, terminals and peripherals — needed to be connected into distributed systems — is too great for any general-purpose network. Again, some systems demand fast response-times or brief interactive transmission, while others can accept delayed but cheap message delivery or batch-transmission of lengthy records and files. Most computer manufactures have network architectures for their particular equipment, such as, the architectures of the Digital Equipment Corporation (DECNET), International Business Machines (IBM-SNA), and Sperry-Univac (DCA). Some networks are designed for specific applications, such as, international electronic funds transfer or airlines reservation. Some networks handle only messages shorter than a certain length, thus considerably simplifying their mechanism.

Some networks are designed to interconnect computers but not terminals, with correct protocols programmed into the software. Some other networks handle specific types of terminals, such as, telex-machines or inexpensive machines which conform to definite protocols. An example is AT & T's Transaction Network System, permitting deployment of telephone devices along with a small display, keyboard and magnetic card-reader. Another example is the British Prestel network (originally called Viewdata) using conventional television sets at home for broadcasting data (comparable to Teletext in Europe).

Network Structures

Computer networks may be viewed as in Fig. 13.1, composed of nodes, — with circuits, channels or links connecting them. A node may vary from a small amount of fixed hardware logic to one of the major computers. Nodes are used to support network connections as "store and forward" computers (i.e., to receive and store messages, and to despatch them along one of the several different routes); as "concentrators" (i.e., to take input characters from a number of slow terminals and assemble them into blocks); and as attachment points for major computers. Physical details of circuits, channels or links (comprising lines, microwave-links, radio-links, cable television or satellites) are of little consequence for computer networks. Relevant parameters for a channel are its maximum data-rate, error characteristics and direction-limitations.

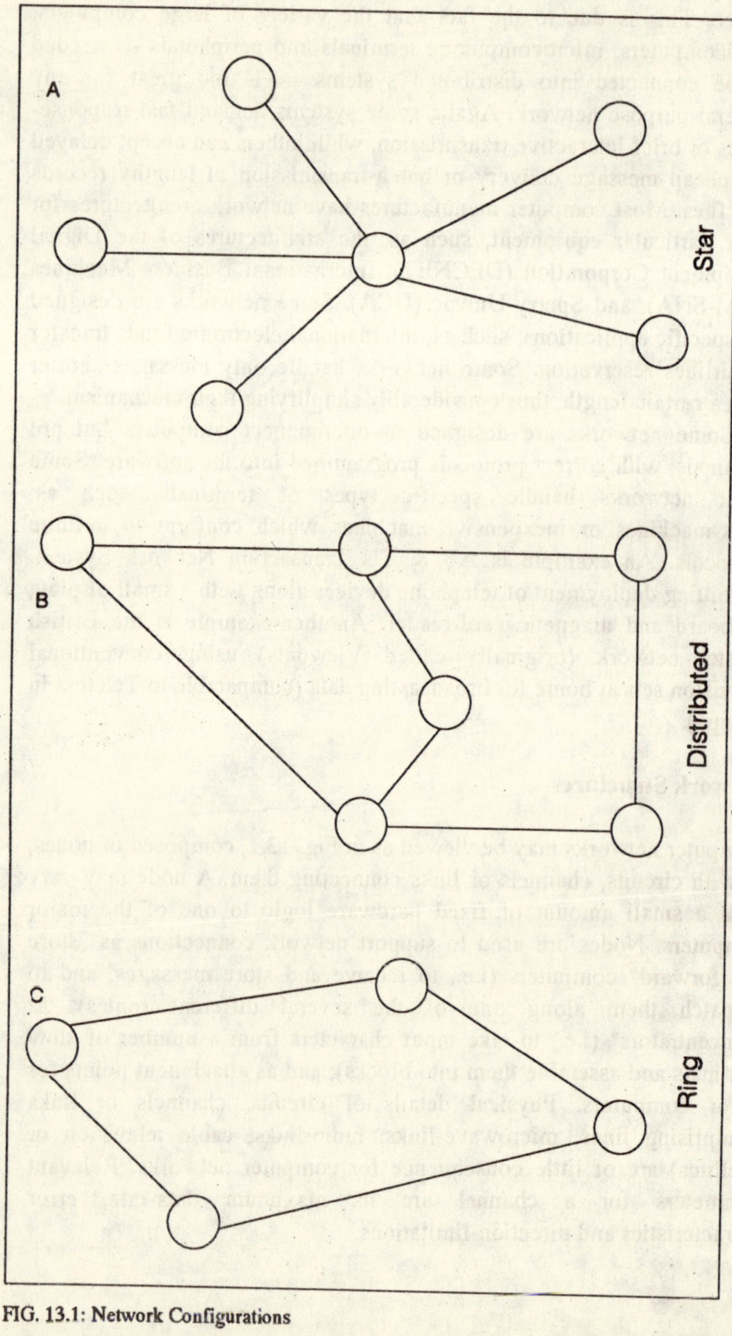

FIG. 13.1: Network Configurations

In each computer network, there is a control mechanism by which the connected computers and terminals share the use of the band-width. A simple control method is multiplexing, i.e., transmission of a number of messages simultaneously over a single circuit. While data-rate in earlier networks using space-division multiplexing was limited to 9600 bits per second (BPS) or so, modern systems with high band-widths employ frequency-division multiplexing (FDM) as well as time-division multiplexing (TDM). In the former, there is a portion of the frequency spectrum of the medium assigned to each point-to-point connection, whereas in the latter, a time-interval is so assigned. Both FDM and TDM techniques are widely used in long-distance transmission.

Early Efforts in India

A local area network (LAN) is a data communication system for interconnecting computers and terminals that are within one building or in several buildings in close proximity (up to a few kilometres). LANS are desirable for the same reason as distributed networks are: they make possible locally the sharing of resources (such as, computing power, data-bases and switching services) by users at diverse locations. The advantage is that it is feasible to implement band-widths or data-rates of several megabits per second (MBPS) in local networks. These higher data-rates are realised in paired, twisted or coaxial cables and in fibre-optic media. Examples of early local "star" networks were the clusters of B-1955 minicomputers around the large B-6806 system as the host computer in TISCO and TELCO (at Jamshedpur and Pune). Here the data and file transfers could take place in any job-operation from any computer.

NCSDCT has earlier developed a close-coupled network (CCN) using a few TDC-316 computers located at IIT, Bombay for further development of software. Another important effort was to develop a "star" network at IIT, Kanpur, with the IBM-1800, TDC-316 and DEC-1090 as the three outer nodes and a microcomputer MICRO-78 (based on INTEL-8080 chip) as the switching centre. The advantages derived by linking all the machines in a computer network were an all-round increase in the computing facility. In particular, the IBM-1800 devices of a card-punch and 7-track magnetic tape unit were made available to DEC-users over the network and old 7-track tapes could be easily converted to 9-track tapes used in the DEC system.

Further, the IBM-1800 provided extensive real-time control facilities and hybrid computing, and these resources were available to a wide class of users over the network. Again, the TDC-316 was used as a RJE station for the DEC system. Finally, the TDC-316 was also used as "Concentrator" for terminals, thus allowing for easy system expansion.

Current Status

Networks, involving similar or disparate computers, have come a long way in India. CMC Ltd., has introduced INDONET which operates with IBM clusters or VAX/PDP clusters at Bombay, Delhi, Calcutta, Madras and Hyderabad, along with many extended terminals for distributed processing in other cities. This is typically a wide-area network (WAN) and provides regional software services.

There are a number of other WANs in operation today. The principal one is the National Informatics Centre Networks (NICNET), having regional centres at Delhi, Bhubaneshwar, Pune and Hyderabad; State and Union Territory capital centres at 32 cities; and district centres in some 461 districts. This is the premiere hierarchical network for the Centre, States and districts for improved information exchange, uniformity of data structure, use of mathematical modelling and, as a whole, efficient Central and State planning.

The other WAN is ONGCNET with the nodal centre at Dehradun, and regional centres at Bombay, Baroda, Calcutta, Nazira (near Jorhat) and Madras. The regional computer centres do routine seismic processing of the data gathered from the line-kilometres of the off-shore and on-land survey ships and survey-teams respectively, leaving the non-routine processing to the Dehradun IBM Computer.

The metropolitan area network (MAN) is confined within a city, such as, NIC's Computer Centres networked for the ASIAD games at different stadiums in and around Delhi city, or, Neyville Lignite Corporation's Computer Centres networked within the Neyville township.

Conclusion

India today is seeing the emergency of a large number of computer networks of varying capacity for resource-sharing (mostly disc-space and printers) and spread over long distances, starting often with LAN.

Indian banks are joining the SWIFT (Society of Worldwide Inter-bank Financial Telecommunication) network, and Indian Airlines and Air India are already members of the SITA (Society for International Traffic in Airways) network on a global basis. The education field has received a filip with the education and research network (ERNET) operating among the five Indian Institutes of Technology, Tata Institute of Fundamental Research, Indian Institute of Science and National Centre for Software Technology. Most of widespread networks are operating through INSAT 1-C satellite whose available channel capacity seems to be one of the limiting factors for the growth of networks.

14

PATTERNS OF INFORMATION MANAGEMENT

Introduction

All modern complex organisations deal with men, material, machinery and, of course, money. This was postulated long ago by Forrester who added information to the list. Information is as vital a component to an organisation as the other four, and is as crucial to its continued viability as the others put together. The analogy is to the genetic code carried by our chromosomes in a highly formal manner, — the sheer regularity and carrying forward is essential for the organism to survive. Any departure can only lead to a cancerous decay process.

Human Analogy

Before we look at our complex organisations managing their information, let us see the human being managing his. An average human being has a fairly healthy system working and maintaining itself with the help of food, drinks and respiratory inputs changing and metabolising their content into matter and energy, and segregating and eliminating the less desirable outputs. In this process, the body continually interacts with the environment and has devised a highly ingenious was to deal with all information. The five senses are in "contact" with outside world, collecting information and sending them to the brain through the nervous channels. The brain processes them and passes control instructions to the motor mechanisms of hand or foot or heart in what usually is a "timely" response. But the body is highly selective in what passes to the brain and what need not. If the sleeping person touches fire, his autonomous reflexes would prompt him to shift his burning limbs, — without the restful brain ever realising it or "remembering" it later. It is obvious that the human body deals with information hierarchically and only the most essential information reaches the highest decision-making quarters, namely, the brain.

Do our organisations have a similar hierarchy of action? We can first describe an organisation's supervisors and clerks as the operational level; divisions, departments and profit-centres as the managerial level; and the top echelon of executives as the corporate or strategic level. Activity-wise, then, the operational level executes decisions and use resources in conformity with rules; the managerial level makes decisions, sets rules and allocates resources, besides measuring performance; and the strategic level sets objectives and determines resources for the organisation.

Hierarchy of Information Flow

Looking at the hierarchy of information now, clearly the information is immediate and real-time, limited to work-centres at the operational level. It is short-term and internal to the organisation at the managerial level. It is long-term and external to the organisation at the corporate level. Nature of information would be precise, readily available and tailor-made for the problems at the bottom; historical and fairly accurate and integrated at the middle; and predictive and imprecise at the top. Use of information would vary from just following directions, through administrative persuasions, to being creatively analytical at the three levels.

It is important to notice that types of decisions that are made at bottom level are highly repetitive and structured, almost "programmed". At the middle, they are still repetitive but not programmed any more. At the top, they are one-time kind and totally unstructured, based largely on qualitative information, as distinct from the accuracy of quantitative information at the supervisory level. In fact, while it is possible to "optimise" one's decision at the lowest level with a judicious use of resources subject to the available constraints, this is possible distinctly less and less as one moves up the hierarchy, and it becomes only a question of compromise among a number of competing and conflicting factors quite sub-optimally, best known as "satisficing".

Selectivity of Information

Having noticed these hierarchical variations, any judicious management of information has to recognise the cardinal principle that information has better be selective at the top in order not to deluge it or, in other words, what body does for the brain is just right to save the top from excessive information. Such considerations have led to a fascinating hypothesis: information is really the knowledge of disorganisation, or, of what is not going right within the organisation, especially as one moves up from routine data full of certainty to a flexible unstructured decision-making in a highly uncertain environment.

Does it add a new angle to handling of information and its selective use in decision-making? Single tasks or operations can cope with all the data available. But in the higher echelons, the whole organisation looms more and more in the view, and a ruthless, limitless process of "eliminating" garbage (does not the body do it?) is the only sane way for the top to confine its attention only to what is erring, i.e., departures from the set norms and targets, exceptions which bring out non-obedience of the rules and, generally, all deviations and aberrations to be rectified and to be put back to the right path.

Corollary Principles

A number of fairly significant principles follow from the above. First of all, since the top manager — with his understanding of the above — would no longer thump the table and ask for "all the information" (since he cannot handle it in the first place), there is a logical case for *delegation.* It lets decisions being taken where it is due based on information available in more details and, in the bargain, satisfy the subordinate's ego. Secondly, it helps to create far less file-bound "cases". More important, the spirit of delegation can go all the way down in terms of only aggregated, reduced or processed information being put up above which satisfy pre-defined yardsticks. For instance, certain "tolerance" limits can be easily specified (body does it again!) and what is controllable can be given attention to, without the wasting of time on what is uncontrollable.

The above enunciation militates against the age-old adage "information is power", and perhaps justly so. If the pathological craving to be "overinformed" is got rid of and the fear of "uninformed" decisions overcome, where is the need for clinging on to every opportunity for monopolising information?

Operational and Managerial Levels

It is precisely at the operational level that computers have helped the most by mechanising routine structured data, and that is how it should be. A lathe operator's acceptance or rejection of a turned-out part, is dependent upon the catalogue and part number, design-specifications, tolerance limits for different design-parameters, and a few other factors. These factors are specified according to prior directions, deterministic in nature and hence easily "programmable" onto a computer. The routine decisions can then be spelt out by the computer and acceptance or rejection takes place mechanically. A bank-clerk's honouring or refusing a cheque is another instance of operational level activity, where the verification of name and account number, amount at credit, signature, etc., can be smoothly entrusted to a computer, — with no qualitative factor involved. A foreman from stores department places a new purchase order for material, based on the re-order level and re-order quantity. The decision rules are so well-formalised that TISCO could use even its second-generation computers to trigger *automatically* new purchase-orders without any human intervention.

At the managerial level, the decisions may veer round a product mix. In an agricultural implements company, the capacity of different machines to produce these implements was determined, grades of skill and number of skilled personnel were assessed, and decision-rules were worked out according to a mathematical programming model for an optimal production plan every month according to upper and lower bounds of known current market-demand for each implement. Quite often, these computer-based decisions were sufficient for managers to control production levels for the best profit-margins. Again, layout of a plant is a typical management-level decision needing many administrative considerations, but a general guideline to locate the physical facilities can be worked out with the help of computer. Recruitment of a group of staff-members can be considerably facilitated by a computerised data-bank on existing personnel (complete with skills, qualifications, experience and career-directions) and identifying the specific gaps to be filled by matching requirement with the availability of outside skills. Designing an advertisement campaign is a smaller management exercise based on both historical and current data on product-profile and customer-profile on computer, and then using qualitative judgement for identifying the best campaign strategy. The point to be noted is that computer usage can be fairly selective in all the above situations, with many interfaces between the human decision and mechanised information.

Conclusion

At the strategic level, decision of an altogether new plant or introduction of a new production technology can all demand corporate attention. In the corporate planning group for TISCO, important decisions were arrived at on the replacement of old plant, establishment of new product-plant and adoption of a new steel-making technology all of which were essentially questions of compromises among a number of competing, conflicting and exceedingly complex factors. Again, in the execution of a collaboration or negotiation of an industry-level labour contract, the role of a computer can only be marginal (in the form of predicting forecasts on implications of adopting different strategies), — with the onus of responsibility lying with the corporate brain alone, as the body will do in carrying out all its "intelligent" activities!

15

EFFECTIVE MANAGEMENT INFORMATION SYSTEM

Introduction

Utility of information in decision-making has always been realised by management. The increasing complexity in modern organisations, growing volume of data ascertained on a large number of parameters and the timeliness of critical decisions on many crucial problems are all phenomena of today, which often necessitate the use of computer. If management information system (MIS) can be defined as the essential capability of access, storage, processing and retrieval of all important information for control, monitoring and planning purposes, — such functions are admirably carried out for small organisations manually. It is only the volume of data, number of calculations and frequency of output reports which decide whether or not a computer need be used for MIS.

Responsibility Levels for Information

Managers at different levels of responsibility hierarchy use information in characteristically different ways. The pre-occupation with day-to-day routine information at the operational level yield grounds to more semi-routine handling of information at managerial levels with less stringent rules for decision-making. At still higher corporate levels, the quality of information is only partly quantitative and the environment of decision-making is a highly flexible one. But at all levels, it is a cardinal management principle to concentrate upon only selective information on "as required" basis. This saves time and prevents a deluge of data which management could get "snowed under".

Let us look at an effective MIS from the above point of view. Most activities (at any level of responsibility mentioned above) can be assigned a pre-set norm or standard value (or budgeted figure) for the way the management expects it to be performed. In real practice, however, quite a few activities are not performed in an ideal manner due to the prevailing circumstances. It is only the deviations for those activities — of the way they have been actually performed from the way they should have been performed — that are of interest to management control for taking corrective action. It is therefore an essential function of MIS to monitor such differences and feed them back to decision-makers, as illustrated in the Fig. 15.1.

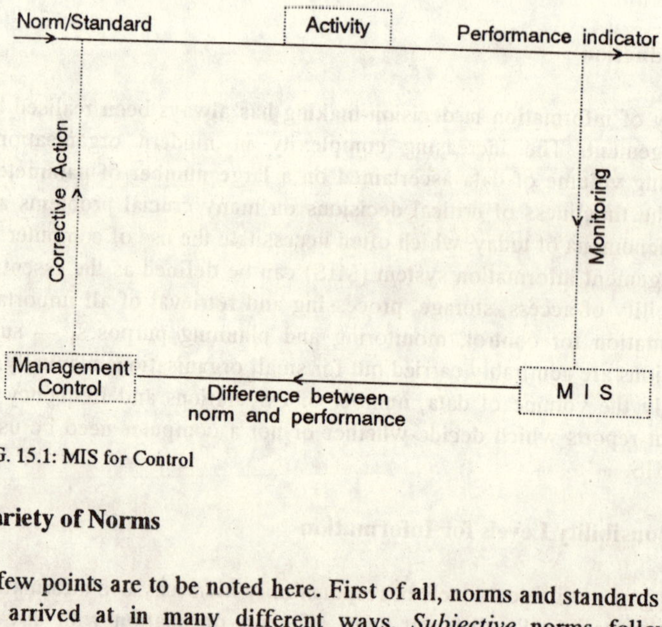

FIG. 15.1: MIS for Control

Variety of Norms

A few points are to be noted here. First of all, norms and standards can be arrived at in many different ways. *Subjective* norms follow a decision-maker's own predilection perhaps followed by mature experience. *Historical* norms fall back upon past records while *analogical* norms draw from the experience of other organisations performing similar activities. *Engineering* norms are outcome of time-and-motion study and *mathematical* norms are derived by using calculations in performing specific activities. The commonly used norm is the *statistical* one which is assembling a large amount of performance data and then finding out the average (mean, median or mode) value, after eliminating the extreme readings. Secondly, the differences between norms and actual performance indicators need not be fed back in their entirety. There can be differences which are small enough to be ignored and a prior management effort to define such tolerable differences can help considerably in reducing the volume of MIS reports. For instance, value-differences in inventory-items were watched every month, as compared to the beginning of financial year, in a large production organisation and were discussed in monthly production-meetings with departmental heads. Once the idea of tolerable differences was accepted with management concurrence, the inventory-value reports became small and very manageable ones. Thirdly, there are certain differences which are controllable, in contrast to certain others which are not so. It would be a futile management exercise to concentrate on the uncontrollable differences at the expense of the controllable ones. For instance again, the inventory-value reports mentioned above were divided into three parts, showing differences due to change in prices in the market, those due to introduction of pre-planned plant and machinery, and those due to change in the stocks going up in the stores department. Obviously, management could do little for the first two types of differences, while the third one demanded all their attention for control purposes. Finally, corrective action is deemed as the decision-making to rectify the performance problems and get back to the originally viewed norms as far as possible. In the above process, MIS is a help but not the final arbiter, as there may be some qualitative factors which are also necessary by way of value-judgement. In TISCO, once the charges levied by a bulk-supplier of some raw material were found very high and were thrown up in MIS as a disparate amount compared to the long-standing supplier-rates. Top management took an unusual corrective action, viz., admitted the high charges, on the value-judgement that the specified supplier, having helped TISCO in the latter's lean days, now needed bailing out from certain industrial- relation problems.

Hierarchy of Outcomes

MIS — with or without computer — should provide for a hierarchy of outcomes. In routine data-handling situations where rules are unambiguous, it can generate almost automatically corrective actions (e.g., placing of purchase orders, etc.). In less routine cases, it can furnish regular exception-based reports (e.g., production scheduling, machine-loading, etc.). At a still higher level of responsibility it can supply specific reports only on demand (e.g., resource analysis and cost allocation for a project management system, etc.). These outcomes apart, MIS can be geared to maintain an information-bank which can be delved into whenever necessary, like the using of a library resource. For computer-based MIS, the first three actions can simply be performed in a batch mode, while the updating of a data-bank and selective retrieval of information are best done on a time-sharing mode.

Implementation of MIS must begin at the output end, by ascertaining what do the user decision-makers do need by way of selective information. Such a requirement analysis can shed new light on many angles of information-needs which are not — or inadequately — catered for in the current handling of information. After requirement analysis has been done, it should become clear as to what items of processed information would be required, by whom, at what level, at what frequency (periodic or ad-hoc or one-time), on what formats and with what details. The last point about details is important as there has to be a balance between the desire for details and the expediency of data-collection.

Study of Information Flow

The next stage is to identify the input data which, when processed and reduced, could give rise to the needed outputs. At the input end, assessment of sources to generate data, agencies to collect data, frequency and format for collection, and level of details are all important considerations. Thereafter, design of permanent and current data-files have to be taken care of, manually or through computer, by adequately trained manpower and processing has to be tried out with sample data and dummy format first. Final implementation should be gone ahead only after successful conducting of trial runs.

If data-volume, calculation-complexity and output-frequency for MIS warrant computerisation, conceptualisation of computer-based system is needed at an early stage. This has to be done after a full scale study of the physical flow of information and in the flow-charts for computer-based MIS, enough provisions have to be built up for integration, modification and any other rationalisation of physical information-flow. The system design should specify through the flow-charts the necessary linkages and validation procedures, and envisage clearly the type and extent of codification needed. The programming action is then to follow in the shape of edit, update, sort, merge, calculate and print programmes, to name an important few. The designed system needs careful desk-check (to see if all the desired logic has gone into it) and thereafter the trial-run should be obtained on computer with test-data. Final implementation may have to wait the above steps being repeatedly performed to achieve complete confidence in the computer-based system.

Conclusion

A few important factors are to be noted for any MIS exercise. First, no MIS is better or worse than the data it is supposed to cater for. Therefore, data-validation procedures (both manual and computer-based) are to be rigorously tested and implemented. Secondly, data-homogeneity has to be ensured to prevent unevenness in data to creep in from different data-sources. Thirdly, the authenticity of both source for data-generation and agency for data-collection is a crucial factor to build up trust in MIS. Fourthly, user education and training has a lot to do with the success of MIS. A "number-taker" of railway wagons in the marshalling yard or a "writer" of crime-records in the police-station or a "munshi" at the colliery-pithead to track the gang- performance below are the pillars of MIS and their familiarity as well as involvement are of paramount importance. Fifthly, data are to be regarded as a consumer non-durable commodity, — to be preserved only till required and to be weeded out thereafter to free their storage-space. Finally, the involvement of corporate management is very desirable right from the decision to implement MIS, to approve the system-design and to clear the test-runs up to the stage of monitoring what has been implemented. The *sine-qua-non* of MIS is its practical usage and any changed perception by the user management must get reflected in it with the least possible delay.

16

EMERGING TRENDS IN MANAGEMENT INFORMATION SYSTEM

Introduction

Useful information had often the dubious distinction of being confused with the raw, unprocessed data. The element of selectivity and aggregation in the data captured in greenfield condition is, although very desirable for higher-level decision-making, not always so obvious. New trends in Management Information System (MIS) have now happily coincided with the ethos behind the Shannon and MaCullogh's mathematical theory of information: the knowledge of disorganisation in an organisation can only be termed information; whatever activities are in a steady, pre-determined state do not give rise to any information.

Clerical Levels for Automated Control

The philosophy behind the above adage can be easily understood if one analyses the decision-making process itself. In any modern and complex organisation, hierarchies are clearly discernible: supervisory or clerical, middle management and top administration. Decisions made at supervisory or clerical levels (for topping "heat" in a steel-melting shop; distributing medicines in an outpatient department; or reconciling credits with debits in a bank) all deal with routine data under well-set rules, instructions and precedents. The data are essentially quantitative and quite short-term. The decision-making environment is pretty definitive and methods for optimisation (to achieve highest production or quickest dispensation of services to patients) can be applied well.

The above level of activities were computerised first in the last couple of decades and there has been no looking back ever since. In fact, the future trends are definitely towards *automated control* at this level, — where processes or services are designed to feed readings from instrument panels to computers which, in turn, draw upon the built-in logic and decision-rules and pass on (without any human intervention) the final instructions to control and regulate the process or the service.

There are examples galore of the automated control in the industry. In Indian steel industry, the nova and eclipse series of computers have been put to use at the steel meeting shops of Rourkela Steel Plant to monitor the end-point carbon and temperature of the incoming pig iron, and combine these readings with the polyvac laboratory analysis of the impurities to activate directly the blowing pressure and angle of the oxygen lance, — so that the right grade of steel can be made from out of the pig iron. Computer-aided manufacturing (CAM) is a recent trend in using automated programming to instruct the job-shop machines for carrying out milling and surfacing operations, apart from the simpler lathe-machine functions. Among the service organisations abroad, automated cash-dispensation is done by inserting cheques (with optically or magnetically sensitive characters) inside the public slot mechanisms connected remotely to the bank. In Indian service organisations, automated control has just started making its appearance, — notable among them being the Overseas Communication Service, where computer control is being used to press in service (or release) free (or occupied) trunk routes for transmitting calls to multiple destinations all over the world, and to indicate visibly the state of occupancy of every single route.

Middle-Management Decisions

Decision made at the middle management levels (for coordinating steel-making shop production in step with the blast-furnace productivity and output frequency; allocating available hospital facilities according to the surgical clinical, radiological and pathological needs; or deciding on the quantum of loans and advances to be disbursed in a bank's branches (with or without collateral support) are distinctive in their being semi-routine in character, — where rules have to be combined with managerial discretions. The data can be partly quantitative and partly qualitative, involving a medium-term time-frame. The environment is fraught with risk and scope of clear-cut optimal solutions becomes increasingly unclear.

The above level of activities came for computerisation much later than the supervisory or clerical activities of a repetitive or accounting kind. The future trend points towards *operator guidance* at this level, — with computer being fed data by men and providing, in turn, a set of alternatives ready-reckoner tables which can be conveniently used by men to arrive at appropriate decisions.

There are many noteworthy examples of operator guidance in the Indian industry. Most on-line production planning and control, material management, and job scheduling systems on computer are of operator guidance kind, needing timely and effective human intervention both at the data-input end, and at the decision-making end. Among service organisations, Air India has now introduced on-line passenger-reservation system — with computer maintaining a data-bank for all flights and intending passengers, and linking them with current cancellations or changes as well as fresh intentions arising from passengers — so that operators can provide an up-to-date reservation service to all passengers. A similar operator guidance system is the Indian Railways plan for an on-line freight-control and wagon movement system, — to monitor movement, loading, unloading and idling of all railway wagons so as to increase their effective utilisation by better planning through human intervention. An interesting application in a public utility like a dam is the monitoring of past meteorological data, current rainfall, tributary-flow, evaporation-loss and catchment-reserve data; linking them with the demand pattern for agricultural as well as hydroelectric water-needs; and providing computerised guidance to engineer-operators for adequate release of water through sluice-gates on a weekly or fortnightly basis. This approach was tried with the Nagarjunasagar Dam operation with very successful results.

Top-Level Decisions

Decisions made at the top administration levels (for deciding on amalgamation or diversification in a firm's activities; planning new hospitals with extended facilities; or opening new branches for a bank) are fairly non-routine in character, being almost entirely discretionary and seldom following any set decision-rules. Data used are largely qualitative, involving long-term time-horizons. Decision-making environment is usually entirely uncertain, with an optimisation efforts being replaced by finding the acceptable satisfaction in the decisions to be made.

Although the top level of administration has come last in using computerisation, — this has been one of the most fruitful areas. Due to the very nature of non-repetitive data and unstructured decision-making, computer applications have to be highly selective. The trends are to provide *decision support* with an integrated MIS and other reports based on aggregation (for routine cases) and exception (for non-routine case). The earlier hypothesis about "information on disorganisation", as it were, comes more fully at play than at any other lower levels. Due to sheer pressure, the top executives cannot cope with "all the information at one's command" but necessarily a much reduced and filtered flow.

Indian examples of very selective MIS for decision support are many, including public administration, such as, Department of Steel and Mines, and Chemicals and Fertilisers which are mainly manual. The current trend in using computer for selective storage and retrieval of information, called from integrated files or data-bases, has started showing up in, for instance, Tata Steel in the private sector and BHEL and Hindustan Zinc in the public sector. A very significant decision support system is use of computer in aid of corporate planning. Formulation of possible corporate strategies, evaluating the various alternatives and arriving at the most preferred strategy can be immensely helped by computer-based simulation technique. The other usage of computer for corporate planning is to provide the return-on-investment (ROI) for various projects conceived, so that the best portfolio can be selected. ROI calculations can be based on simple project pay-back, discounted cash flow (for arriving at the present worth), the simple rate of return or the internal rate of return, — all on the computer, as done during the Tata Steel modernisation plan.

Conclusion

The interesting now development taking place abroad is to go in for *expert systems* which could use the entire knowledge-base and provide almost tailor-made decisions. For such services as medical ones, diagnostic aids combined with the past pathological history, can lead on to therapeutic prescriptions after searching through a vast array of medical facts and syndromes, and after matching with drug directories, among others. Such knowledge-based systems would eventually combine the automated control at the execution level and operator guidance at the monitoring level, — and lead to far more efficient decision support systems using the "expert" status of the computer. Fifth-generation computer development plans in both Japan and the USA are poised for this kind of break-through.

PART TWO

REAL-LIFE APPLICATIONS

17

ACCOUNTING SYSTEMS

Introduction

Perhaps the most popular, and historically the first, applications on the computer have been the accounting systems. Beginning from the common practice of double-entry book-keeping in main accounts up to the most elaborate inter-bank reconciliations of global fund transfers, computers have played an increasingly important role in handling accounting systems, in different organisations. A little less significant role played by the computers has been to elevate these routine clerical systems into computer-aided decision-making at senior managerial levels. Some of these systems can be examined in the areas of financial management, personnel management, materials management, maintenance management, project management, production management and marketing management.

Financial Management

At the routine level, inputs to a clerical system and transactions revenue or capital in nature, which involve all financial instruments or ready cash. The actual transaction may include receipts, issues, returns, rejections, interests, taxes, depreciations, and so on.

Computers are used by user organisations (by each division, if the organisation is large) — to prepare ledgers under several hundred or thousand account heads. These ledgers or sub-ledgers lead on to jounalisation of entries and, in turn, to simple income and expenditure statements for service organisations. For commercial organisations, profit and loss statements and balance sheets are derived further apart from loan accounts, fixed deposit accounts and tax registers.

At the decision-making level, managers need to carry out cash-flow planning (with adjustments between cash in-flows and out-flows); credit planning (to stretch to the limit the organisation's credit-giving on services rendered or products sold); profit planning (by forecasting potential profits); and infrastructure planning (on the investment into infrastructure facilities). Computer-aided decision-making can help as follows through regular MIS reporting:

(a) *by retrieving selective information*

- Receivable statements
- Payable statements
- Ageing reports for outstanding debtors

(b) *by retrieving analysed information*

- Management ratios
- Management trends and patterns
- Management forecasts

(c) *by retrieving inter-related information*

- Linking finance with inventory
- Linking finance with marketing
- Linking finance with production costs
- Linking finance with personnel

(d) *by retrieving integrated information*

- Total credit
- Total profit (product-wise)
- Total tax liability

Personnel Management

The personnel accounting systems involve clerical level transactions shown in Table 17.1.

The clerical systems cover the employee services which form the staple of personnel management. The data can be stored for computer-aided decision-making as follows:

(a) *Post recruitment financial planning*: for salary scales, allowances, provident fund recoveries, increments, promotions, rewards, bonus, incentives, etc.

(b) *Pre-retirement financial planning*: for pension, gratuity, annuity, insurance entitlements and commutations.

TABLE 17.1: Personnel Accounting System Involve Clerical Level

	System	*Permanent/current transactions*		*Outputs*
(a)	Payroll	Name, designation, pay, allowances	Leave/absentee memo, presentee statement	Salary slip Cheque Leave register
(b)	Provident Fund	Rates, interests	Changes, if any	Provident fund schedules (annual, monthly, individual, collective)
(c)	Loans and Advances	Loans recovery rates	Changes, if any	Recovery schedules (as above)
(d)	Income tax	Recovery rate	Changes, if any	Tax schedules (as above)

Some specific cases of evaluated information can be mentioned here. In the Air Force, 400 cases of leave without pay were selected as exception-based reports centre-wise, trade-wise, grade-wise, age group-wise, etc., amongst the airmen, to assess the reasons for such leaves and their remedies. As regards analysed information, wage-board negotiations can often be helped by analysing the financial implications of the trade-union demands on one side and the management offers on the other, before finding the final compromise. Such efforts bore fruit in the cases of Andhra Pradesh State Road Transport Corporation (APSRTC) and Indian Oxygen. Regarding integrated information, possibility of policy-making was enhanced by computer-based promotion-planning for SAIL and BHEL, and transfer planning for MP State teachers, after using both financial and non-financial data.

Materials Management

As will be illustrated in Chapter 18, materials control is built on the materials accounting system. The inputs to such a system can comprise material receipts, issues, their rates, inspection notes, return notes and so on. The clerical outputs from the computer can be priced-store ledger, stock purchase registers, purchase debit/credit notes, purchase bifurcation by purchase codes, etc.

The purchase data base can be built up, for the vendors, commodities, quality of supply, timeliness of supply, rejections, etc. Combining the physical data with the financial data, inventory database can also be created, alongwith analytically defined re-order levels and re-order quantities. These data bases can lead on to purchase system (from automatic requisitions to orders), vendor rating, slow-moving analysis, dead-stock analysis, age analysis, fast-moving analysis, cost-criticality analysis, etc.

Maintenance Management

Maintenance accounting system is part of a larger approach to computerisation of maintenance management. The financial data needed for controls are the direct cost of maintaining each equipment or facility; the value of inventories and procured materials for maintenance; cost of manhours spent including overtime; maintenance contribution to the unit manufacturing cost; etc.

While accounting for break-down maintenance is difficult except after the event, the preventive maintenance costs can be computed for planning purposes for, say, "re-lining" blast furnaces of the steel plant under SAIL; dry-dock maintenance for Mazgaon docks; shut-down of the Madras thermal refinery; etc., which have all been attempted in practice. Outputs in terms of resource levelling reports, manpower cost reports, excess stock reports, surplus reports, etc., can contribute to managerial control of maintenance expenditure craft-wise, equipment-wise and facility-wise.

Project Management

Project accounting system comprises the expenditure and revenue items of any project, including the cost of direct labour, direct material, indirect labour and material, other overheads, and any revenues earned. These apart, capital budgetting can be an important aspect of project accounting, involving capital funding and investment.

Combining physical data with financial data, project accounting system can be elevated into providing support for decision-making to management as follows:

(a) *Project Selection*

- Financial appraisal (present net worth discounted cashflow)
- Resource Appraisal

(b) *Project Monitoring*

- Project schedule (including cost under-run and over-run for critical path analysis)
- Schedule monitoring (cost revision)

(c) *Project Performance*

- Objectives, targets, achievements

Production Management

Production accounting forms only a miniscule part of the vast area of production management. These are primarily the cost data and includes the direct labour, direct material, indirect material and labour, and other overheads like the project management, but covering much wider span. The individual cost data can extend to a large number of production items and figure in as many accounts. There can be also a few control accounts for allocation purposes and eventual transfer to the financial accounts.

On-Line Transaction Processing (OLTP), which allows data-logging direct into the CPU from the keyboard and interaction with the CPU for instruction-transmission and control, has become an integral part of production management in a number of industries. While these relate to the conversion rates, fields, ratios and rejection percentages in the process industry and bill-of-material explosion in the engineering industry, on-line help for the cost data — which come much later in any case — is not yet feasible to a great extent.

Cost data relating to the work-in-progress inventory and finished goods inventory are part of the industrial scene. Computer-aided accounting in these two areas has become established in some professionally run industries.

Marketing Management

Major inputs for the marketing accounting system can be from the sales onwards. Beginning with finished goods notes, inspection notes and railway receipt notes for despatch, the computer can help in sales invoicers, sales registers and sales debit/credit notes.

At a decision-making level, the above may generate periodic MIS reports as follows:

(a) Linkage between sales invoicing and order processing systems, so that the placing of an order can be followed up to the maturing of the order and despatch of the product or delivery of the service, involving financial data with physical data;
(b) Sales monitoring, spread over a large number of sales depots, often in a network like TISCONET or SAILNET;
(c) Credit monitoring, involving (i) introduction of new items, (ii) bulk-purchase incentives, (iii) lifting of the accumulated stock, and (iv) involuntary credit;
(d) Cash-flow monitoring, arising out of cash-sales and credit-sales.

While marketing is a long-term strategy for sales and production, marketing accounting system is essentially keeping track of the expenses of various promotional moves, advertisement campaign, incentive schemes, reward systems, and so on. Watching actual expenditure against targets is the common financial exercise although monitoring the financial achievement of the marketing exercise can be a distant dream.

Conclusion

For some time now, computer-aids are available for the accounting systems in the form of available application packages which are (i) menu-driven, (ii) user-friendly and user-oriented, (iii) simple to use, (iv) fast and accurate, (v) secure through passwords, (vi) with auto-check for data-protection, (vii) with internal locking, (viii) with on-line validations for data-entry, (ix) with on-line query facility for any ledger accounts, and (x) flexible for enhancement. Some software vendors, like Tata Consultancy Services (TCS), have been pioneers with MASTERKEY and PRISM packages in the management areas described earlier, and the market is decidedly supportive of the users to a large extent.

18

MATERIALS CONTROL

Introduction

Handling of materials in most large organisations (whether industrial enterprises like a steel plant or public sector utilities like a state electricity board) has two important characteristics. First, the accounting procedures for procurement and consumption of materials are usually well laid down due to their cash implications. Secondly, the volume of data, arising out of materials transactions, tend to be large. Both these characteristics have been responsible for introducing computerisation in many other areas (like payroll, or financial systems), as computers serve best when logic is standardised and data-volume is large as well as repetitive. It is no wonder that materials handling departments (including stores and purchase) in most large organisations have been among the fore-runners of computer usage in India, coming after the accounts and finance departments.

In its essence, materials accounting consists of only the accounting operations for the materials received by the store, issues made by the store, recording these transactions in a stores ledger (with or without prices), and valuing the closing stock at the end of the accounting period (say, a year). These are book-keeping functions, a simple extension of which is to analyse the material consumption at various cost-centres or profit-centres to enable simple comparison to be made with norms and then to analyse variance. Such accounting activities, put early on the computer, have been helping a lot the finance and audit functions, but higher-level help to management planning and control functions needs a more integrated approach.

Materials Flow

Materials can be regarded, in most service or production organisations, as part of a birth-to-death process. From the time a purchase-requisition is initiated and thereafter an order is placed, the birth-process is set on. The arrival of the consignment from the supplier or vendor, its inception and acceptance, and its allocation to the store-bins is as much part of the organic process as is the item being indented for consumption, issued (without return) to the destination point, consumed for the purpose indented and eventually struck off from the store-ledger and a new balance arrived at. One can also view it as a flow-process where the store (or inventory) can be visualised as a vast reservoir where materials pour in from the manufacturers and vendors through a supply pipe-line. The consumers (the plants or service departments) draw from the bottom of the inventory-pit through another pipe-line and whatever is not consumed in the computer-pit is either drained off as scrap or re-conditioned for use as spares for being put back into the inventory. From the latter reservoir, there is also a siphoning out of the excess, obsolete and dead-stock items for ultimate auctioning and disposal.

In the materials flow-process as above, control action can be introduced through some imaginary taps : one on the supply pipe-line between vendors and inventory; one on the consumption pipe-line between inventory and consumer-pit; one on the re-conditioning pipe-line; and one on the siphoning out pipe-line. All management controls can now be viewed as operating these taps in a judicious manner, i.e., monitoring the flow-process through a series of exception-reports and policy-reviews. These are described below.

It is first necessary to identify 'A' class items in terms of high cost and high-consumption pattern as well as 'V' class items in terms of high-criticality and high-consumption pattern. After this is done both 'A' and 'V' classes are best put on an annual ordering system and the deliveries scheduled on the computer. It is possible to establish a dynamic control, with the help of the computer, by re-scheduling deliveries based upon *actual* stocks and *expected* changes in consumption over the subsequent period. This is the nearest approximation to a minimal stock-control for such items. As regards 'B' and 'C' classes of items (on cost-consumption criteria) or 'E' and 'D' classes (on criticality-consumption criteria), it would pay to control them using an optimal policy curve. The latter can be based on the economic-order quantity method, which allocates orders to each item so that minimum stock-holding is achieved, without increasing the total number of orders and without the probability of stock-outs.

Exception-Reporting

The above considerations apply to all stores materials which do not require any special treatment, namely, due to some pre-scheduled maintenance, acquisition of pre-planned new items of budgetted capital projects. In general, exception-reporting can now be applied to flow of materials in order to bring out differences between laid-down norms (or standards) and actual performances and in order to highlight conditions for corrective action. Examples of the exception reports that can be printed by the computer periodically are given below:

(a) *Stock-outs and potential stock-outs* — after taking into account the quantity in store and the quantity on the pipe-line, against the quantity indented — these can be part of a well-orchestrated warning system set up to monitor conditions one fortnight, one month or one quarter in advance, and can help tremendously to follow up with suppliers;

(b) *Over-stocks and potential over-stocks* — on the same lines as (a) above. Such a warning system can open up investigation into reasons for excess stocks, such as, wrong ordering, suppliers not following the delivery schedules, wrong demand forecast (due to one-time usage, etc.), long material life (due to improved maintenance practice, material specification and spare-quality) and consequent drop in projected consumption;

(c) *Obsolete and dead stock* — the former due to changes introduced in equipment, parts, design and processes and the latter (non-moving) due to closure of some production-lines or handling facilities. Control in advance on their procurement can stop such accumulation;

(d) *Purchase-order follow-up* — for items falling below order-level which need to be re-ordered of where excessive ordering has to be prevented for changes in the consumption pattern. This is linked with (a) & (b) above;

(e) *Vendor rating* — for vendors whose performance indices in respect of price, delivery schedules and quality of delivery can be drawn up. Such rating can be used to eliminate the ones below the standard;

(f) *Suppliers' pending bills (or bills payable)* — for an age analysis when the payable bills are over-due, beyond a specific period after the satisfactory receipt of goods. The control action in payment clearance can be synchronised with the organisation's own cash in-flow, as part of the liquidity management.

Two more aspects of exception-reporting deserve attention. First, such reporting presumes that norms are stipulated in the initial stage and the feed-back obtained at regular intervals would enable better appreciation of the changing situation. For example, ABC analysis or VED analysis, if monitored periodically, can show movement of an item from one class to another, and hence the need for a change in the control mechanism for the specific item. Need for such changes is an established fact in most industries. Secondly, the difference between norms laid down and performance achieved can be made more meaningful for laying down certain tolerance-limits within which no monitoring need be done. In an integrated steel plant where tens of thousands of items are in the store, comparisons made between values of inventory at the year-beginning and those at the starting of any subsequent month can be made manageably brief by ignoring small (and tolerable) differences and concentrating upon large deviations. Similarly, differences between norm and actual performance can choose to omit the uncontrollable factors (e.g., price escalation) and to highlight only the controllable factors (e.g., change in value due to increase in inventory-volume). These are some variations possible on the theme of exception-reporting.

Policy-Reviews

Management control by way of policy-reviews can follow by looking at exception-reports from the computer over a period of time. Such policy-reviews can include the following:

(a) *Lead-time pattern vis-a-vis consumption pattern* — to regulate the delivery schedules in tune with the changes in consumption for 'A' class items (re-classified, if necessary);
(b) *Lead-time pattern vis-a-vis criticality pattern* — to regulate, as above, in tune with the changes in criticality for 'V' class items (re-classified, if needed);
(c) *Excess-stock and under-stock patterns* — to regulate any significant variations in the inventory held and to correct the exception conditions.

The computer inputs are specifications of material items, standard rates, names and addresses of suppliers, addition or deletion of items, changes in material-specifications and suppliers, receipts, issues, inter-store transfers, rejections and returns, indents and orders, supplier bills, etc. The computer prices receipts and issues, updates inventory-quantity and values order status, suppliers names and addresses, material specifications, etc., analyses inventory situation to trigger control actions, and prints out exception reports and policy-reviews. The computer outputs are stores ledger, creditors ledger, supplier performance, items to be ordered, stock-outs and potential stock-outs, over-stocks and potential over-stocks, critical items follow-up, matched bills and bills overdue, bank-cheques and projected cash-outflow, material cost allocation, consumption and quality exception, and incentive items.

Integrated System

For organisations producing to service or to sell, there is also process inventory and product inventory. An integrated marketing and inventory control system on computer can link order processing system, invoicing system, performance reporting system, sales accounting system, stock accounting system and sundry debtors system, thus connecting sales, production, store, purchase and accounts departments. While only large main-frame computers can sustain such an integrated system, the materials accounting, exception-reporting and policy-review are feasible on mini and micro-computers as dedicated applications.

An integrated system in the materials control area encompasses the entire gamut of activities from requirement planning through ordering, procurement, consumption and despatch of finished goods. Modern on-line interactive computer systems are ideally suited to run such an integrated system to make available information to the user on a continual basis, based on input-data provided to the computer at each step of the material procurement, handling and consumption process. Normal benefits of computerisation are timely and accurate monitoring of stock-value, highlighting exception-conditions (such as, below order-level, above maximum inventory level, etc.) and following up of purchase-orders to prevent excessive ordering.

Conclusion

By using the facility of enquiry into the data stored on the computer from on-line terminals, the ultimate benefit is a stricter control on the entire material management function through a constant step-by-step monitoring. This can result in optimal levels of inventory being held at various stages and avoidance of both stock-outs and excess stocking, leading to reduction in the working capital and a release of additional funds for other productive purposes.

19

INDUSTRIAL PRODUCTIVITY

Introduction

Productivity considerations have been mainly to assess how organisations function to provide the products or services (according to their founder-fathers' objectives), given the efforts to run them. Computers today have come to help organisations in doing a timely and tireless monitoring of their functions, no matter what the volume of work is. Here we look at the essential role of organisations and examine systematically how computers can be a useful tool in the field of productivity at various levels.

Complexity — Organisational and Environmental

Most large and complex modern organisations have a few common features. First, they have a definite content, — which normally relates to converting certain inputs into more socially desirable outputs. Secondly, they have an organisational structure, — hierarchical or otherwise. Thirdly, they have well-defined channels of communication, for flow of information both within and without. Finally, they all have a built-in control mechanism by which they can almost consciously map out their growth patterns and remain usable even under changed circumstances.

Such large and complex organisations cannot be independent of the socio-economic environment under which they function. The environmental influence is particularly manifest in the expectations of the government in the over-all functioning, besides the guidelines from some central authorities (e.g., SAIL for steel industry, RBI for banking industry and so on), aspirations of the share-holders (for any private-sector undertaking) and the legitimate hopes of the public being served (for any public utility system). As environmental conditions differ from organisation to organisation, each organisation can devise its own plan of action to improve productivity in the light of its strengths and weaknesses, to determine its priorities and to initiate specific measures for improving its performance. The priorities, however, do not remain a constant factor and the organisation has to revise them from time to time and effect appropriate changes.

Translated in managerial terms, such a plan of action may begin with a target and a strategy for reaching it. A budget can then be worked out on what the plan would cost and a time-table for maintaining it. The management has to ensure that the plan ends with the attainment of the target or with an acceptable explanation for falling short of it. It is usually a result-oriented exercise in which procedural rules are only means to an end.

As distinct from administration problems (of, say, different districts of the country which all can be administered more or less with the same procedure indicated by tradition and dictated by equity), management is far from being uniform in all organisations. Producing steel needs an approach different from insuring lives. Again, running an airlines is vastly different from distributing petroleum or marketing wrist-watches or banking money. Environmental conditions can also be quite varied. While organisations like Indian Airlines are monopolies, others like the general insurance have competitions in the public sector, and yet others like the banks and Air India have to compete with both the public and private sector, — Indian or foreign.

Utility of Computer

It would be fairly obvious that a managerial plan of action is severely dependent on the existence of an information system, which stores all planning and control information relating to the organisation and processes such information in order to retrieve meaningful indicators regarding performance of the organisation. An effective information system has basically three components: general historical records, timely access to current information, and meaningful communication functions.

General historical records have raw or reduced data, and partly processed information, obtained from various master documents according to established procedures or on demand. They are kept in a general data-bank as a repository of information which may be referred to when needed or systematically scanned from time to time.

Current information comprises live data obtained in time, — to be combined and processed with historical records after updating, or stored for further references. There has to be a proper machinery for capturing such data from appropriate sources and transferring them to be stored and processed in the general data-bank.

Communication functions embrace output reports in the form of information analysis — obtained continuously, periodically, on ad-hoc basis or only on one-time basis — for use by management in their plan of action, for controlling, coordinating and monitoring the activities of the organisation.

With their exceedingly fast processing capability (of both arithmetic and logical kind) and with very considerable storage capacity, computers have come to the fare to help management in carrying out the communication functions based on stored mass of records, linkages with currently incoming data on retrieval of selective information. The utility of the above kind has further gone up with a rapidly decreasing cost of the computing machines.

At different level of management, computer usage has been quite diverse. At a low level, computer can be entrusted with the entire implementation based on rules well-framed in advance, such as, triggering action for placing purchase-orders on specified suppliers based on re-order quantities and levels. At the middle level, computers can be quite useful to generate regular exception-based reports, say, differences of inventory-values from the year-beginning values above a specified margin. Alternatively, computer can generate reports on demand, such as, whenever warning is needed about fast-moding items which have gone below a week's (or a fortnight's) consumption level. Lastly, at the top level, computer's main function can be as an information-bank to be tapped only when necessary or for any analysis which has become the crying need of the moment.

Using the above approach, a general methodology can be visualised for a plan of action to use computer for formulating and monitoring productivity on the following lines:

(a) Organisations are listed as production industry, service organisation, public utility, etc., and their normal and special features identified;

(b) Information-flow within the organisation is studied to explain both the general historic process and currently in-coming data, and also the communication functions are selected;

(c) Objectives for each organised activity in the operating division or departments are listed;
(d) Objective-wise performance indicators are formulated on quantitative basis;
(e) Objective-wise standard norms are obtained from past knowledge and experience;
(f) For each division or department, objective-wise formats for output reports are prepared, comprising both performance indicators and standard norms;
(g) Input data are identified at appropriate aggregate levels which would help to generate the output reports in the designed manner;
(h) Formats are prepared for collection and storage of input data from specified source-documents; and
(i) Input data are codified and programmes are developed for building up the data-bank, updating the same and generating the output information reports.

At every stage, provision has to be kept for updating of objectives and the organised activities, so that the computer-based planning and monitoring system can remain flexible, and cope with changes.

Productivity of Industrial Organisation

Although industrial organisations vary from one to the other in their complexity, their development has imbibed some common activities. It is possible to bring out some general purpose productivity indicators for these common activities applicable to a variety of industrial organisations. A list of common activities is attempted in the Table 19.1 together with objectives as well as productivity indicators formulated for the activities.

Measures of Productivity

For individual industries, productivity measures would vary at different managerial levels. Steel industry, for instance, can have the following computer-based productivity-indices at the level of general manager:

(a) *Production division* — yield; rejection; fuel consumption; scrap utilisation; coke consumption; production of hot metal; billet;

standard-grade steel; special steel; tested steel; off-grade steel and structural steel; palette consumption; steel quality; and delay;

(b) *Services division* — transport cost; material handling cost; demurrage; relining cost; work-order; turn-over; off loaded hours; maintenance cost and hours, and maintenance performance;

(c) *Sales division* — sales cost; booking; direction of sales effort; market-share; special steel booking; and stockyard cost and sales;

(d) *Materials division* — general stores stock; spares stock; off-loading, delivery performance; ordering cost; supplier quality performance; and supplier performance rating;

(e) *Accounts division* — bill payment performance; cash-collection; cash-flow; debit; debtors turnover; and capital investment; and

(f) *Manpower division* — grade-wise turnover; recruitment efficiency; grade-wise recruitment/promotion/retirement; temporary/permanent manpower and standard force.

TABLE 19.1: Illustrative Common Activities, Objectives and Productivity Indicators for Industries

Activities	Objectives	Indicators
1	2	3
1. Planning	To optimise the utilisation of existing capacity under the personal bottlenecks, also remove them to the possible extent.	1. Utilisation of capacity; 2. Bottlenecks; 3. Achievements in the five year plan; 4. Supplies to different government sectors region-wise; 5. Order-book position; 6. Gestation period; 7. Per-capita consumption of India and other countries.
2. Capacity creation	To meet indigenous and export demand	1. Demand forecasts; 2. Existing production capacity

Contd.

TABLE 19.1 *Contd.*

1	2	3
3. Target setting	To advise about the increasing of capacity to meet the estimated demand economically and to find substitution of imported components.	1. Desirable licensing pattern year by year; 2. Economic plant-size; 3. Norms of consumption; 4. Substitution of imported components.
4. Industrial licensing	Apprising the licensing authority of the facts and figures to help in taking decision about the issuing of licenses.	1. Licensing policy; 2. Existing capacity; 3. Upcoming capacity; 4. Production; 5. Norms of consumption of raw material (DGTD); 6. Industrial average; 7. Consumption.
5. Investment	To depict the comparative picture of profitability and the investment structure of the factory together with their sources of finance.	1. In case of public sector units proportion of profits to — (a) Total assets; (b) Production; (c) Raw Material(RM); (d) Paid-up capital; (e) Loans; (f) Installed capacity; 2. Proportion of production to RM and dividend; 3. Proportion of reserves and dividend to paid-up capital.
6. Import	To apprise the concerned authorities about the facts and figures about collaboration, raw material and capital goods (CG) for taking decision on setting up of an industry with foreign collaboration.	1. Policy of collaboration; 2. Norms of Export obligation; 3. Standing of collaboration; 4. Category of industry; 5. Norms of CG requirement; 6. Nature of priority for import assistance in case of RM; 7. Import policy for the entire product; 8. DGTD Norms for RM consumption and components consumption; 9. Industry's average consumption of raw material per unit of production.

Contd.

TABLE 19.1 *Contd.*

1	2	3
7. Production	To study the production trend State-wise and industry-wise and the reasons (bottlenecks) for the fall or stagnation in their production.	1. Proportion of production produced this month out of the total production up to this month; 2. Comparison with corresponding quarter's production of last year; 3. Proportion of this production to that planned for next month; 4. Production/man-hour; 5. Down-time/man-hour; 6. Percentage of — (i) Electricity received; (ii) Transport facility; (iii) Fuel; (iv) Raw Materials.
8. Inventory Control	To estimate the time at which an industry should get the Raw Material. To keep the supply of the finished good smoothly or to estimate the time at which the production should be reduced to avoid stocking difficulty.	1. Critical stock level of Raw Material; 2. Stock level of the finished goods.
9. Exports	To study the self sufficiency level of the industry	1. Export/import at constant prices.
10. Research and Development	To study the research and development efforts and achievements in various industries.	1. Amount spent on research and development per unit of production; 2. Proportion of investment in research and development.
11. Foreign Exchange allocation	To estimate the allocation of foreign exchange for the next 3 years.	1. Actual consumption of foreign exchange in the previous year; 2. Allotment proposal for the current year.
12. Manpower	1. To estimate the manpower requirement region-wise and state-wise in different categories; 2. To study the availability of personnel of different categories; 3. To study how effectively the training facilities are utilised.	1. Proportion of number of persons actually employed to: (a) Capacity; (b) Annual production; (c) Standard norm; (d) Industrial average; 2. Proportion of number of trained to untrained personnel.

For the same industry, important productivity parameters like cumulative production; actual production; average cost per tonne; and actual cost per tonne can be watched on computer every month at managing director's level, — for production division alone, apart from others. Similarly the critical productivity parameters at the board-of-directors level can include the following:

(i) *Purchase and inventory* — inventory levels; carrying costs; rejection percentages; and late deliveries;
(ii) *Sales* — order density; order transmission for production; order status; and goods despatch and invoice density; and
(iii) *Production* — manufacturing cycle; turn-over; process-inventory levels; and idle man/machine time.

In contrast, the corporate-level productivity considerations for an engineering industry, like the scooter industry, can be quite different. These considerations can encompass the following at managing director's level:

(a) *Funds* — release of payment to suppliers; quality and performance of suppliers;
(b) *Material* — development of alternative sources; procurement vis-a-vis production;
(c) *Equipment* —balancing of capacity; funds for balancing; critical breakdowns; preventive maintenance; machine-failures; and
(d) *Personnel* — work-order utilisation; idle-time.

An integrated production, planning and control system can be easily visualised on computer for productivity monitoring in the scooter industry.

Productivity of Service Organisation and Public Utility

Quantification problems are of prime importance in considerations of productivity for a service organisation. While considering banking service to the Integrated Rural Development Programme (IRDP), Chairman of the State Bank of India —one of the largest banking networks in the world with 7200 branches and above 3000 in deposits — came recently to certain interesting conclusions. According to him, there should be no target-oriented approach to IRDP in covering a minimum number of beneficiaries per block and the number should depend upon the potential existing in a particular area. Further, there are implications of the concessional rate of interest and the massive quantum of loans for IRDP on the overall profitability of the banks; problems of entrepreneurial development for the lowest strata of the rural poor; and difficulties in administration for above one crore additional loan accounts (during Eighth plan period) in the areas of accounting, control and supervision, involving a considerable degree of advance planning and training of field staff. A degree of mechanisation and computerisation was thought to be inevitable to make banking productivity a success for IRDP.

At the regional management level, productivity in the banking industry would be reflected quantitatively in the per-employee deposits, advances, other business and profits, — after taking into account the inter-branch and inter-bank comparison year-wise for coverage in the fields of agriculture, small-scale industry and small business. In order to indicate the levels of productivity, the above parameters have to be qualitatively supplemented through value-judgement, — about the improvement in customer service, the quality of lending and recovery of loans, the state of internal house-keeping, and the morals and motivation of employees. Still, there is a paramount need of an efficiently-run computer-based management information system.

In another service organisation such as the airlines, passenger-miles per day for passenger traffic and tonne-miles per day for goods traffic can be effective measures of the ultimate service. Number of passengers flown or tonnage of goods carried can be compared to the corresponding number or tonnage refused or kept waiting and would make a good productivity indicator for the *potential for service* with respect to a specific period or a particular area. Productivity indices can also be framed with the amount of aviation fuel, number of employees and number of wait-listed passengers, and used on computer at a managerial level.

Productivity concepts in the railways, the country's foremost transportation organisation, are far more complex as they involve locomotives, wagons and passenger-coaches as distinct units of rolling stock. They run different types of trains every day, connect far-flung stations, use several marshalling yards and serve hundreds of commodity groups. Earlier computer applications in the Indian Railways were largely confined to passenger and goods accounting, maintenance of stores accounts, pay-roll services and wagon movement reporting at the inter-change points. Current computer applications envisage better utilisation of locomotives and wagons; planning and design of marshalling and line-capacity works; and a global marshalling strategy, — involving a large number of productivity parameters relating to wagon-delays in marshalling yards; facilities for long-distance marshalling; empty haulage of wagons; unloading, loading and sake-formation of wagons; locomotive utilisation and idle-time on inter-railway basis; number of reception, departure and classification lines; line and yard capacity works with varying traffic patterns; and a host of others. An on-line system of monitoring on computer for wagon movement and freight control with the first few productivity parameters is an imperative need for the railways, already becoming operational over seven railway headquarters.

Hospitals form an important service organisation. Number of patient-days is an important productivity measure for bed-occupancy, average length of patient-stay, expenditure on hospital staff and cost of medical stores and services. Since the hospitals exist to give an early and effective treatment, the number of patient-days may be modified to take into account the patient service-days (i.e., the actual number of patients admitted X number of days of bed-occupancy) in proportion to the patient waiting-days (i.e., the actual number of patients waiting to get admitted into the hospital X number of days of waiting) in each patient-category. Such measures can be usefully adopted by directors of health services in the States for all hospitals above Taluk level and by the Director General of Armed Forces Medical Services for the Military hospital network at the command, base and forward levels, with the aid of available computers.

Central and State PWDs construct and maintain the national highways and the state roads. Similarly, Border Roads Organisation have been responsible over last two decades for building and maintaining roads at high attitudes and remote areas under some eight projects. "Cost per mile" is a productivity parameter for both project management and financial authorities to review performance and evolve a tool for planning and control. Such a concept takes into account the inputs, e.g., costs of labour, plant and machinery, and material consumed; as also outputs of mileage of a road built or maintained up to a given specification, in a particular environment and having a certain traffic capability. For the output side, such factors as terrain condition (number of spurs and re-entrants); altitude (height); strata (ratio of sedimentary to non-sedimentary rocks); composition of soil (ratio of hard to soft rocks); climatic condition (number of inches of rainfall); geometrics ("design speed" in miles per hour); traffic (average number of vehicles plying per day); and lead from the nearest rail-head (distance) are important to consider, further to mileage concept. Usage of computer in the above domain can lead to an effective management aid to monitor productivity on a comprehensive basis.

Conclusion

The above provides a brief illustrative view of computer applications to measure and monitor productivity in some important industrial and service organisation, and public utilities. A number of important factors should be kept in view, before applying the above concepts:

(a) Norms and standards should be carefully formed and used as a comparative yardsticks, wherever feasible;

(b) Top management should be involved at both conceptualisation and implementation stages for computer-based productivity monitoring;

(c) Data should be properly validated, after ensuring their accuracy and source-agency authenticity;

(d) Users should be thoroughly trained and familiarised with the applications at operational levels; and

(e) All data should be treated as non-durable consumer goods, and examined periodically for updating or deleting purposes in keeping with changes in practice.

The main point is that under the changed environment of easy availability of powerful computers, existence of trained manpower and the government's encouragement to computer applications in all non-labour saving areas, — a happy match can be obtained between the computing capability in the country and the rapid growth in the industrialisation, public utilities and service facilities. Productivity is the right direction to train our available computing power on, for achieving substantial results.

20

NATURAL RESOURCES SECTOR – REMOTE SENSING

Introduction

India is a country rich in its resources. Almost every conceivable natural or mineral resource finds its place here. It is wonderful to speculate what the country could do, — if full knowledge were available of all its crops, forests, waters, minerals, fish and ocean-bed wealth and if there could be detailed district-level planning to make use of each of these resources!

This is precisely what is going to happen now. There is a National Natural Resource Management System (NNRMS) which has been drawn up by the nodal agency of Department of Space in the Government of India in cooperation with several other concerned agencies and organisations. The NNRMS scheme is now linked with Natural Resource Data Management System (NRDMS) as a pilot project which has the country's districts as its potential beneficiaries.

Natural Resources

What are the natural resources that are going to be monitored and what is the monitoring mechanism? Indian Remote Sensing Satellites (IRS-IB) had gone up in 1988 and 1991, and are now orbiting at heights of 900 km from the earth to scan the complete surface of the Indian sub-continent once in every 22 days. The remote sensing images are to be received back and thereafter interpreted in digital form as well mapped for specific areas.

The idea of satellite imagery for remote sensing data can be given in terms of image-frame, frequency, resolution, cost and data capacity, — as shown in the Table 20.1 for the French SPOT and the American LANDSAT satellite being used by India so long:

TABLE 20.1: Satellite Imagery

	SPOT (FRANCE)		LANDSAT (USA)
Frame	60 km × 60 km		180 km × 180 km
Frequency	26 days		16 days
Resolution	10 m. — black & white		80 m. — false colour composite
	20 m. — false colour composite		30 m. — false colour composite
	5 m. — black & white or false colour composite		
Cost	$ 2500	10 m. or 20 m. resolution	$ 1500 30 m. resolution $ 1000 80 m. resolution
Capacity	90mb. for 10 m. resolution 90mb. for 20 m. resolution		30mb. for 80 m. resolution 250mb. for 30 m. resolution

With IRS-IA and IRS-IB, the expectations are running high today and the satellite imagery from India's own systems are definitely more cost-effective than from the French and American systems.

Among the large number of inter-departmental and cross-disciplinary task-forces supervising the acquisition and analysis of data on our natural resources, first and the foremost is the glacial resource which supplies water to all our snow-fed rivers. Knowledge about the timing and extent of glacial melting is vital for flood forecasting and irrigation purposes. Second is the surface water resource in dams, barrages, reservoirs, canals, ponds, lakes and rivers, — to give an idea of the current status of water in the country.

The third is the cropping resource. The main crops, their seasonal variations, the experiments in cash crops and the inter-cropping are all very important to determine the progress on the country's food-front. The fourth is the forest resource: showing both the forest wealth and the deforested areas. The fifth is the underground water, — lying as aquifers under the entire Indo-Gangetic plain and elsewhere. This knowledge is essential for solving the potable water problem: to provide drinking water to all.

The sixth is the underground mineral resource, revealing the country's immense mineral wealth on both sides of the Vindhyas. By the way, for both the underground water and underground minerals, infra-red photography is used to make out imagery with false colour composites.

The seventh is the sea-fish resource. For our fishermen from West Bengal, Orissa, Andhra, Tamil Nadu, Kerala, Karnataka, Maharashtra,

Goa and so on, it is most rewarding to know, for instance, that schools of Tuna fish come to the shallow waters near the coast in the twilight hours between 3 and 5 p.m., — to ensure their bountiful catch!

The eighth and the last is the ocean-bed mineral resources. There are rare deposits of iron, copper, manganese, nickel, tin and cobalt in the dark recesses underwater which can be explored and exploited, for augmenting our mineral resources. Otherwise, it is more than likely that the developed countries would not merely find out about them, but also send seabed-sweeping submarines to take them away.

Computing Facilities and Pilot Districts

In order to do justice to the flow of data from the sky — as something like 36,000 pages of a book every hour — there are VAX computers with graphic facilities at computer centres at IIT, Kharagpur funded by Department of Science and Technology; at the Indian Institute of Remote Sensing, Dehra Dun funded by Department of Space; at the Central Arid Zone Research Institute, Jodhpur funded by Departments of Science and Technology, and Space; at the Geological Survey of India, Bangalore funded by Department of Mines; and at the National Bureau for Soil Survey and Land Use Planning, Nagpur funded by Indian Council and Agricultural Research. These centres apart, the Annamalai University at Madras; the National Remote Sensing Agency at Hyderabad; and the Indian Agricultural Research Statistics Institute at Delhi have got their computer capacity augmented.

All these data are available to help our districts in the NRDMS scheme. Drawn by the Department of Science and Technology, the scheme operated on participation by some six districts, to start with. Vishakhapatnam district in Andhra Pradesh is working with the National Coastal Research Institute in the same city; Sultanpur district in the UP with Aligarh Muslim University; Gurgaon district in Haryana with the National Institute of Science and Technology Development Studies, Delhi; Koraput district in Orissa with Operations Research Group of Baroda; and Khera district in Gujarat with IIT, Bombay. One district in Manipur has recently been added to the list of pilot districts.

These pilot districts are planning to make out blue-prints for development, — combining the NRDMS data with the existing census data; National Sample Survey Organisation's data; and ad-hoc field data. Perhaps many other districts will join soon.

Aims of NRDMS

The main aim of NRDMS is to facilitate conductance of area-specific and decentralised planning and monitoring exercises by providing data at various levels — village, block and district. The project seeks to :

- establish an area-specific data management system for decentralised planning;
- adapt the methodology for island system, such as natural disasters in specific areas other ecologically sensitive areas;
- establish linkage with the programmes of National Natural Resources Management System, National Informatics Centre Network and other sectoral information systems;
- generate development profiles of different regions; and
- support specific studies to develop regional development perspectives using NRDMS as an aid.

The NRDMS file structure consists of data files on different types of natural resources (forests, land, minerals, meteorology, environment, etc.) and socio-economic characteristics (agriculture, industry, demography, infrastructure, etc.). It also contains separate files of remote sensing data (satellite imagery and aerial photographs).

A standardised comprehensive computerised data-base is created and updated from two types of data sources: (i) conventional – statistical and survey reports, etc., and (ii) technological – remote sensing, computer-aided and digital processing and instrumentation surveys. Sophisticated methods have been developed for use in NRDMS for rapid storage, retrieval, aggregation and analysis of data. Spatially oriented thematic atlases and multiple-atribute interactive data structures are generated as the decision support system for developments planning.

While data collection, processing and entry has been planned, the analysis of data is to be undertaken for theme generation and for identifying sectoral trends. The creation of the following file structure is in progress, for instance, in Gurgaon district : (1) natural resources, (2) energy, (3) environment, (4) demography, (5) agro-economic, (6) socio-economic (7) remote sensing, (8) sectoral, (9) infrastructure, (10) block information, (11) village information, and (12) household information.

NRDMS Software

The integrated composite software package for NRDMS called "GRIDS" stands for "Geo-Encoded Resource Integrated Data System". This is a special software package which is operational on a cost-effective microprocessor-based system. GRIDS takes into its fold the conventional database which are available at various State and Central levels coupled with data generated from the canvassing of structured questionnaires at various levels for specific studies. An innovation in the system is the integration of high technology like remote sensing, computer-aided data processing, compugraphics and instrumentation surveys with the classical data sources. The package develops spatially oriented thematic maps, multiple interactive data structures and details out computerised planning priority decisions which have area-specifity as the underlying theme. Further, the package is capable of monitoring and evaluating a programme. Compatibility, rapid updation, quick retrieval and aggregation of multiple attributes, and spatially oriented structured data are some of the advantages of this package. The package consists of a number of programmes which may be classified into four categories : (i) thematic map generation for different sets of data like natural resources, demography, agro-economy, socio-economy, infrastructure, remote sensing, etc.; (ii) selection of areas suitable for specific applications of developmental programmes; (iii) determination for development indices and potential indices for blocks of districts; (iv) remote sensing application programmes; (iv) analysis programmes for geophysical parameters for such essential purposes as ground water evaluation.

Usefulness and Current Status of NRDMS

NRDMS is expected to be handy in :

- providing a sound information base for a district at one point for decision-making;
- facilitating assessment of resource potential and extent of development of different sectors in different regions;
- making available the resource and opportunity profiles in different sectors for entrepreneurial initiatives;
- assisting in the identification of target groups, specific locations and situations;

– supplying information for taking suitable measures for managing natural disasters such as droughts, floods, earthquakes cyclones, landslides and avalanches;
– assisting in agro-economic services by providing ready information on commodity prices and their trends, crop yields, cropping pattern, soil characteristics, moisture content, etc.;
– helping in district-level planning taking into consideration clusters of blocks and villages; and
– creating conditions for hierarchical planning from district level to State and national levels and vice-versa.

The ultimate goal of NRDMS is to provide linkages of micro and district level planning with macro level planning. It is expected to help in undertaking monitoring and evaluation exercises. The uniqueness of NRDMS lies in the prompt supply of grass-root information to the users — government, NGOs, researchers, specialists and people at large. The major achievements of the project are : (i) formats for recording data on natural resources and socio-economic parameters have been developed and provision has been made to store about 225 attributes in computer; (ii) software packages for analysis and retrieval of data have been developed; (iii) NRDMS application test studies have been undertaken. Some studies already completed are:

– Block planning exercise in Similiguda block;
– District planning exercise in Medak district;
– Wastelands in Vishakhapatnam district;
– Selection of harbour site — case of Goa;
– Operational Research (OR) studies on water management and industrial potential of an area; and
– A multiple database study in the Ghaghra-Gandak area of the eastern Uttar Pradesh to study parameters related to flood plain zoning.

Decision Support Systems from NRDMS

The district databases as conceived are expected to find applications of far-reaching significance in the areas of decentralised planning and decision-making. Some of them may even be of non-conventional type. It has, therefore, to have the requisite level of flexibility and comprehensiveness, so that it can cater to a wide variety of requirements. The following are typical of the applications tnat can be visualised as decision-support systems, using the computer actively to arrive at rational decision:

(i) *Establishment of a Veterinary Centre in the Gurgaon District*

To get a rational decision in this respect, the database should provide the name of an appropriate village in the district, after applying the following tentative criteria:

(a) Block-wise list of villages not having veterinary centres within a radius of 8 km.;
(b) Cattle population in these villages;
(c) Human population in these villages; and
(d) Availability of water in the villages situated within a radius of 1-2 km.

(ii) *Setting up of an Industrial Estate in the Gurgaon District*

The parameters relevant to this topic may be as follows:

(a) Wasteland available in different parts of the district;
(b) Availability of water in these locations;
(c) Distance of these locations from the major sources of raw materials;
(d) Distance of these locations from the major marketing centres for the products; and
(e) Estimated cost of developing the wasteland for making it suitable for industrial use.

The database should identify locations on the basis of the above tentative parameters and thus aid in decision-making through decision-support systems using the computer.

Conclusion

The exciting situation today is that if good quality resolution is available in the NRDMS data, very good soil maps and mineral maps of districts can be prepared, – as indeed is the case today. The potential is vast, – with 20 metres or 10 metres resolution, when there is no confusion to interpret the resource data and no mixing with the intermittent clouds.

If one adds judiciously the above data to the aerial photography data (which is age-old in India), one can have the most effective planning blue-prints. Districts like Gurgaon, Khera and Sultanpur are already showing the way. Before long the experiment should include other districts, especially in the Himalayan and the North Eastern region, – to achieve micrc planning of districts so dear to our Prime Minister's heart.

21

AGRICULTURAL SECTOR – CASE OF MARKETING FOR AGRICULTURAL PRODUCE

Introduction

Marketing of agricultural produces is basically dependent on a buyer-seller relationship. Assuming in most developing countries that sellers form, by and large, the weaker communities with little precise knowledge of market mechanism, institutions have grown up to provide them some protection in the face of stronger buying parties. It is only appropriate that legal provision such as Agricultural Produce Marketing Regulation Act, exist to look after transactions in almost all commodities in the States.

Commissioned agencies operate today under the aegis of Mandi Parishads to deal with sales of agricultural produces. The sales are normally by auction or tendering of negotiation, with weighting supervised by weighment committees. Prices are arranged to be paid within the same day, with the arrangement that agency commissions (around 2 per cent for cereals and higher percentage for other crops) are paid by the seller. Penalties are imposed for certain non-permitted types of sales.

Government of India has a Directorate of Marketing and Inspection which operates a Market Planning and Design Centre (MPDC). The latter conducts sample surveys from time to time to decide on the location of markets, prices of different commodities and quantity of a produce to be channeled through specified markets. Such surveys need an intensive round-the-clock coverage of all market movements: both incoming (of produce brought by the sellers) and outgoing (of produce taken over by the buyers). As regards time, daily and hourly movements are brought out in a week long survey. Although seasonal movements, too affect the markets, short-term variations are usually more revealing of the type of details needed for improving operational aspects and for designing new facilities, than long-term data.

A typical survey was carried out by MPDC in Delhi, India for the neighbouring New Azadpur market attracting daily 2,450 tonnes of fresh fruit, potatoes, onions, and vegetables. The market served primarily as a fresh fruits and vegetables, and secondly, as a terminal wholesale market for around 80 per cent of Delhi's metropolitan consumers through retailers and retail-jobbers. The survey was based on a planned approach to make the loose market network into a more coherent market system – with the progressive segregation of the wholesale from the semi-wholesale and retail functions; transformation of multi-purpose markets into more specialised Centres of trade; and creation of new markets. The long-term objectives were two-fold: (a) to reduce the margin between producers' and consumers' prices; and (b) to introduce an element of stability into the section of perishable produce through the availability of alternate choices at competitive prices.

New Azadpur's organisation as a transit market and commercial outlet was of vital importance to farmers in many states as well as consumers in many other cities. In fact, a shift and effective transformation of the New Azadpur Complex from a Delhi bazar to one of the most important wholesale markets in India was needed in terms of the rural interests at stake in the apple trade.

Other Asian Examples

Marketing of agricultural produce has been given a lot of attention in the neighbouring Asian countries.

Indonesia

Early Dutch collaboration let to be development of many marketing plans. Jakarta has been intensively surveyed, leading to its being developed as an ideal market, comparable to New Azadpur Complex of Delhi. Communication on marketable produces and their prices is pretty frequent, through radio broadcasts and market bulletins. Collection of information takes place by "market inspectors" on a country-wide basis. Computerisation of information is on its way.

South Korea

Market "intelligence" is collected regularly and intensively, with a wide-ranging arrangement of dissemination of information. At the capital Seoul, for instance, there is a telephone-dial system available and connected to a computer.

Japan

A very advanced computer-based system is operating in Japan on forecasting and communication in this field. Market plans are regularly cast on areas to be covered, period of coverage, extent of coverage, quantity of a produce to be marketed and prices to be changed. Such plans are able to advise agricultural sellers as to when to arrange to stock and when not to sell in specific markets to avoid losses. Communication is through telex, teleprinter, radio and television. A small buyers' co-operative manage the above functions, with a lot of attention given to daily marketing phenomenon: periodicity (which hours of the day); seasonality (which seasons carrying which days); Prices (highest, average and lowest); and produces (say, five types of orange quality with a price for each).

There is obviously a high quality of survey data available to back up the Japanese kind of approach. General levels of awareness contribute considerably to the success of such a system.

Survey Methodology

The growth in survey research activity has resulted in many more people, than in the past, coming into contact with surveys. They may have to assist in the design of the survey as a part of their work or education, to commission and supervise survey, to evaluate a method used, or to interpret and apply survey results. Although none of these tasks can be properly carried out without a working knowledge of survey methods, most people, who are temporarily involved, have neither the time nor the inclination to undertake a detailed study of the considerable amount of literature on sample surveys, which draws its techniques from a very wide range of disciplines including statistics, psychology, sociology, anthropology, economics and computer-sciences.

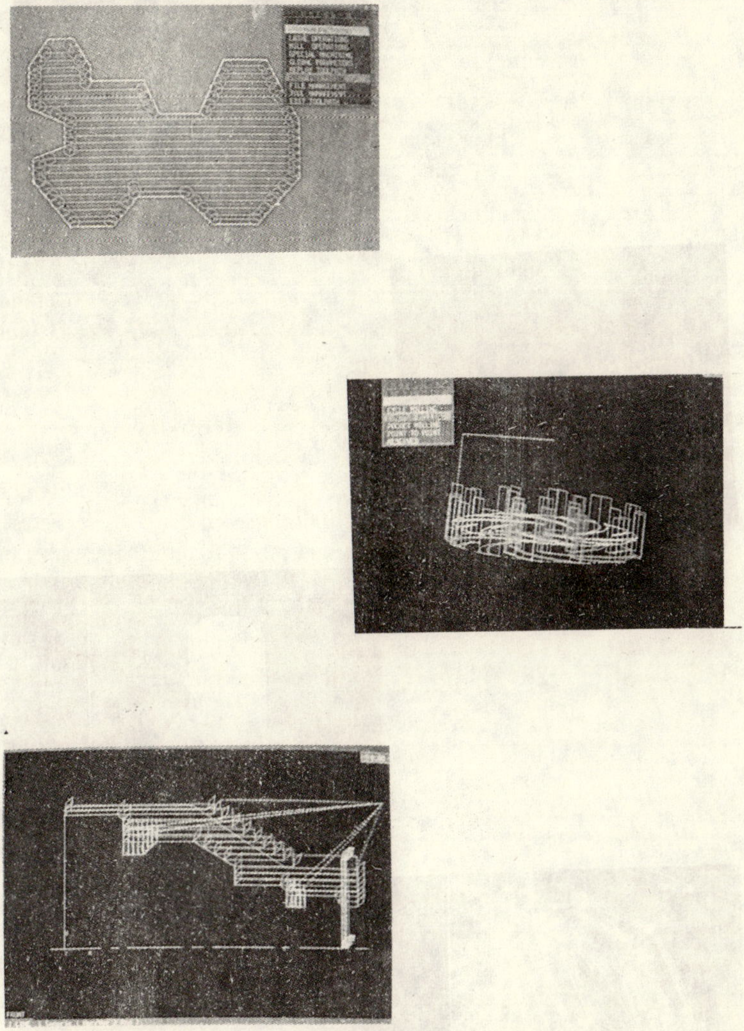

Numerical Control Machines on Computer

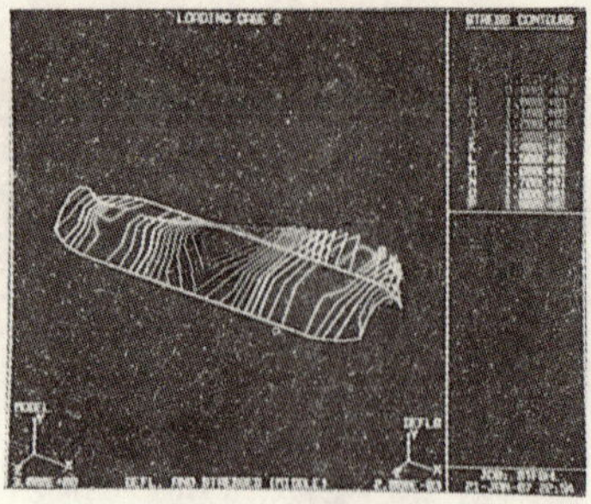

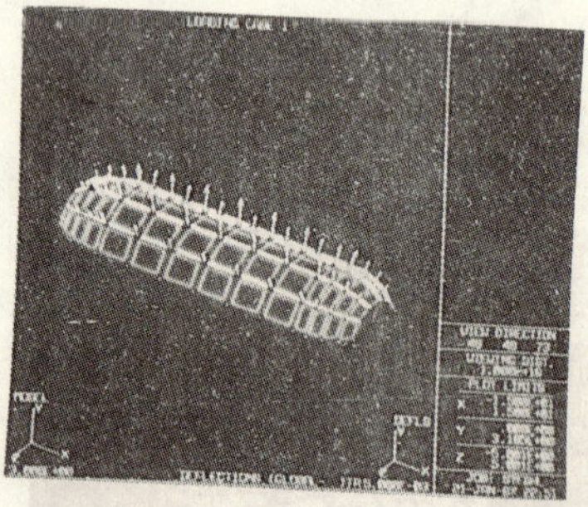

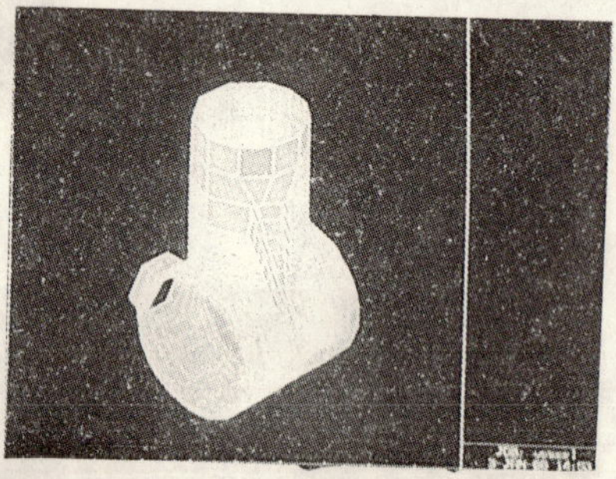

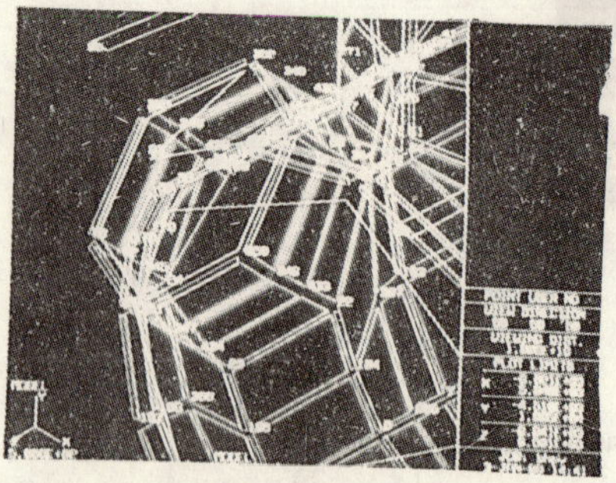

Finite Element Modelling and Analysis on Computer

The need for a survey can arise in many different situations. A survey may be required to provide the solution to a problem of public policy or to a produce data needed for business management or to update a continuing series of trend measurement or to test hypothesis developed by social scientists.

The basic concept of a survey is to take a random and unbiased sample keeping in mind that the sample should represent the whole population (thereby avoiding investigation for all the population).

Area

In our case, we have to select a few vegetable markets as a sample. The selection should be unbiased. Selection should be made of those markets which serve or cover most of the population of Delhi. The need is to collect information about these markets.

Objective

The objective in this case is to plan for an improved market with proper infrastructure and sanitation. Chaos created by inflow of the heavy traffic is to be minimised. Other measures may include: connecting the drainage canal with the main drain; provision of adequate water supply; installation of a public telephone system; and installation of a daily waste disposal service.

Data Collection

Data collection for any survey depends upon the scope of work and the objective of the survey. Usually, a team of trained interviewers need to be used to carry out the field work. The success of the interview will depend as much on the performance of this team as on the design of the questionnaire. In short, performance will depend on the way the interview team sets about its task. At a pre-field work briefing, the leader can explain the purpose of the survey, describe the survey method and introduce the questionnaire. The written project instructions can be outlined and some practice with the questionnaires can be given around briefing table. The interviewer, however, needs time to absorb its information and to become familiar with the project.

The sampling instructions and filtering instructions in the questionnaires and special definitions have all to be mastered. The interviewer should be given proper addresses before going to the field.

The interviewer has to locate sample addresses and find out whether they are occupied. Difficulties over addresses can often be resolved with the help of local residents or shop-keepers. When the interviewer comes across an unoccupied address, there are two options which he may adopt. Either he may mark it as empty or he may intelligently choose an alternate address.

In case it is decided that the survey data will be processed by a computer, special attention needs to be given to the design of the interview lay-out and upon the feedback of the interview. The answers should be in a specific coded form. For example, if age is required to be filled in the sample questionnaire, it may be provided in ranges say at 5-year intervals. Each interval should be given individual codes as 1, 2, 3, – or A, B, C, –. This will facilitate computer processing.

Survey team

The survey team should be made up of experienced persons or should at least be headed by a person having good experience in such type of surveys in order to prevent biased information from being collected in the survey. Care must be taken so that base data, i.e., raw data should be unbiased.

The manpower required depends upon the following:

(a) Scope of survey;
(b) Volume of data collection; and
(c) Number of stations under survey,

Theoretical training of the team or general instructions to Investigators

What to collect, what the prime areas of importance are and how to covert many qualitative measures (involved in data collection) into quantitative measures, depend on various factors. These points must be clearly discussed and understood before going into the field. The objective of the survey too must be clear to everyone. For example, if the surveyor wants to find out the condition of the traffic at its worst during peak hours, further care must be taken in collection of data during peak hours. Leaving out information during this period can result in a high degree of inaccuracy, whereas in case the surveyor is interested in seasonal changes, this error will not cause much inaccuracy.

Main information to be collected for such surveys – (Vegetable/fruit markets)

(1) area of sample;
(2) number of units in the sample;
(3) approximate population serviced by the market;
(4) incoming vegetable/fruit load at any particular time;
(5) daily incoming load;
(6) traffic at any given time, i.e., number of trucks, cars and carts;
(7) maximum and minimum road width and condition of roads;
(8) covered area and parking area;
(9) uploading facilities;
(10) peak arrivals; and
(11) sanitary arrangements.

Processing

There are several ways of processing the collected questionnaire. In all the surveys, some manual intervention is definitely required such as to check the incomplete questionnaires and to code them correctly. The final processing may be carried out manually or through computerisation. In either case, the data will have to be coded in an appropriate form. If the amount of coding in each questionnaire is limited, the editing and coding may be combined, the editors can scan the questionnaires for errors and commissions, but for a survey involving a lot of coding, it will be more efficient to separate the functions and treat coding as a specialist's task. The coding techniques will have to be designed according to the type of processing being adopted.

In certain cases, time may be more important than cost. For example, manual processing can be more time consuming and equally costly, because by the time result of the survey is obtained, it may become obsolete. So it is upto the group leader to choose the processing technique which suits the project requirements, such as time versus cost. The technique to be adopted generally depends upon the nature of the survey, i.e., whether the survey is one time of recurring. If it is a one-time survey, it is advisable to adopt manual processing and in case it is recurring, computer processing is advised.

Manual Processing

Manual processing requires quite a few statisticians and, therefore, a strategy must be adopted to break up the whole project into feasible steps. Doing the complete project break up, simultaneously is usually not possible. Appropriate formulae should be designed for the project while strictly keeping the objective of the survey in mind. Before giving the final shape to these formulae, in-depth discussions are necessary, in order to make sure that all relevant factors have been taken into account.

Actually, the whole data is further divided into sub-samples, depending on the volume of data and the number of statisticians and their subordinates, so that they can all work on the sub-sample. Later on, these separate results are merged appropriately to get the final result.

Care must be taken while making any observation, because a little error at any step leads to an absurd result and one can never know where it occurred. It is better if intermediate error-check formulae can be thought off or designed. The final result is erroneous if the statistician is careless and commits a mistake. The situation becomes serious when a statistician forgets to include a variable and another statistician duplicates a record in his calculation. The final result then appears to be correct but it is definitely biased and such errors cannot be treated. This process depends totally on human understanding and human errors are quite possible. Therefore, the probability of erroneous results is very high. Also, every time the input data changes, one has to recalculate the variables. While in computerising the processing, once a system is designed, any input data can be processed any number of times. Thus it gives more flexibility to the user.

Computerised Processing

The computer can deal with small as well as voluminous data but the main point to be considered is proper input data formats and system design. Some of the important points are highlighted below:

(a) input format design;
(b) input/output responsibilities;
(c) system design – (i) developing new programmes; and
(ii) using existing statistical packages.

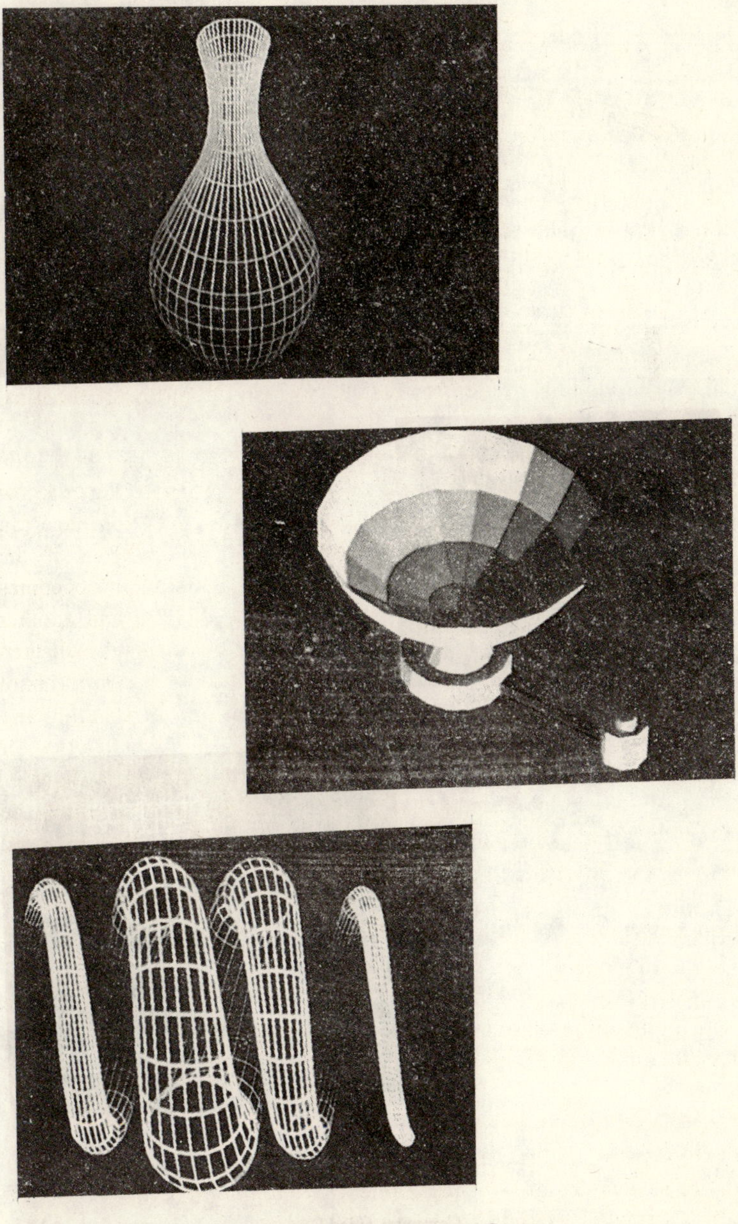

Three-dimensional Drafting on Computer

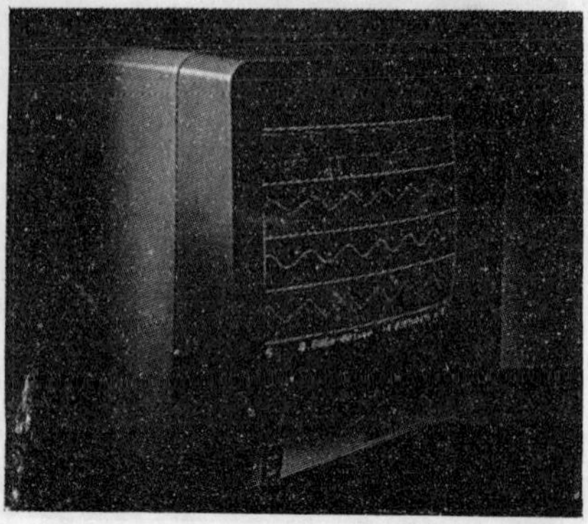

Computer-aided Design

A. *Input/output design*

All companies, having computer facilities whether small or large and whether they deal with small volumes of data or huge volumes of data, have to keep in mind the importance of the following while computerising the same:

(a) input document(s);
(b) input format;
(c) proper schedule; and
(d) output responsibility.

(a) *Input documents*

The most important thing is input data. It must contain an identification number/batch number for the entire batch, which will remain constant for the complete batch and will not be repeated for the next batch. The length of the field must be mentioned on the input documents. Proper tabulation is necessary to differentiate the field and to provide easy access to the variables of any field length.

(b) *Input format*

The input format is most vital. When the length of field is variable, it is important to design the input format in such manner that it is easily accessible, *whether* it is an *alpha field, numeric field* or an *alpha-numeric field.* While designing the input formats, project leader/programmer should keep in mind that the card code is always numeric with the provision to punch the identification number/batch number. The detailed description of variable positions must be defined clearly in the input format. Some extra bytes (space) should be kept for further development or for future requirements. A sample of input format design is given below for reference purpose:

(Serial No./Card Col./field/No. of Cols./detailed description)

The input format design should be completed from column 1 to column 30 with all detailed instructions. Modifications (if any) in format should be intimated to the concerned department with the new input format design and the detailed description, by the project leader/programmer.

(c) *Proper schedule*

The schedule for the input data must be already discussed with the users/customers according to convenience of both (monthly, fortnightly or weekly). Similarly, the processing schedule must also be understood before implementing it. If check-listing is required, check-list delivery data and, after check-list correction, output delivery data must be decided upon.

(d) *Output responsibility*

Output responsibility is also a vital part of the computer processing. Some of the important points given below should be kept in mind before handing over the output to customer/user:

1. the reports should be segregated by removing the extra sheets;
2. the reports must be checked for quality printing;
3. the various totals must be cross-checked (if necessary);
4. the selective reports (if any) must be printed; and
5. proper challan must be made for the delivery of the outputs.

B. *System analysis and design*

At the outset, the problem needs to be clearly identified and then analysed. At this point, the objective and scope of the survey must be strictly adhered to. This analysis is a very important part and, therefore, extreme care must be taken. Whilc analysing a problem, extensive discussion with the customer would be beneficial to derive successful survey results. After analysing the problem carefully, one has to design a foolproof system. This may be done in two days, i.e. either by designing a new system (which needs a set of programme) or using existing statistical packages.

C. *New system*

The whole system consists of many programmes that may vary according to the requirements of the projects.

All the required formulae should be discussed and must be given a final shape before writing the programme. The programmes should be developed in a modular, flexible and generalised manner so that they may operate on different kinds of data. Some editing programmes must be included to edit and update the erroneous data present on the file. All programmes should highlight incorrect result through a separate report. Test data must be prepared and the programmes tested thoroughly before using them for production. However, this is a very lengthy process and it may take months to develop such system. So it is advisable to use already existing packages as far as possible.

Statistical Package Usage

As several statistical packages already exist and they have been thoroughly tested on various statistical applications, it is much better to use such packages.

To use statistical packages, one has to arrange data in such a manner that it is suitable as input for the package programmes. The manpower required is very much less. However, only experienced people should use the package. The desired result can be obtained by simply using a few control cards. Moreover, as most of the packages provide levels of significance, the need to manually look up 'F' Tables is eliminated. The run time is also reduced considerably because the package programmes are developed by very experienced and expert people.

All packages have their own specific reporting systems. The user must, therefore, become familiar with the various reports and the understanding of the reports. However, the output reports produced by a package are very clear and simple, and each observation has its importance because these packages produce highly precise reports for all types of statistics. The user can produce any report at will by suppressing the not required statistics. Statistical packages generally can do the following:

A. *Frequencies and condescriptive*

This can produce one-way frequency distribution, measure of central tendency and dispersions. Data on which these procedures can operate can be of interval and scalers.

B. *Cross table and breakdown*

This procedure can produce relationship (*chi-square*) between two or more variables, and a variety of non-parametric statistics.

C. *Correlations*

These procedures can produce different type of correlations such as:

(i) partial correlations; and
(ii) multiple correlation and regression.

D. *Discriminant analysis*

The effect of a collection of interval-level independent variables on a nominal dependent variable is calculated. Discriminant-function coefficients and classification-functions coefficients are printed. All independent variables may be entered into the discriminant functions.

E. *Factor analysis*

The major use of factor analysis by social scientists is to locate a smaller number of valid dimensions, clusters or factors contained in a large set of independent variables.

F. *Canonical correlation*

Multiple regression is a technique for examining the relationship among several independent variables and a single dependent variables. Factor analysis is a technique of data reduction that locates the fewer underlying dimensions in which no distinction has been made between independent and dependent variables. Canonical correlation is in some respect combination of two alternate multivariable techniques. It contains data reduction capabilities similar to factor analysis, as the user is required to divide the variables into two sets it also accesses the relationship between the two sets of factors.

A large variety of reports can be produced for any system but all the reports are not always useful. Check-list reports must be given at all points to help in cross-checking the result. The information in the output reports must be precise as well as concise. The design of the output report must give a clear picture of the results at a glance. The report heading should also be explicit. The information in the output reports must be self explanatory.

Costs

The cost factor depends on the method of data processing chosen and it is directly proportional to the volume of data. However, the cost of market survey remains the same for all options. The costing features can be summarised as follows (example is taken of an ideal project consisting of 3 data-sets each having about 10,000 records and each record having 200 variables):

A. *Manual processing*

The cost of manual processing is directly proportional to the number of man hours and in manual processing the number of persons required are very large. It is also required that all the persons must have a sound knowledge of statistics and a few of them must also be experienced enough to lead the project. The wages above would amount to approximately Rs. 60,000. In addition, there would be the cost of space, furniture, calculators, rental and other facilities. The total cost of the project would be approximately Rs. 85,000.

B. *Computer processing*

Two types of computer processing options, as described below, are available (but in both the cases, the cost of card punching and card-to-tape or direct key-to-tape data entry will remain fixed):

(i) *New programme development*

In this the manpower requirement is definitely less than in the manual processing, but the persons handling the project must have very good knowledge of system analysis, programming and statistics. Here the cost include wages of the persons involved as well as the cost of computer time. For developing a system and testing it on the computer and the processing of data, the cost would be around Rs. 70,000. However, once the package has been developed, the cost of subsequent run would be much less. The processing charges are approximately 25 per cent of the system development cost. However, designing such a system is very time consuming. It may take months to develop a system and to test it on the computer.

(ii) *Standard package usage*

The cost of the project can be heavily reduced by using the already available statistical packages. The charges for the usage of such packages are very high. However, the cost of programme development and testing time and manpower requirements are considerably minimised. Here, the overall cost of wages and the cost of wrong runs is reduced. Using such packages, very little additional system design is required and the cost of the first run should be approximately Rs. 30,000. The cost of subsequent runs would be much less, approximately Rs. 15,000. The processing is, therefore, the cheapest and the easiest to implement and it is most convenient for both the users as well as the computer agencies.

Availability of Equipment and Software

In India, almost every big city has computer facilities. There are a number of regional computer centres and besides there are a large number of computer consultancy companies. Almost all big computer centres have some good statistical package, e.g., GSARS (Generalised Statistical Application and Reporting System), equivalent to SPSS. The other statistical packages available are: SPSS, SAS, SSP, etc., some of which run on PCs.

Trained Manpower and Speed of Processing

A. *Manual processing*

It requires at least 4 good experienced statisticians and 15 to 20 subordinates having good knowledge of statistics. Manpower requirement may be less or more depending upon the volume of data and the coverage of the survey. The speed of the survey depends upon the skills of the manpower involved and is limited only by human capabilities. The survey analysis should take from 6 months to one year. However, all the 4 statisticians are not always involved for the length of the project, but they are definitely needed at the time of initiation of the project.

B. *Computer processing*

(i) *New Programme development*

For systems development, the manpower requirement would be one system analyst, two good statisticians having good knowledge of programming as well (they may be needed to assist the system analyst) and four other programmers. Part-time production people are also needed.

The speed of the processing depends upon the experience of the team people. System design can take one month or two months and the programme development and testing time will be around two to three months. Once the system and programmes are developed, the processing time may be a fortnight or less depending on the input schedules and, of course, on the computer time availability.

(ii) *Package usage*

The manpower required is a system analyst and two other experienced persons knowing how to use the package. A programmer may be needed in some cases. In this case, the speed of processing is very fast as it depends on the input receipt schedule only. In some cases, minor system design modification may be required which can take about a month.

Conclusion

The above gives a brief outline of both manual and computerised processing of survey results for agricultural markets. While Japan and South Korea have gone ahead in using and implementing sophisticated survey, a beginning in India has to be made with caution. For example, weekly wholesale price of 130 standardised agricultural commodities received from over 500 markets are regularly processed on the computer at IASRI. This involves checking of prices of individual commodities with those obtaining in the previous weeks as in the surrounding markets, and editing the data properly before such prices are published. Statistics of arrivals of foodgrains in different markets and studies in trends of area, production and yields of crops are conducted at national and district levels to identify regional imbalances and to take corrective measures. The following factors are to be kept in mind:

(a) general population dealing with agricultural produce are not too familiar with survey methodology. Hence the possibility of getting highly skewed data;
(b) quality of social science research being field techniques is not often very high, leading to undependable survey results;
(c) people are generally used to conservative nature of enquiry and responses. Conversion of such habits to formality of survey need be done continuously; and
(d) discrepancies are known to occur between the survey data and those obtained from the market committees.

Even in the above framework, Food and Agriculture Organisation of the United Nations is interested to introduce limited survey as pilot studies in Indian Agricultural markets and observe the results based on computerised processing. A phased introduction of survey methodology and computerisation in the Indian scene is certainly likely to lead to analytical insights into agricultural markets and be of benefit for planning improved markets; for designing standards for market infrastructure (with emphasis on cost efficiency); and for financial planning of new market projects, market ownerships, and market fees and services.

22

EDUCATION SECTOR

Introduction

The world's first ever computer ENIAC I was born in a university. Although the war-time efforts of rapid calculation with an enormous amount of data relating to the defence forces were the cause — the result was an electronic calculating and memorising machine created in the academic world.

Changing Status

The first to benefit was also the academic community. The research scholars benefited by the ease and accuracy with which the computer could solve abstruse mathematical problems. Calculation of the value of *pie* — circumference divided by diameter for any circle — was one of the early tasks assigned to the computer. This way at the behest of the astronomers who needed to apply it for measuring the coordinates of the heavenly spheres to arrive at the time and place of the eclipses and other celestial phenomena.

In India, too, the first computer came to Tata Institute of Fundamental Research. In collaboration with the Indian Statistical Institute, Calcutta, Jadavpur University developed a small computer system in the late fifties for academic purposes. Since then a number of universities have gone ahead either to procure their own computers or obtain computer time from the neighbouring service centres to assist in the studies and research-investigation. Such universities number around more than 100.

In particular, Indian Institutes of Technologies have played a leading role. IIT, Madras has a large computer IBM 370/155 upgraded further to help in their education process. IIT, Bombay and IIT, Kharagpur had both EC-1030 computers obtained from USSR replaced by much larger Cyber Computers. IIT, Delhi has today an

ICL computer 2950 as gift from the UK enhanced much further. IIT, Kanpur had a cluster of computers — DEC-10, TDC-312 and Micro-78 — being made into a network. All the IITs have since considerably upgraded their computer resources with most advanced computers from CDC, IBM, ICL and other vendors with scores of upper-terminals. Next to IITs, regional engineering colleges have acquired for their own computers. Motilal Nehru Regional Engineering College at Allahabad and others had been early in using computers and have since replaced them with much larger ones.

A novel idea to encourage computers in the education sector is to build regional computer centres with the tri-lateral participation of Central and State Governments and the local universities. The first to come into being was Region Computer Centre at the Jadavpur University campus in Calcutta, followed by those at the Roorkee University campus and Pune University campus. Some more at Chandigarh and elsewhere followed suit. Often large academic research institutions also play a leading role in this matter. Tata Institute of Fundamental Research at Bombay, for instance, has been using DEC-10 and PDP-11 computers earlier and has now a CYBER-173 system exclusively earmarked for academic and research purposes. Indian Institute of Science at Bangalore has similarly been rendering yomen service to the academic community, and is now the centre for research on parallel processing for fifth generation computer architecture.

Variety of Usage

A recent trend in the use of computers for universities and examination boards has been for educational management. Such managerial application of computer resource has been in diverse fields. First, where a large number of theoretical classes, tutorials and laboratory sessions are involved with limited availability of halls, rooms and laboratories apart from the faculty, computer has helped in drawing suitable time-tables keeping all resource-constraints as well as student-requirements in view. Secondly, faculty recruitment has been resorted to after a computer-based matching of the academic needs with the available and potential faculty-profiles and then filling up the gap. Thirdly, large data-banks have been created on computer to keep track of the enrolment of students in different grades and classes, and then link these records with their annual and other periodic performance tests, tutorial assessments and classroom outturns. Fourthly, universities function with a large amount of financial resources and need a close watch of their academic and non-academic budgets. A judicious planning and control of such resources is possible by a computer-based financial monitoring system.

In the Indian context, while some of the above management applications are understandably catching attention in the education field, a popular use of computer is in the processing of examination results. Various examinations are held by secondary boards, intermediate boards, universities, medical and engineering colleges on different dates and literally hundreds of thousands of candidates are involved in most of them. With the deplorable tendency of influencing examiners, tampering with marks and manipulating results is apparent today in all its manifestations and is the less controllable in manual operations. An arrangement of codified mark-script and a computerised processing of results at the post-examination stage (preferably away from the examination-centres) has found to be of great use by many Indian universities and institutions. While the computer-usage has not reached as quick and rational management as in the West, the general feeling is veering more and more towards computerisation in most large examining bodies.

An important off-shoot from the above system is its extension for socio-economic analysis. If the examination-candidates are allowed to indicate their communities, parental education and income, and if such data are built up over a few years, a great deal of systematic analysis is feasible of far-reaching impact. For instance, it should be possible to find out the quality of teaching subject-wise, institution-wise and area-wise; levels of student-performance community-wise; and the need for extra faculty, teaching facility and validity for instituting special stipends and grants for specific groups of students and subjects. Educational planners and decision-makers are agreeable that such analysis would be of great interest in regional planning for the education sector.

Objective types of testing are the order of the day. Especially where very large numbers of examinees are involved, a quick scrutiny of the mental faculties for comprehension, retention and assimilation is a difficult task in the preliminary rounds of elimination. Along with computers, optical scanners are used today to carry out quickly such bulk objective tests for both literary and numerical kind and to declare the results in the shortest possible time.

An extremely important application of computer in education field is the very personal touch it can provide in the basic learning process. The scene is quite common in the West today where little children are seen in small cubicles or with just desk-top terminals, — resembling a keyboard and a television-like screen. Through a process of pressing button and eliciting answers, a computer is able to provide a totally personalised service suited to the need of an individual child. Apart from the cases of very gifted children, the others particularly benefiting from such a system are children of the retarded kind (with physical or mental handicaps) and those from the backward communities. Through a series of questions and answers, computer is able to provide a very patient and personal guide to the child's learning process.

In India, apart from such computer-terminals being prohibitively costly in the average learning situations, there is the additional problem of a plethora of languages and the suitability of India scripts for computer recognition and reproduction. A lot of valuable work is being done to overcome these difficulties in the IIT, Madras, IIT Kanpur, and TIFR, Bombay. The pioneering work done at National Centre for Software Technology (NCST) on VIDURA project with Indian and Roman scripts suitable for desk-top developing and on GIST hardware Card at Centre for Development of Advanced Computing (C-DAC) and remarkable for their pre-review.

Courseware

A special boon in this area is the advent of personal computers. Apples II and III, Plato and Micro-plato, Commodore-Pet, Radio-Shack and Hatari are just a few examples of the competing brands. Glittering exhibition held during the World Congress on Computers in Education have showed the enormous amount of development that is taking place and the easy availability of ready-made teaching and learning packages — called "courseware" — based on small computers on an inexpensive scale.

India is well-poised to enter this area in a big way. The peculiar necessity in the Indian case is not just standard "courseware" in conventional education, but the enormous range of utilitarian "courseware" that can be used both in formal and informal education in the vast rural area. Surely one can think of small electric-pluggable computers carrying many such "courseware" lessons on magnetic tapes and floppies and moving from one electrified town or village to another, after many prolonged sessions of group learning. If the State governments come forward and make such experiments possible in different languages, one can imagine lively situations of portable computer resources holding captive an enthralled audience in a learning process and grappling with the adult illiteracy problem in a very practical and potentially useful manner. A general-education and utility-education resources unit like this, abbreviated as "GURU", can literally spread the gospel of education and create many Japans of hundred per cent literacy within a short time!

Conclusion

An interesting possibility for India is a general-purpose computer-network among universities, where each computer keeps its own data without any common relationship, and a user can access any computer on the network. This is similar to a very well-known resource-sharing network ARPANET in the USA interconnecting more than 50 university and research computer centres, including a few in Europe. Many universities have interesting and sometimes unique computer facilities. These become more valuable if they can be employed by a large community of users from amongst professors and students. The seed has been sown already in the ERNET project, connecting the 5 IITs, TIFR, NCST, IISC and Department of Electronics, which also has a daily gateway connecting them through the Unix platforms network to the US Universities. The ERNET now is getting linked with other premier Indian institutions on a nominal payment basis.

Another development worth noting recently is the use of BBC Acorn computers, followed by our ESPL's Unicorn computers (both being 8-bit microcomputers), in the Computerised Literacy and Studies in Schools (CLASS) project which is going on in a few thousand Indian schools, initiating the students from the few higher secondary standards into the computer mystique. No wonder, many bright students have already become developers of quality software!

The latest entrants in the field are some professional computer training institutions (such as NIIT, ICS, ISCT, etc.) which have either adopted schools or launched for them various computer-related education programmes. These are laudable efforts by the private sector and seem to be finding favour with the Government, as they can help in a big way to bring in computer literacy in the education sector in its most impressionable phase.

23

HEALTH SECTOR

Introduction

Computer applications in the health sector have increased phenomenally in the seventies all over the world. A number of sophisticated medical applications are currently in operation throughout North America, Europe, Japan, Singapore and Australia. It is, however, in the recent times that the developing countries have shown any degree of interest in the computer-based health information systems that can play a role in helping a health administration to meet the needs within their limited available resources.

Public Health Care System

While public health services relate to the health problems of a community as a whole, medical services concern each individual within that community. The decision-making by public health authorities follow four stages: identification and evaluation of the community's health needs; selection, collection and processing of pertinent data; planning and implementation of public health policies; and assessment of the results achieved by these policies.

In the field of medicine alone, the 3,000 diseases and 12,000 medical terms recognised in 1900 increased ten-fold by the end of seventies. According to an American feasibility study for a universal computerised consultation system, some two million medical facts have to be mastered by anyone practicing general medicine today. Such an abundance of information can prove negative for the physician who does not properly master it in making diagnostic and therapeutic decisions. Medical information poses not only quantitative problems involving excesses and gaps, but also organisational problems related to procedures for evaluation, decision and action, and to methods for planning research and collective health management.

A major health care system in teaching hospital has a *consultation sub-system*, resulting from contact with the patient and developed by a medical team through diagnoses and examinations apart from its experience. The resulting medical files can form a major feedback loop of medical knowledge through treatment evaluation, and clinical and epidemiological research. Medical activity is also backed by a *hospital logistics sub-system* which includes allotment of beds, management of hospitalisation period, laboratory requests, pharmacy management, control of food-stocks and filing of personal medical records. New technologies applied to health care system can lead to three *information sub-systems:* aid to fundamental diagnostic decision-making; research and prevention, including statistical and epidemiological applications; and the hierarchic evaluation of the activities of the health care system.

Health Information System in the West

Most computer-based health information systems in the West make it possible to organise and rationalise the analysis of patient and hospital data, the collection of test results, cross-checking (the task of the physician), filing and billing. The personal medical file is typically composed of a *first* group of relatively standard data, such as, identification-background (personal, social and family), personal profile (disease-susceptibility and habits), and an overview of different physical functions; and a *second* group of data relating to the patient's current health problems. Standard data play the major role in a normal check-up, while the second type is relevant to deal with emergency cases.

Some health information systems currently available handle accounting administration (e.g., GAMM). Others handle descriptive statistics in epidemiology (e.g., OTARIE). Still others handle hospital logistics and communication (e.g., TMIS). Some document-based systems facilitate the handling of medical files (e.g., DOSTAM and MAYO). There are systems to monitor a group of patients suffering from a specific and chronic pathology (e.g., CHRONOSS, for dialysis and hypertension); for coordinating in-patient treatment (e.g., COSTAR); for carrying out interactive check-ups by proposing appropriate analyses and treatments (e.g, PAOMIS); and for clinical and epidemiological research (e.g., AIDE-PLD and PASTIS). Pharmacological and toxicological data-banks also exist (e.g.,

MEDIPHOR, BIAM and INSERM). Such aids to medical decision-making have caused a revolution in techniques and improved the selection process among a plethora of tests, the doctor-patient relationship, the role played by the medical staff, the relationship between general practitioners and specialists, and even medical teaching.

A particularly interesting example is the clinical data system (CDS) used in the UK. Records stored on computer allow any information to be quickly referred to on a video-terminal screen and updated on the keyboard. It is also programmed to analyse records and produce graphs which give the doctor an immediate indication of the patient's condition. CDS is in use in the renal units of 12 hospitals, where renal transplant or renal dialysis cases are regularly monitored (for the whole of patient's life) in terms of 40 different parameters relating to the patient's bio-chemistry, harmatology, blood pressure and transplant therapy.

Developing Country Problems

Computer-supported total medical information systems in the West are backed by nearly unlimited financial and skilled manpower resources, and are hardly suitable for the developing countries. Such systems require not only highly trained managers and scientists, who would have to be trained in the First or Second World, but also personnel to perform data collection and data entry procedures. All such people are not easily available. These apart, experts recorded the problems of implementing health information systems in developing countries as: lack of infrastructure; lack of priority to health budget; relative high cost for short-term returns; novelty of the large-scale information technology; absence of policies for data protection and communication; lack of communication between health and computer professionals; neglected social and cultural values; excessive significance attached to hardware; and inappropriate transfer of technology.

Indian Status

Studies of the Comprehensive Rural Operations Society (CROSS) showed that input data can have assured reliability, provided, these are based on the primary medical documents collected from the local health care personnel. Although the Institute for Medical Statistics Research uses second and third generation computers for statistical data processing, computers have not really found their way into Indian hospitals. There are more than 6,000 hospitals overburdened with patients and 5,000 rural centres for preventive care. But the considerable amount of information coming from them is hardly analysed on computer before government and public decisions are made on health matters.

The computer-based management information system (MIS) for health, sponsored earlier by Electronics Commission of India and undertaken by the Administrative Staff College of India for the health directorate of Andhra State, identified the major sub-systems of health as disease control, medical care, promotional services and resources. The *disease control sub-system* comprised national programmes to control and eradicate such communicable diseases as Malaria, Tuberculosis, Smallpox, Cholera, Leprosy and Filaria. The MIS was planned to support monitoring of critical parameters of field operations to ensure proper implementation of programme guidelines and would provide statistical methodology, which could be used by the health administration in making best use of available resources to prevent the spread of the disease.

The *medical care sub-system* comprised the allopathic system of medical care through primary health centres, taluk hospitals, district headquarters hospitals, and teaching and speciality hospitals. The MIS was planned to support the studies of utilisation of different categories of hospitals, disease-trends in different regions, and projection of bed-needs and other services, — with the flow of data from a sample of hospitals covering both inpatient and outpatient care. The *resource sub-system* comprised major resources utilised by the health department, such as, personnel, drugs, buildings and equipment. The MIS was planned to support monitoring utilisation of various resources and projecting requirements of different regions, — with operational systems developed for personal postings and transfers. The *promotional services sub-system* was not covered by the MIS at the current stage.

Centre for Railway Information System (CRIS) has developed a comprehensive Hospital Management System on computer for the railway hospitals. Other hospital monitoring systems developed in India include the software packages by the Regional Computer Centre of Chandigarh and Applied Computer Services of Hyderabad.

Malaria Eradication

The monitoring system of surveillance, treatment and spraying operations in National Malaria Eradication Programme (NMEP) was undertaken based on 10 years' data from 565 villages of the Araku Valley, one of epidemic areas in Andhra Pradesh. Data used in the system covered blood smears according to sex, age, etc.; details of all positive cases of disease; insecticide spray details; and climate data on rainfall, temperature and humidity. The system used techniques of trend analysis to determine periodicity of malaria out-breaks; regression analysis to relate the number of malaria incidences to the climatic variables; and spread analysis to develop a statistical model capable of predicting spread of malaria from village to village. Many interesting results were thrown up and the monitoring system was fully implemented.

Dialetic clinic problems in handling patients was studied in a hospital by Regional Computer Centre of Calcutta, with a view to ensuring optimal resource utilisation and provision of highly efficient medical care, by using INQUIRY language of Burroughs 6,700 computer. Queuing problems in peak hours in a TELCO hospital and medicine inventory problems (with due regard to shelf-life) in a TISCO hospital were also interesting studies yielding practically useful results.

Conclusion

To summarise, India as a developing country needs a unified and decentralised national health service, supported by a health information system to encourage health care planning. A comparable health information system (HIS) in Italy includes networks for the speedy reporting of the outbreak of a communicable disease; collection of data on health service efficiency; nation-wide standardisation of medical files; rationalisation of infant mortality data; comparison of data on pregnancies, miscarriages, abortions, still births, congenital malformations and infant care, and so on. A similar approach to the Indian scene is certainly worth considering for managing the public health care sector.

A new study under UN funding undertaken for the Himachal Pradesh health services has a comprehensive approach for nearly 5000 eligible couples for pre-natal, neo-natal and post-natal health awareness and nearly 300 villages from each of the 12 districts and 69 blocks. The survey covers the role of health communication through mass media; printed media and other modes from these couples, formal and informal leaders and village statistics; help to computer-based statistical processing using frequency distribution; cross-tabulation and regression analysis; and promising interesting results.

24

BANKING SECTOR*

Introduction

Computers have had a major impact on the banking industry. The computer has not only affected the accounting and operating operations required by the traditional bank services but has also influenced the form and extent of all such services and made possible a variety of new "computer services". The computer is playing an even more decisive role in the operation of many banks through its use in financial models and other management science applications.

Banking Services

Traditional and new banking services that can be computerised include the following:

A. *Demand Deposits Accounting*

This application involves the automation of checking account processing. This was the first and most widely used utilised computer application in banking. It depends heavily on the use of magnetic ink character reader (MICR) coded cheques and deposit slips, and the use of MICR reader-softers to automate the capture of input data. Output of this system includes special reports concerning such items as new accounts, overdrawn accounts, etc. and monthly customer statements.

---

* Contributed by Prof. A.K. Nayak, Head, Department of Computer Sciences, Indian Institute of Business Management, Patna.

B. *Savings*

Most banks can have some form of computerised savings account processing. Some banks still use batch processing systems to process the deposits and withdrawals, and post them to their proper accounts on a daily basis. Other banks utilise a real-time savings application which use data communications terminals at the teller's windows and automated remote "teller terminals" which are electrically linked to the computers in the bank. Such terminals are really special-purpose micro-computers or "intelligent terminals" which automatically update a customer's balance on the computer and perform various banking services for the bank customer. Manual savings and loan associations are other major user's of computers for real-time banking applications.

C. *Consumer, Commercial and Mortgage Loan*

Banks can be computerised mainly in respect of data processing required by their lending activities to consumers and business firm. The widespread development of bank credit-card plans has greatly increased the use of computers to process the multitude of transactions generated by millions of bank credit-card holders. Banks also lend money on a long-term basis for real-estate mortgages and are the major sources of short-term credit for many business firms. Most banks utilise punched card, MICR and optical character reader (OCR) source documents to automate the capture of input transaction data into their computerised loan system. Output of this application includes monthly customer statements, interest and fax reports, and various loan analysis reports.

D. *Trust Application*

The trust function of banks involves the management of corporate trusts, personal trust, pension funds, and health and welfare funds. The computer is utilised to handle a wide variety of accounting chores and produce management report and legal documents. Advanced trust applications involve the use of computerised security analysis and portfolio selection applications.

E. *Advanced Application*

Many large banks can utilise computerised financial performance models for internal planning and control, and to evaluate the financial condition and financing requirements of bank customers. Banks can utilise many other tools of operations research that require the computational power of the computer.

The computer can also be considered as the primary component of future electronic fund transfer system (EFTS) which will replace cash and cheques as the primary method of payment. The banking industry is in the forefront of efforts to develop the related hardware and software. Automated teller machines (ATMs), point-of-sale (POS) terminals and computerised pay-by-phone systems will be the evidence of this development.

Many banks can offer computer services to their customers that are quite different from the traditional banking services. Through the use of computers, banks can offer a wide variety of services to other banks and financial institutions, business and professional firms, government and public organisations, and individuals. Some banks can spin off their EDP departments into separate EDP service subsidiaries that compete with independent computer service bureaus. Banks offering computer services must operate within specific legal restrictions but still manage to offer a wide variety of services.

Regional and Head Office Level Computerisation

Applications that can be undertaken at the head office level are: (a) administrative, (b) performance monitoring, including budgetary control, (c) credit information, (d) consolidation of certain information for feed back of HO and (e) external agencies including RBI, returns.

Requirement at regional levels are: (a) methods and frequency of collection of data, (b) coding structure, (c) output formats screen layouts and (d) various reports including headquarters enquiries.

Most of the banks have achieved their success to a considerable extent in computerising the above-mentioned functions at head office and regional level. A lot of benefits can be derived from the latest tools of the information technology by streamlining the functions at both these levels.

In the classical approach, much work has already been done for Indian banks. In the system study area, work has been done by several committees as follows:

(a) Reserve Bank of India — Committee on Mechanisation in

Banking Industry;

(b) Indian Bank Association — Committee on Rationalisation of Returns;

(c) Government of India — Working Group on Customer Service to Banks;

(d) Indian Banks Association — Committee on Computerisation and Mechanisation in the Banking Industry.

These committees have studied the banking system in depth and highlighted the problem areas. As a result, a three-tier appropriate information management has been undertaken as follows:

(a) Head office level,

(b) Regional office level, and

(c) Branch office level.

Cheque Clearance

Cheques clearance in India operates through clearing houses, and about 60,000 branches of banks participate in clearing. On the average, 200,000 cheques are cleared everyday. 69 per cent of the clearing load is handled by clearing housing of Bombay, Delhi, Madras and Calcutta. In terms of the volumes of instruments being processed, there is a great need to computerise the cheque processing system.

The introduction of MICR technology of cheque processing has emerged as the most logical step in this direction. The working group, appointed the Reserve Bank of India at the instance of Government of India, considered the modalities of introducing national clearing of outstation cheques and the feasibility of introducing mechanised processing of cheques. The Committee recommended adoption of magnetic ink character recognition (MICR) technology for facilitation mechanised cheque processing by the banking industry in India.

MICR Implementation in India

Mechanised processing of instruments has been initially introduced in Bombay, Delhi, Calcutta and Madras; and will be extended in phases to other State capitals and major centres. Thereafter in the final phase, the system will move to GRID concept.

MICR is the technique of using ink containing magnetised particles (ferrous oxide) to print characters on cheques, drafts, travellers cheques and other paper documents which can be translated into machine-level language by a device that senses magnetisation. When the magnetised portion of the instrument is placed below the electrical field, the magnetisation generates certain wave patterns which are interpreted as characters, then decoded by the machine to obtain required information regarding document numbers, amount, etc. Reader/Sorter can be programmed to sort documents by city, bank, branch or any other desired parametre.

In addition, the document data can be captured on computer-compatible media like magnetic tapes and disks for further processing, such as, obtaining listings of instruments branchwise. Batches of instruments can be simultaneously sorted and balanced with control totals. Thus mechanised sorting, listing and balancing is possible with the use of MICR equipment.

Standardisation of Size

For mechanised processing, instruments have been standardised to the following two sizes:

1. Saving bank cheque, travellers cheques: $6^1/_2$" X $2^3/_4$";
2. Current account cheques, drafts, dividend interest warrants, etc.: 8" X 3-2/2".

MICR Equipments

Basic MICR equipment consists of the following: (i) Encoders; and (ii) Reader-Sorters.

(i) *Encoders*

These are small table-top machines that print in MICR font, i.e., in a specified type set, the required information on the instrument. Encoders use special MICR ribbons. Encoders have a key-board similar to that of a typewriter. They are manually operated and can be run at a speed of approximately 1000 to 2000 documents per hour. Some encoders have a display unit and also allow for auto-feed,

(ii) *Reader-Sorters*

A reader reads the information printed in MICR ink and translates it into machine language. Reader-Sorters are available with sorting speeds, ranging from 20 to 2000 documents per minute, and with up to 36 packets. Computer sort programmes are designed to ensure complete sorting of inward and outward instruments in a minimum number of parses on the machine.

To enable the clearing instruments to be 'read' by machine, the required information relating to the instrument, viz., cheque/ instrument No./city/bank/branch on which drawn, account No., transaction type, and amount of instrument are printed (enclosed) in coded form in the bottom 5/8" band of the instrument reserved for the MICR code line. Codes have been allotted to the four major cities and to banks and their branches participating in clearing in the cities. The transaction types, e.g., saving accounts, current account, travellers cheque, dividend, etc., have also been coded.

Branch Mechanisation

The Rangarajan Committee identified the application areas and test centres based on size, location and ability of the branch very clearly. It also identified the outputs to be generated from the system, keeping in mind that all branches would not be computerised. As a result, branch mechanisation at present is confirmed to the installation of advanced ledger posting machines (ALPMs) in the branches.

This system would ultimately replace manual procedure of making entries in the primary ledgers relating to consumer accounts, such as, saving accounts, current accounts, cash credit, time-deposits and loan accounts with the help of ALPM can handle the following:

(i) 2000 saving bank account,
(ii) 750 term deposit accounts,
(iii) 750 current accounts, and
(iv) 1000 loan accounts.

Apart from the above, it can also handle the following:

– Recurring deposits,
– Cash credit accounts,

– General ledger accounts.

The ALPM has in-built security features to prevent misuse/ unauthorised use of machine. A hierarchy of passwords is maintained by the machines allowing access only to authorised personnel at various levels within the branch. These machines automatically carry out the following functions:

(a) Casting the balance in the accounts,
(b) Working out products,
(c) Calculation of interests,
(d) Printing of lists of all transactions as and when they are entered for checking purposes,
(e) Printing statement of accounts of customers periodically,
(f) Listing of daily standing instructions,
(g) Printing of advices for customers, if required,
(h) Cautioning the ledger-keeper in respect of accounts where care is to be exercised,
(i) Refusing to accept entries with regard to cheques stopped for payment, and
(j) Printing of various supplementary reports.

Each unit of these machines has the following hardware:

(i) *One typewriter like key board*: This contains numeric, alphanumeric and special function keys for entering data and commands and look like the typewriter key-board;
(ii) *Two floppy disk drive*: A floppy disk or floppy resembles a gramophone record. It is made of a plastic disk with magnetic coating on both sides. It is enclosed in a sealed jacket which has elliptical openings on both sides for reading/writing information (data) from/into it. Floppies are used to store information pertaining to ledgers, accounting details and daily transactions. Handling a floppy disk carefully is of extreme importance.
(iii) *Printer*: This is used to print information being processed on the ALPM-like reports, statements, advices, ledger, interest provision, etc. Speed of the printer is independent of the speed of the keying in at the key-board and paper feed in continuous from the roller stack.
(iv) *Video Screen*: The screen heips the user to physically see the

contents of the data entered by him and ensure that right data has been fed into the machine. It also displays comments to be followed by the operator and the information processed by the machine. This unit resemble a TV screen.

Conclusion

Indian banking industry must look forward for the following technological advancement: (a) Electronic fund transfer, (b) Automated teller terminals, (c) One-point service counter, (d) 24-hour banking, (e) Customer data-base, and (f) Customer information services.

The resistance to computerisation from different trade unions and employees associations should be overcome by arranging extensive training and awareness programme both in-house and outside agencies to ensure their speedy exposure. They should be informed about their job security and care should be taken to increase their interests to use the computer for productivity and better efficiency in order to provide prompt customer service as well as to help in national development as a whole.

25

RAILWAY SECTOR — COST VERSUS BENEFIT

Introduction

The announcement that the Indian Railways' proposal for one of its computer project for an amount of Rs. 500 crores was accepted at the highest level had raised many skeptical eyebrows. The amount was purported to include the cost of developing Railways' own telecommunication network as well as other infrastructural facilities. But the nagging question was still whether deployment of such a large fund would yield value for the money invested.

Railway Computerisation

The first point was that mechanisation has not been a new feature for the Railways. Statistical compilation on punched cards started way back in 1924 with Hollerith machines, — used by the accounts branch for audit and accounting of revenue earnings, and by the statistical branch for compiling revenue statistics. IBM unit record equipment (with plugged circuits and limited data storage) came in 1963-64 for all the Zonal Railways. These machines helped to evolve an integrated system of accounting and compilation of revenue statistics directly from the source document of invoices. Investment in modernisation and expansion in the scale of operations in the Second and Third Plan periods led to replacement of unit record equipment with second-generation computers (with transistors). IBM 1401 computers came first at the production units in 1966 — one each at Chittaranjan Locomotive Works in West Bengal, the Integral Coach Factory at Madras and the Diesel Locomotive Works at Varanasi — to handle accounting applications like payroll, stores and materials, and costing as well as sophisticated applications like production scheduling and machine loading. By 1970, IBM 1401 computers were installed at the 9 Zonal Railways with a centralised computer in the Railway Board at Delhi. The zonal computers took on freight and fare accounting, fuel accounting, stores accounting, statistical compilation of operating performance, general payroll and financial accounting. The Railway Board computer was fed from 41 interchange points and 7 yards to keep track of the interchanging of broad-gauge wagons and to monitor the movement of special stock like petrol-tank wagons, acid wagons, etc. In addition, one computer was put at the Mughal Sarai marshalling yard to deal with wagons received and marshalled in its vast network of reception, departure and classification lines. A small analog computer in the Research, Designs and Standards Organisation at Lucknow was used for calculating the running of trains with varying parameters of load, rolling resistance gradients and speed restrictions in order to frame Railway Time Tables. All these computers are now under phased replacement with much higher computing power.

Railway Capital Assets

The second point is that the Indian Railways have evolved into a gigantic system spreading all over India with costly capital assets such as locomotives, wagons and coaches. They cover a route of nearly 60,000 kilometres running more than 10,000 trains per day and connecting about 7,000 stations and 45 major marshalling yards. The capital rolling stock has around 10,000 steam, 1,400 diesel and 600 electric locomotives which operate 400,000 goods wagons and 35,000 passenger coaches, — with a total mobile asset value of around Rs. 4,000 crores. A primary role of the Railways is an efficient utilisation of the above rolling stock and an availability of wagons for the movement of coal, petroleum, steel, cement, iron ore, foodgrains and fertilisers: all in the core sectors of the national economy. Such efficient utilisation is possible only with an information system having a reliable and extensive telecommunication network, and powerful computer facilities which can process the reported data into timely information for meeting the day-to-day needs of operation as well as managerial decision-making.

Clearly the earlier 14 second-generation computer — with limited memory and slow peripherals — could not meet the above needs. Railways in the advanced countries are already using fourth-generation computers (with large-scale integrated circuits) having capabilities of real-time operations and multiple task performed simultaneously: for supply of empty wagons to match requirement with minimum delay; for reservation of berths to intending passengers; for timely assignment of locomotives; and for a host of other jobs. Examples are the Japanese Railways, Canadian National Railways, British Rail, SNCF of France, Deutsche Bundesbahn of West Germany and Southern Pacific of the USA, — which the Indian Railways are now set to emulate with the latest computer project. The economics of the project are fairly straightforward.

Freight Information and Operation System (FIOS)

One important application envisaged is an on-line computer-based wagon movement and freight control system. It is a striking fact that out of 24 hours in a day, a wagon is on the move only for an average $4^1/_2$ hours and detained for the remaining $19^1/_2$ hours in marshalling yards, sick lines and repair shops. The other fact is that wagons are loaded and unloaded on individual basis, whereas they are transported only as a train with a single or multiple rakes (22 wagons each). In order to reduce detention of wagons in transit at the marshalling yards, to ensure elimination of intermediate marshalling and to enhance empty haulage of wagons from release points to demand points, there is the need of a real-time information system capable of sophisticated analysis and using mathematical programming techniques. Assuming an improvement of even 10 per cent in the effective utilisation of wagons, this is equivalent to an additional supply of 40,000 wagons, the manufacturing cost of which is about Rs. 150 crores. The entire amount can be taken as the annual saving, — with the additional advantage of not increasing the physical holding of wagons which would have increased the turn-round time and reduced utilisation.

Other Railway Applications and Ensuing Benefits

A second important application is the computer-based all-India locomotive utilisation strategy. Diesel and electric locomotives move with a cruising range of about 1000 miles and extend over more than one Zonal Railway. In order to anticipate arrival times of long-hauling locomotives and to plan for their most efficient utilisation, there is the need of telecommunications and timely analysis of linear programming kind. Assuming an improvement of only 10 per cent in locomotive utilisation, this is equivalent to adding 140 diesel and 60 electric locomotives to the total fleet. Unit costs of diesel and electrical locomotives being Rs. 27 and 22 lakhs respectively, this tantamounts to adding Rs. 38 crores plus Rs. 13 crores to our total capital asset, i.e., Rs. 51 crores of annual saving.

A third important application is the computer-based all-India marshalling strategy. Although marshalling is a key element of railway operation, the present Indian marshalling rules have evolved historically through trial and error. With a massive increase of traffic in the Fifth, Sixth and Seventh Plans, a global marshalling strategy has been the needs to be formulated for alternative traffic patterns by using mathematical modelling and simulation techniques. RITES, for instance, had conducted such a study by using the Inter-data computer of the Planning Commission. These studies need continuous revision and updating on the behaviour of traffic streams with alternative patterns, — under alternative investment plans in terms of line capacity and yard capacity. If this leads to reduction of wagon detention by another 5 per cent (over and above the earlier 10%), the notional increase in utilised wages resources would be of the order of Rs. 75 crores per year.

A fourth corollary application is the computer-based traffic facility analysis. So far, the Indian Railways have been spending about Rs. 75 crores every year on traffic works for augmenting the reception, departure and classification lines, apart from the different types of yards. The methods of determination have been mostly ad-hoc kind, except some yards like Mughal Sarai where simulation techniques was applied. If the Railways make extensive usage of Monte Carlo simulation for the project planning of both line capacity and yard capacity works, scarce resources are likely to be far better utilised in the works projects than under the thumb-rules now. Assuming 10 per cent more efficiency would mean a notional availability of Rs. 7.5 crores every year in terms of marginal investment.

The tally in the above benefit analysis is Rs. 150, Rs. 51, Rs. 75 and Rs. 7.5 crores, i.e., Rs. 283.5 crores in all. On an investment of Rs. 500 crores, this is 56.7 per cent return per annum, on an conservative estimation of 10 per cent (or less) improvement in efficiency. This is a more moderate projection than the declared 15 per cent rise in efficiency which, if achieved, would lead to even more solid results in terms of returns on investment.

Conclusion

The above financial calculation does not present the social benefit to the population by increasing efficiency or the multiplier effect in the core sectors of economy by additional availability of rolling stock of wagons. There is also the prevailing computer application for on-line passenger reservation system in the railway stations of the metropolitan cities starting with Delhi, Bombay, Calcutta, Madras and Hyderabad cities, with often far-flung terminals to provide a passenger's choice of any train any day, any class, any destination and any priorities: quite a tall order. This is comparable to the use of computer terminals for airlines reservation and is also a common sight in the large railway stations overseas. In spite of sheer complexity of the Indian situation in terms of classes of railway passenger accommodation, the pressures from privilege groups and the prevailing illiteracy of the commuting masses, success of such a system is emerging beyond doubt. Even the other applications make the computer project of the Railways very much worthwhile.

26

STEEL SECTOR – DECISION-MAKING

Introduction

Decision-making has been variously defined, particularly as translating information into executive action. It is interesting to go back a century or so, when at the wake of industrial revolution, decision-making was confined to fixing wages and time periods, rewards and incentives, and keeping account of men and material. For today's managers, these are routine decision-making, best relegated to lower-down clerks. With progress in industrialisation came needs for decision-making in man power planning, inventory control and materials management, marketing research, and project management. These were areas of semi-routine decision-making involving both set logic and value judgement, thus involving high level managers, but not all the way. Last to emerge on the scene were corporate decisions on long-term planning, investment appraisal and others of this genre.

Decision-Making

Interestingly enough, usage of computers can be based on the above delegation in decision-making. First applications to merit computerisation were, pay-roll, incentive scheme, and the whole gamut of financial accounting and analysis. Later, computers took in their stride project control systems, man power planning, marketing information systems and others of the ilk.

An important distinction has all along existed in decision-making, — between structured decision and unstructured ones. In repetitive functions, decision is usually structured involving known rules and their careful operations, with a vigilant eye on performance against target or norms. Computer is happily suited to help managers for the bulk of structured decisions. Unstructured decision is a different game, in the form of judgement for action tempered with experience and value judgement, with objective rationale going hand-in-hand with subjective criteria.

Decision-making in steel have gone through all the above processes of gradual mechanisation and growth in computer applications for more and more non-routine areas. As Steel making is an age-old process so is the decision-making for Steel, — far more structured than in more recent technologies.

World Steel

Steel has almost a global distribution, — with Western Europe earlier contributing 26.3 per cent, U.S.S.R. and Eastern Europe 26.1 per cent, Asia 22.3 per cent, North America 20.5 per cent and others 4.8 per cent. Nippon Steel leads the field in raw steel output above 40 million tonnes, with U.S. Steel, British Steel and Bethlehem Steel following close upon its heels, with others making up a total world output in excess of two hundred million tonnes in the middle of this decade.

Requirement of Steel industry are vast and differ substantially from chemical industries where most fluids are processed, and temperature and environmental conditions do not exist in great extremes. Steel plans process solids and molten metals where even sampling raw materials and products is a major problem in itself, apart from their analyses. One needs sensors to measure weights (100–500 tonnes vessel), temperature (1200°C–1800°C), dimensions (length, width and thickness of red-hot moving object), and velocities of rolled products (hot and cold), rotations and rolls in mills, and levels of molten metal in vessels (pouring height), to mention only a few. Contactless and non-destructive sensors are increasingly needed but are often a management's despair.

Computer in World Steel

Cost and productivity, replacement and expansion of capacity, environmental protection are all rapidly growing and demanding market information which is a part of the ever-changing pattern of problems faced by today's major steel producers. Dynamic changes are in evidence in wage rates, productivity, etc., taking place all over the West, which sharpen demands for fast information, flows and easily accessible data banks which contain updated and concentrated information. High quality management often results from priorities assigned for investment in information systems. Table 26.1 presents the earlier distribution of data processing applications in steel industry, in the middle of the seventies. Table 26.2 shows such applications for specified objectives. Japan, apart from being the world's largest steel producer, had many distinctive computer applications among the first ten. Table 26.3 shows the then computers in Japanese steel industry.

TABLE 26.1: Earlier Distribution of Data Processing Application in Steel Industry (1975)

(*Percentages*)

	U S A	Western Europe	Japan
Production Planning and Control	45	55	75
Commercial and Administrative	40	30	15
Process Control	10	10	5
Corporate Planning	5	5	5

TABLE 26.2: Earlier Data Processing Applications for Steel Industry Objectives

Steel Industry Objectives	Data Processing Applications
Higher Serviceability	Order entry and tracking Production planning and control
High quality	Process control Quality control
Minimal or optimal production costs	Production planning and control Material movement. Process control
Budget and finance control	Finance planning simulations.

TABLE 26.3: Earlier Computers in Japanese Steel Industry

Steel	No. of Makers	General Purpose	Process Control	Total
Blast Furnace	9	107	403	510
Open Health & Electric Furnaces	25	53	26	79
Others	9	18	10	28
Total	43	178	439	617

Earlier data processing systems in the steel industry in U.S.A., Western Europe and Japan are reflected in Fig. 26.1. It is interesting to contrast the distribution of data processing applications in steel against the earlier world wide on-line computer installations, as reflected in Table 26.4. Historically, Japan took the pride with its process control computers, as shown in Table 26.5.

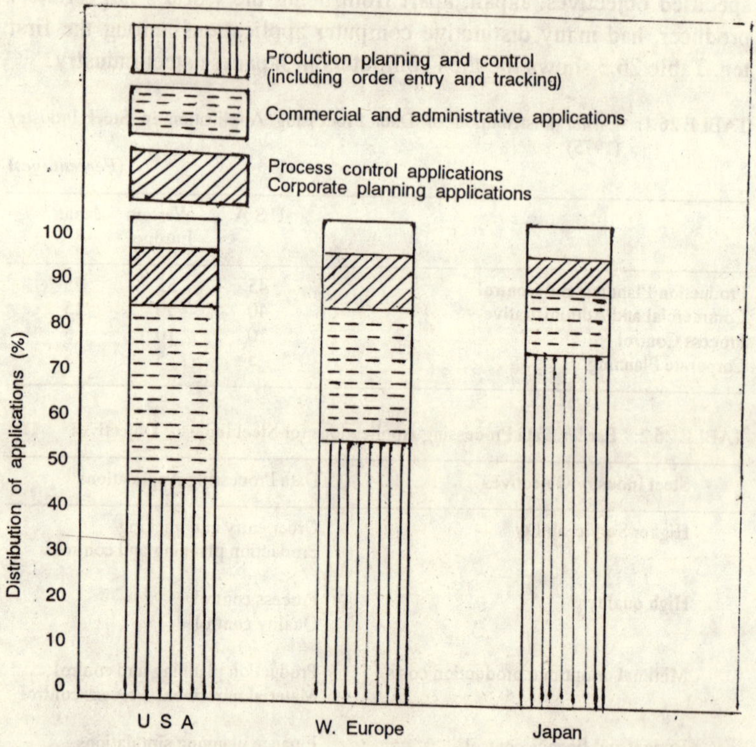

FIG. 26.1: Distrubution of Data Processing Systems Applications in Steel Industries

In the Russian Steel industry, computer applications can be divided into two groups: Management Control Systems and Operational Control Systems. The first group aims at raising the efficiency of management, by solving operational and long-term problems; through planning of plant output; planning accounting of raw material, supply and consumption; financial control of production; and planning of equipment repair. The second group tackles blast furnace heating systems, control systems for stores control system for metal cutting in rolling mills and automatic control systems for metal consumption of the finished products. There are both on-line control systems and off-line control systems for providing operator guidance, most of which have since become on-line transaction processing (OLTP) on computers.

TABLE 26.4: Earlier Online Computer Installations (Worldwide)

Date	Gas, Chemical, Petroleum, Paper, Cement	Power	Metals (Mostly I&S)	Miscellaneous	Total
March, 1961	16	11	10	—	37
May, 1962	45	66	23	23	159
Sept., 1963	92	117	55	76	340
Aug., 1965	212	203	144	236	795
Sept., 1966	336	289	242	485	1352
March, 1967	386	324	260	601	1571
July, 1968	—	—	—	—	2890

TABLE 26.5: Earlier Installation of Process Computers in Japan

Process			No. of Computers	
Raw Materials	:	Ore Pretreatment	1	
		Sintering	14	
		Pelleting	2	
		Coke Oven	2	
Iron Making	:	Blast Furnace	36	(Total Blast furnace in operation — 58 in 1971)
Steel-making	:	Basic Oxygen Furnace	24	(Total LD Vessels — 88)
		Open Hearth Furnace	1	
		Electric Furnace	1	
		Continuous Casting	2	
Rolling	:	Slabs and Blooms	15	
		Hot rolled sheets	15	
		Cold Rolled sheets	8	
		Plates	11	
		Shapes	7	
		Wire rods	2	
		Pipe and tubes	2	
		Annealing	4	
Others	:	Energy control	10	
		Analysing	10	
		Others	8	
Total as on Jan., 1971			175	(at 88.5 Million tonnes of of Steel)
Total as on Jan., 1974			328	

Indian Environment

Indian Steel plants were studded with instruments of late fifties vintage. While other countries had gone in for instrumentation based on integrated circuitry and LSI, steel making in our country was until lately an art for which production and quality varied with operators.

Management control and operations control are still needed in the above environments which aim less at process control but detailed operator guidance and general management control, with specific objectives and tasks. The summary of objectives and tasks for various functional areas in Indian Steel are illustrated as follows based on the current computer applications:

A. *Production*

To render assistance in improving production efficiency.

Objectives	Tasks
(a) To assist in Production Planning	Product profitability reports.
(b) To assist in Production Scheduling	Despatch programmes and updating.
(c) To watch production performance	Production reports based on aggregated performance.
(d) Meeting despatch targets	Preparation of despatch performance against programme.
(e) To investigate production problems	O.R. and Statistical reports.
(f) To optimise conflicting interests and working under different limitations	Product mix studies, Yield optimisation studies, optimal distribution of hot metal etc.
(g) To introduce S Q C (statistical quality control)	Preparation of S Q C reports.
(h) To assist in improved maintenance management	Eventual preparation of equipment failure analysis and reports on availability of components and spares.
(i) To assist in management of computers and spare parts	Preparation of machine loading and shop scheduling reports and monitoring off-loaded items.

B. *Marketing and Sales*

To render better customer service on short and long-term basis.

Objectives	Tasks
(a) To assist in sales invoicing	Preparation of sales invoices for ex-plant despatches.
(b) To assist in sales accounting	Preparation of net realisation and other accounting reports.
(c) To assist in watching stockyard performance	Preparation of stock statements ledger balances and inter stock yard transfer statements.
(d) To assist in watching sales performance	Preparation of profit performance and tonnage performance reports.
(e) To assist in marketing information system	Preparation of customer, industry and product profiles.
(f) To assist in efficient credit management	Preparation of credit analysis.
(g) To assist in investigation of various marketing problems	Rationalisation of documentation, watching advertisement expenditure against business generated, etc.

C. *Materials*

To reduce inventory (to generate more working capital).

Objectives	Tasks
(a) To indent when and where required	Preparation of automatic indents after timely review action.
(b) To assist in physical stock-keeping	Preparation of storewise inventory documents.
(c) To watch physical stocks against targets	Preparation of central inventory control reports.
(d) To review indenting and stock policies	Preparation of review reports.
(e) To assist in timely action in emergency situations in marketing areas	Preparation of raw stock and high stock statements and furnishing exception reports.
(f) To watch supplier performance	Preparation of vendor rating reports.
(g) To assist in integrating control over direct materials	Eventual preparation of indent stock posting and review reports.

D. *Finance*

To assist in efficient financial accounting and management.

Objectives	Tasks
(a) To assist in timely wage payment	Preparation of pay slips
(b) To assist in accounting of production expenses	Departmental production and cost figures
(c) To assist in accounting of sales expenses	Preparation of sales accounting documents
(d) To assist in accounting of material expenses	Preparation of material cost statements
(e) To assist in various employee services	Preparation of annual fixed deposit, P.F., income tax, gratuity, etc. statements
(f) To assist in accounting of capital expenditure	Preparation of capital expenditure statements
(g) To assist in accounting of town expenditure	Statements on dairy farm, local invoice, housing
(h) To assist in accounting of labour expenses	Labour cost statements
(i) To assist in assigning priorities to capital projects	Preparation of capital invoice analysis (Risk & D C F)
(j) To assist in improved cash management	Net cash-flow statements and investigative studies on operation of credit policy and rebate policy

E. *Engineering*

To render help in improved project performance.

Objectives	Tasks
(a) To assist in project management	Preparation of critical path analysis reports
(b) To watch performance of capital budget schemes	Capital budget studies
(c) To assist in risk analysis of major	Eventual preparation of risk analysis reports
(d) To assist in civil engineering design and construction problems	Preparation of optimal design studies
(e) To assist in updating schedule of rates and estimate of equipment prices	Use of microprocessors and desk calculators for the purpose

F. *Services*

To render aid for efficient services in hospital, town and other civic amenity areas.

Objectives	Tasks
(a) To assist in hospital management by better therapeutic planning	Eventual preparation of disease control cards and other hospital documents
(b) To assist in town management	Preparation of investigative reports
(c) To assist in sanitation and public health management	Preparation of investigative reports

Computer in Indian Steel

In keeping with the world-wide trend computerisation in India, too, came through accounting applications first of a routine decision-making kind. Soon they got on with semi-routine applications involving managerial decision-making on integrated project control, man power planning, maintenance management, and so on. Computers already provide help in non-routine decision-making to Indian managers apart from taking on, to a large extent, the operational control problems.

Two points need emphasis here. First, as shown in Fig. 26.2, computation speed and density of stored information have made rapid progress in the last few decades and go on unabated. In fact, average cost of central processing unit came down rapidly, as shown in Table 26.6. In consequence, cost of computer systems started falling lower and lower as shown in Table 26.7. Secondly, even using the earlier technology, each Steel plant built up rapidly its utilisation of computer power, as shown in Table 26.8.

If we take into account the response time needed for computer systems for various categories of data processing, we can visualise management decision-making distinctive application areas, as reflected in Table 26.9.

The following characteristics emerge clearly from the changing levels of computerisation in the Indian Steel scene:

(a) From the late sixties, second generation computers started being used as a replacement of unit record equipment and were mostly placed under the control of the Finance authorities, in each steel plant;

(b) The utilisation of computers gradually built up in each case and reached the peak of around 500 hours. In fact, in a plant like TISCO, the peak has been marginally above 500 hours owing to proper user maintenance;

(c) By virtue of second generation technology the usage of computers were entirely in batch processing mode and communications of data through terminals were not feasible for that technology;

(d) As a large number of batch mode applications had been clamouring for time in a computer even while being run round the clock, the response time could never be less than half a day. In fact, in most applications, response time had been inevitably more than 24 hours; and

(e) Introduction of fourth-generation computers with a distributed hierarchy of mini-computer, PC, and dumb terminal, have made possible on-line transaction processing today integrated with a variety of management information systems and decision support systems.

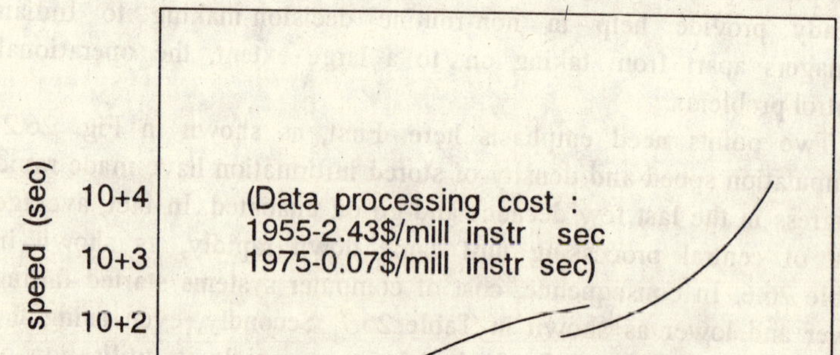

FIG. 26.2: Development of Data Processing Systems

TABLE 26.6: Average Cost of Central Processing Unit

Year	Average cost of computer (price of CPU)
1960	$ 1,00,000
1968	$ 60,000
1977	$ 10,000

TABLE 26.7: Earlier Cost of Computer Systems

Computer System	Cost	Year First delivered
TDC - 312	Rs. 1,600,000	1972
IBM - 1800	$ 250,000	1975
HP - 1000	$ 120,000	1976
DEC PDP - 1145	$ 135,000	1976
VARIAN 77 - 600	$ 85,000	1977

TABLE 26.8: Earlier Monthly Utilisation of Second Generation Computer Meter Hours

Year	Average per month
1968-69	139.20 meter hours
1969-70	194.00 meter hours
1970-71	200.66 meter hours
1971-72	232.71 meter hours
1972-73	277.80 meter hours
1973-74	283.92 meter hours
1974-75	323.86 meter hours
1975-76	345.63 meter hours
1976-77	375.58 meter hours

Computerisation in Steel Plant consistently keep the following aims in view:

1. To retain user credibility by constant efforts at increasing efficiency of computerised systems and by rationalising computer time by optimal system design.
2. To cover emergency situations and give management quick need-based analysis for high-silicon heats, e.g., cost-benefit analysis for procurement of coal from diverse sources, given to TISCO management.

3. To review, on a continued basis, the utility of computer systems and follow up their progress and acceptability to management.

TABLE 26.9: Emerging Data Processing Categories and Applications

Data Processing category	System response time	Data storage complexity	Applications
Level 1 Batch	Processing once in 8 hours, or on user's request	Very complex	Corporate planning, payroll, budget and costs, personnel billing, invoicing material balances etc.
Level 2 On-line	> 5 sec	Complex	Order entry and tracking, material movement, production planning and scheduling, dynamic rescheduling
Level 3 real-time interactive	> 5 sec	Relatively simple	Production control: Guidance and production data collection, stores control.
Level 4 Event-driven automatic processing	> 1 sec	Simple	Process control: Direct digital control, supervisory control, data acquisition.

Nature of Applications

Both on a current and potential basis, every Steel Plant in India has mapped its computer applications. Table 26.10 reflects major areas of computer applications where groups A and B give the current applications and group C indicates potential applications to be taken on with more advanced and powerful computers of third and fourth generation technology, coming on to the scene.

Applications under group A and B play a significant role in providing systems support in different areas of management control and offer scope for substantial pay-off in terms of tangible benefits. In Bokaro Steel Plant, the basic systems design is sufficiently broad-based to have provided for progressive integration of data computer applications, as follows:

(a) Minimum changes in the input documents to facilitate quick changeover from manual to mechanised system ensuring adequate data accuracy;

(b) Comprehensive pickup of relevant data from each input documents so that duplication is avoided;

(c) Well designed coding of control fields to facilitate variety of analysis for control purposes and also for providing scope for integration of applications, avoiding redundancy in processing; and

(d) Well planned computer file layouts to ensure scope for adequate statistical data analysis and also to ensure smooth transition to data-base concepts with the upgradation of the computer installation.

Current Range of Applications

A. *Production*

Almost in every Steel Plant, production planning and scheduling system has been in operation in jobbing shops on a recurring basis. Often shop scheduling and off-loading systems have been linked with the above, both for work centre loading and for progress-reporting purposes.

TABLE 26.10: Current Major Areas of Computer Applications

Data Processing Applications	Management Control Applications	
Group A	Group B	Group C
Off-Line	Off-Line	On-Line & Real-Time
1. Pay-roll 2. Reward/incentive 3. Financial accounts & analysis 4. Works & stores accounting 5. Estate accounting 6. Sales invoicing & accounts 7. Costing 8. Budgetary control 9. Project cost estimates 10. Integrated management accounting	1. Integrated project control system (a) Network planning (b) Equipment procurement and followup. (c) Pre-order monitoring 2. Capital repairs for major equipment 3. Manpower planning 4. Sales order processing 5. Operational statistics and report generation	1. Integrated inventory Control system 2. Process control (Operator guidance system) (a) Steel melting (b) Blast furnace operation 3. Raw material handling and blending 4. Production planning & control (a) Soaking pit scheduling (b) Mills scheduling (c) Production reports

An interesting off-shoot from the above is a rolling stock movement and utilisation system for tracking, locating and moving wagons within the Steel Plant. At two million tonne level and above, TISCO handles daily an exchange of thirteen hundred wagons, whereas at 1.7 million tonne level the Bokaro Steel Plant handled sixteen hundred ingoing and outgoing wagons daily, with another two thousand additional wagons in the plant. A benefit from planning and control of such a large number of wagons and locomotives is from reduced demurrage. Even a mere 10 per cent reduction saves Rs. 20 lakhs per year, by tracking and locating wayward wagons tucked away in forgotten corners. Non-recurring applications are profitability reports, which are updated as and when needed and can be linked with product-mix studies for maximising contribution towards fixed cost. An important application is optimisation in yield, in strip mills, etc., tried out in TISCO and other steel plant (Table 26.11).

TABLE 26.11: Current Application of Operation Research in Production Problems in Steel Industry

Application stage	Areas of application nature of problem	Techniques used (or likely to be used)
Stage 1. Early 50's	Open-hearth charging, preventive maintenance statistical investigation of blast furnace production data, discharging ore in blast furnace bunkers. Determination of slab mill capacity.	Simple statistical analysis. Linear regression. Hand simulation.
Stage 2. Late 50's and early 60's	Track time and soaking pit availability. Material handling of fabrication works. Blast furnace burdening. Slab-yard reorganisation. Repair of open hearths.	Queuing theory. Computer simulation. Linear programming. Critical path analysis.
Stage 3. Late 60's	Economic models for production planning. Capital investment models, In-process inventories. Overage policies. Static control models.	Large scale simulation by high speed computer. Larger linear programming models. Multiple regression.
Stage 4. 70's and 80's	Sophisticated models for dynamic control of processes. Large scale models of information and decision systems, etc.	Large simulation models. Control theory. Dynamic programming. Decision theory. Mathematics of probability.

B. *Marketing and Sales*

Recurring applications of this genre have integrated, order processing, performance monitoring and sales invoicing system. One can visualise this as an interlinked order processing and production planning system.

Non-recurring applications in this area are based on marketing information system which can provide customer profile, industry profile and product profile, as segments of marketing information needed on a long-term basis to decide on the popular product-mix for a Steel Plant. Other applications are credit management system to find efficacy of credit allowed to customers for boosting up sales and publicity management to assess linkage of sales with expenditure incurred on advertisement and publicity.

C. *Material*

Recurring applications here are integrated procurement, stock posting and review system, already tried out and working in TISCO. The system generated many 'alerts' for exceptions, mainly delayed supplies, low-stock levels, excessive inventory and holding of non-moving and well-moving items beyond specified tolerance limit.

Non-recurring applications are maintenance management systems tried out at Durgapur Steel Plant, study of procurement policy and stock posting policy, etc. The last two can be spin-off benefits from the integrated materials management system, mentioned above.

D. *Finance*

Recurring applications in this area relate to employee services, involving 60,000 or so employees and nearly two lakh transactions in a plant like TISCO. These applications also cover main accounts, financial accounts and stock sheets. An off-shoot is an accounts payable system involving, say, six thousand bills per month, which keeps track of delay in paying creditors beyond stipulated periods.

Non-recurring applications in finance relate to alternative capital investments tried out in plant like TISCO.

E. *Engineering*

Recurring applications in this area relate to capital budgeting system and project control networks. Both these help major construction projects of fairly big size for the purpose of project control, so that adequate and reasonable lead time and opportunity are available for corrective measures.

Non-recurring applications are designed culminations for civil and mechanical work.

F. *Services*

Recurring application is budgeting system for town and civic facilities.

Non-recurring applications relate to hospital management, town management, and so on.

Investigative Applications of O.R. Kind

Table 26.11 gives an idea of applications of O.R. kind in production problems in the Steel industry.

In our steel plant, these applications have been for optimisation in different mills (including yield as mentioned earlier); optimal product-mix for individual mills and for the entire plant; simulation of logistic problems such as, blast furnace ladles; hot metal distribution and scrap charging.

Implementation of Applications

Most Steel Plant applications have the following angles before implementation:

(a) *Top Management* – They should support the computer applications right from the beginning, perhaps by ensuring the idea themselves. Later on, they should remain involved throughout the design; development and implementation processes. Finally they should watch the results after implementation;

All these three stages are best ensured through a computer coordination committee involving the Managing Director or General Manager as its Chairman and Divisional Managers as its members. One such committee is functioning with great success at TISCO;

(b) *Line Management* – The need for computer applications should be accepted by them, they should also be prepared to suggest modifications from time to time. In other words, their involvement is of great importance for the implementation of computer applications;

(c) *Workers* – They should be able to provide 'healthy criticism' whenever a computer application does not deliver the necessary needs, for instance, errors pointed out in pay-roll can lead to check in computer allocation and tightening of input control;

(d) *Users in general* – User should be concerned with continued benefits from computer applications. One way of ensuring this is to float review questionnaires, tried out at TISCO.

Impact of Applications

One can visualise the impact of computer applications as follows:

Systems Impact = System Confidence × System Credibility

1. System confidence depends on user acceptance, this should be a function of achieved/desired speed factor; achieved/desired accuracy; achieved/desired complexity; and achieved/desired volume. This should also depend on favourability of management environment; functional area and time.
2. System credibility depends on user reliance; this should be a function of achieved/desired errors volume; achieved/desired timeliness; achieved/desired output-quality; and achieved/desired output-quantity. This should also depend on capability for automation, review and exception.

A qualitative formulation of system impact is possible based on the above available factors and dependent co-efficients.

Current Growth

As was indicated in Table 26.10, on-line and real-time applications for management control are contributing for future growth in the Indian steel scene. Some of these are described below:

(a) *On-line Inventory Control*

In TISCO, more than 1,00,000 items are handled at Jamshedpur, 20,000 at mines and 20,000 at collieries. This gives rise to nearly

40,000 transactions per month. At Bokaro Steel Plant, over 1,20,000 items of inventory are maintained with transactions nearing 15,000 per month. At both these Plant, terminals are located in the stores to collect details of transactions and generate alerts for exceptions. This facilitates minimum corrective action and provide facility for controlling inventory level and cutting out excessive lead-time. A benefit of around Rs. 1 crore is achieved per annum for each plant by reducing lead-time and bringing down stocks.

(b) *Process Control*

For billet cutting operations at Bhilai Steel Plant, process control applications on computer have been implemented. This involved input length calculations; output length estimation; control signal generation for minimum end-crop; determination of actual output length; and update elongation factor. The response time in controlling the flying shear motor by computer is around one minute for every red-hot, 7 tonne ingot rolled into a billet which is 120/130 metres long and is to be cut into 6±. 1 metre pieces. The cost of computerisation has been around Rs. 10.5 lakhs, other than the cost of the computer. Benefits are around Rs. 1 crore each year, through decrease in net-crop lengths.

At Bokaro Steel Plant, L.D. process of steel making has been computerised, using IBM-1800 computer. This process uses knowledge of weight and composition of inputs such as, molten metal, fluxes and scraps, and measures continuously, temperature of steel (especially at culmination of oxygen blowing) and end-point carbon. The control helps in blowing oxygen on molten pig-iron in order to oxidise carbon, silicon, sulphur and phosphorus at a temperature of 1500°-1600°C inside the L.D. vessel, while adding fluxes through hoppers. The response time of the entire process is 20–25 minutes. The cost of the system including all peripherals is Rs. 54 lakhs at 1.7 million tonne level. The saving in terms of improved performance and production is around Rs. 1 crore per year, through reduction in tap-to-tap time, reduction of redblows, reduction in consumption of ferro-alloys and reduction in off-heats. The process computer control also provides management information to the mainframe computer there.

At Bhilai Steel Plant, the coiler control for wire-rod mill is implemented with a micro-processor based system. This helps in varying speed of the coiler periodically so as to form coils within the limit, systematically. This also help to form a linear-spiral in each layer in the coiler and give rise to substantial benefits.

(c) *On-line Raw Material Control*

This system has terminals at the planning yard, coal storage silos and inward exchange yard. Based on wagon arrivals, material analysis and wagon details are transmitted by computer, to predict blend and composition of material going to sinter plants and blast furnace. Even one per cent improvement in productivity of the blast furnace results in 20,000 tonnes of additional production per year.

(d) *On-line Production Planning and Control*

This is used at the slabbing mills, hot rolling mills and cold rolling mills for effective order process; improvement of yield; reduction in mix-up of finished material and in-process inventory and optimum planning for quality and size in rolling progress. Effective benefits were as follows at Bokaro Steel Plant:

(a) 1.3 per cent yield improvement;
(b) 10,000 tonnes reduction in mix-up losses;
(c) 20 per cent reduction in work-in-progress inventory; and
(d) Reduced fuel consumption in furnaces, improved ingot mould and roll-life.

Conclusion

The above is a bird's-eye view of the computer applications in steel industry in the world and the same in India. Obviously, a long way is to be covered here. But, as has been brought out, with the reduction in computer prices and with the enhancement in computing power (including that of micro-processor), India today is using a new opportunity to leap-frog into sophisticated areas of computer applications in the steel industry. This can only provide a fillip to improved decision-making.

27

STATE ADMINISTRATION

Introduction

India appears to be truly poised to usher in the computer revolution. Thanks to the thinking of the Government, what had been a distant rumbling on the industrial horizon of the country has become a thunderous roar echoing in all fields of activities. The dramatic reduction in the cost of computing power, accompanied by the rapid advances in the technology of micro-electronics, seems to have happened not a day too soon. The convergence of computers with tele-communication networks is going to make possible the unleashing of the tidal wave of technological innovation the like of which the country has never seen.

Emerging Status

Computerisation in Public Administration had begun earlier in a similar way. Many States such as Tamil Nadu, Karnataka, Maharashtra, Madhya Pradesh, etc., had started installing their second and third generation computers mainly for routine applications of accounting kind. Uttar Pradesh took a quantum leap and went for a large fourth generation computer under its planning department. In addition, 11 States, followed by 2 more, were given third generation indigenous computers, in their police departments to deal with crime-criminal information systems and finger print formation systems, apart from the routine pay-roll materials accounting and licencing records applications.

To cap it all, National Informatics Centre (NIC) was set up in Delhi to have access and retrieval capability of the Central Government information, belonging to various ministries, departments and organisations, based on one of the country's largest fourth generation computers. NIC has already shown almost spectacular results by

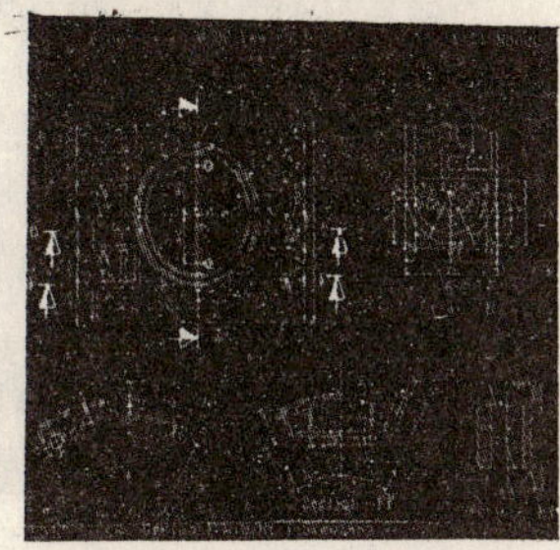

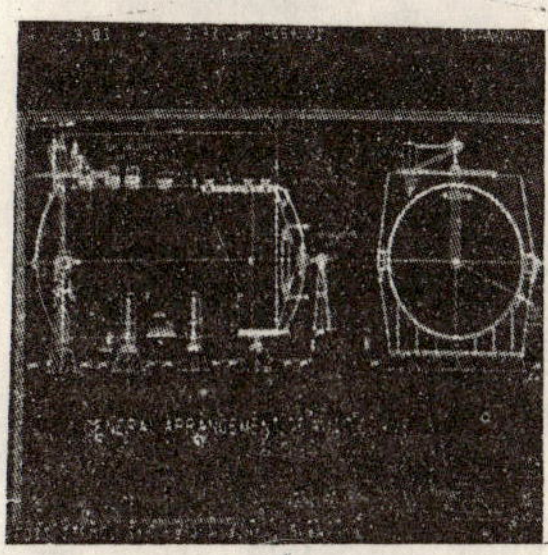

Two-dimensional Drafting on Computer

Magnetic Ink Character Reader (MICR), going with Computer for Banks

extending its helping hand to more than 60 departments and many more to come and having successfully handled more areas, such as, Asian Games. NIC has four near super-computers on its network at Delhi, Bhubaneshwar, Pune and Hyderabad, NIC has also reached the 25 State capitals and 7 Union Territorry capitals to establish a meaningful link between States and the Centre on such areas as agriculture, health, industry, demography and education. NIC has also linked more than 460 districts to this hierarchical network. Police computers, on their own, would similarly get inter-connected in a police-net to enable themselves to exchange vital social defence information within the country.

Computer in Government

Almost all vital aspects of social welfare, health, education, energy, communication and transport, to name just a few, are under the control of the State or its agencies in India. This imposes a heavy responsibility on the Government departments, both at the Centre and the States, to initiate and implement measures which would ensure a rapid socio-economic growth, and that the benefits of such measures reach the lower strata of society. The administrative machinery tends to slow down owing to the enormity of data that it has to deal with and difficulties in retrieving specific information at short notice. Furthermore, the process of decision-making is getting more and more complex.

Computers are finding increasing use in Government departments essentially on account of their ability to store vast amounts of data, retrieve them quickly, conduct a variety of analytical exercises with ease, examine a host of alternatives, and present factual reports in a summarised fashion. All this could significantly speed up the tasks of senior administrators — planning, directing, coordinating and controlling. Owing to their versatility, computers have been used in varied fields from missile-flight control to treasury accounting, and flood control to inventory management.

At the national level, Indian Railways have the largest number of computers and are in the process of further acquiring several third generation computers. Movement of their rolling stock on a national network of tracks is monitored on the computers. Their future planning is for a massive computerisation at Railway Board, connecting Zones, divisions and lower levels starting from on-line real-time wagon movement and freight control, and on-line passenger reservation systems, going up to a number of batch-processing applications involving materials management, financial planning and control, and production management. Theirs is one of the most ambitious fields of computer applications in India today. Indian defence services use the latest computers for a variety of purposes, including planning (with operations and intelligence), administration (with financial budgeting, personnel training and health), logistics (with food and transportation), and production control purposes. Some typical examples are project evaluation, planning of management responsibilities in terms of departmental levels; statistical applications for army vehicles, etc.; inventory problems including imports and high lead-times; production scheduling for naval dockyard; and personnel management system for career planning, placement training. All the steel plants have their own computers to optimise their production and inventory stocks, Shipping, Civil Aviation and Banking are among the several other areas benefiting from computerised applications. Police administrations all over the country adopt computers to assist them in crime detection. They have ambitious plans of developing a national hook-up of computers to benefit from police information across the country.

State Governments, too, have not lagged behind and are adopting computers as an aid to efficient administration. Almost all State Governments have set up their computer centres with the help of NIC and others are in the process of acquiring their computers. Availability of indigenously manufactured computers in the country has substantially contributed to the use of computers in administration. Some of the areas where computers have found wide adoption are briefly discussed below:

(a) *Planning Department*

The department plays a pivotal role in formulating annual plans and monitoring the progress of all developmental projects. It has to coordinate the activities of different departments and executing agencies to provide the thrust for planned growth. The department has to deal with an enormous volume of information coming from various on-going projects, data on physical progress, financial status, spill-over expenditure, etc. Corrective measures have to be initiated to ensure timely completion of projects. Computers assist in monitoring project-wise progress and identifying critical areas calling for attention. Performance statistics and variance reports are generated. The data base, regularly updated with process of work, serves as an aid to plan formulation. Once plans are finalised, computers assist in projecting manpower and other resource requirements. Thus, computers, can provide substantial aid in all aspects of the department's work-plan formulations, monitoring and evaluation.

In the UP, for instance, the projects-data under their planning department, have been computerised. Using a new scheme of 13-digit codification, the project expenditures are classified and monitored to watch performance against target figures. The UPDESCO computer is used for this purpose.

(b) *Finance Department*

Computers are ideally suited for a wide range of applications in the Finance Department due to their speed and accuracy in numerical computations. Computers can assist in budget formulations, tax administration and treasury accounting.

The Department has to deal with a stupendous pile of data on receipts and expenditure, classified under thousands of account heads, emanating from various State treasury offices. Further, this has to be reconciled with the figures available with the Accountant General's Office. Manually handled, this effort could significantly delay consolidation and reconciliation work. Several State Governments are taking the assistance of computers in tackling the problems of treasury accounting. Tax management is another area where computers are used. Sales and Entertainment taxes provide a big chunk of the State revenue and, as such, call for close monitoring to ensure effective collections and to check tax-evasion. Keeping records of important dealers on the computer and processing their advance payments can greatly facilitate generation of tax assessment, balance recovery statements, tax refund reports, statutory reports to Central Government, cases of tax-evasion etc. Computers assist in building a data-base of commodity revenue, prices, income dealers, productions and trade statistics which would aid in tax planning. In the case of entertainment tax, details of all cinema-houses can be held on computers to keep track of daily sale of tickets and tax due from feature and advertisement films.

Other areas which can benefit from computerised accounting and monitoring are the administration of excise duty and other state taxes, and also in maintaining records of land holdings and land revenue.

Karnataka, for instance, has computerised commercial tax records. From their own information system, outputs are generated on tax recoverable and tax recovered for each category and period. This has given the State a powerful weapon to stem-tax evasion. Uttar Pradesh has computerised the sales-tax form-31 which gives exemption to inter-state vehicles to ply without paying sales-tax. Earlier records were sordid where these forms could not be logged in registers in time, thus keeping open the loophole for a tax evasion at the sales-tax outposts. The current records show substantial improvement in collection of tax revenue by eliminating corruption in a large way.

(c) *Bureau of Economic and Statistics*

In several States, the Bureau is entrusted with the task of conducting socio-economic surveys and analysing the data collected to help the administration formulate policies. Population census, agricultural census, economic census, National Sample Surveys, price statistics, etc., are the major areas of the work of the Bureau.

Speed and accuracy are the primary reasons for the use of

computers in analysing the data collected during the surveys. Forecasts on agricultural and industrial production, formulation of price indices, demographic statistics and analysis of other specific surveys are easily possible on the computers. Data so collected can be conveniently retained as data-bank over long periods to undertake studies in trend analysis.

An early effort was launched in Andhra Pradesh through Indo-French Compu-Graphics and Planning Project to help their Bureau in modernising their storage of data, methods of analysis and presentation of results. After 6 years, the following objectives were realised:

(i) regular publications contained several dozen maps, graphs and diagrams which facilitate the study of the statistics presented;

(ii) The Bureau of Economics and Statistics carried out studies requiring high level statistical analysis;

(iii) the Compu-Graphic Laboratory was regularly solicited to carry out processing on a large scale;

(iv) the Bureau of Economics and Statistics confidently started on the installation of a unit for data entry and the processing of its censuses which functioned with its own internal staff; and

(v) numerous data banks were at the disposal of the Government and of the public, and a system of statistical documentation permitted easy access and updating of the information.

(d) *Agriculture*

The agriculture department has to deal with data on rainfalls, area under different crops, irrigation, number of wells etc. in each village. Based on these, the department forecasts the crop productions and plans for the supply of seeds, fertilisers, pesticides, etc., and evolves policies on credit facilities to farmers. The department also conducts several agronomic and agro-economic surveys to help formulate policies. Computers can assist in production forecasts, procurement and distribution planning for chemicals and fertilisers, and procurement of outputs. The yearly data can be retained for historical purposes and also to undertake trend analysis.

A pilot Project in Karnataka was prepared by the NIC to explore the possibility of computerisation of land records and crop-based data with the following objectives:

(i) The Land Records were maintained and updated properly and accurately;

(ii) The records were accessible in the shortest possible span of time; and

(iii) It was also envisaged that the system should be able to evolve ownership records (Patta) of the land and credit details if availed of through any co-operative Bank.

Notebook Computer

Several other districts have now taken up the work on computerisation of land records at the block/tehsil and district levels.

(e) *Irrigation*

Computers can significantly assist the Irrigation Department in management of on-going projects in terms of their physical progress, cost control, manpower planning, stores accounting, materials management and inventory control, etc. Management of water resources (both surface and groundwater) is also assisted through computers.

High-speed Ultra-Compact PC

Andhra Pradesh had been running a computer-based minor irrigation scheme information system for some years. The system visualised execution of projects and monitoring of both cost over-runs and under-runs. The system also reviewed performance in providing irrigational facility with reference to target figures based on data collected at source.

(f) *Public Works*

PWD looks after the maintenance of roads and bridges, construction of buildings for Government departments and other public works. The main areas where computers can assist in the functions of the department are stores accounting, materials management, project monitoring and requirement planning. As in the Irrigation Department, on-going projects can be effectively monitored for physical progress and cost control. Timely completion of projects would check cost escalations.

In Uttar Pradesh, a personnel information system was implemented for PWD, mainly to facilitate transfer planning. The system recorded individual qualifications, service experience and other relevant data and used such information for planning transfer based on management needs and existing vacancies.

(g) *Transportation*

Almost all States have Road Transport Corporations to plan and provide for transportation facilities. Due to complexity of their operations, computers have been widely used by several such Corporations in areas such as spare-parts management and maintenance scheduling. Computers can also assist in optimisation of bus routes, tariff fixation, forecasts of future traffic loads and requirements planning.

For Delhi Administration, a route planning was done for transport for both circular and radial services, which has been successfully implemented.

(i) *Health*

As stated earlier, implementation of various health programmes, curative (medical), preventive (public health) and promotional (family welfare), is carried out by the Directorate of Health and Family Welfare. Monitoring performance of Hospitals in terms of utilisation and cost is aided by computers. Planning for Hospital services requires a vast amount of data on community health needs, existing hospital services and their utilisation, population characteristics and environmental factors. Computers greatly assist in building a data-base for Hospital services planning.

In Andhra Pradesh, an Information System was developed for the malaria disease based on such data as incidence of disease, its spread through men and cattle, soil condition, stagnation of waters, parasite breeding and so on. The system predicted incidence of malaria in surrounding region so that remedial action could be taken in advance.

(j) *Education and Social Welfare*

It was stated earlier that several States have adopted computers in examination results processing at high school and intermediate levels to handle the several lakhs of students appearing for such examinations annually. Accuracy and speed of processing enables fast publication of results and accrues confidence in the results. Analysis of socio-economic background of the students has also been attempted on computer to help formulate policies. In the area of social welfare, various surveys are conducted to study the conditions of a community of a group like tribal communities, backward classes, etc. Computers assist in analysing the data collected and this greatly assists in welfare measures being formulated.

In Madhya Pradesh, a teachers' data bank was built from which transfer planning of teachers could be done based on their personal data and the need of the education department. A similar data bank approach was planned in U.P.

Need for Computerisation

According to experts, computerisation in public administration is characterised by a few factors as follows:

(a) *Complexity of function*: Various social, economic and political forces constantly interact with industry and create extensive demands from the Government. Rapid growth of population, industries and limited resources poses a serious challenge to the administration. Law enforcement problem, for example, once solely within bounds of police departments, impinge on such fields as education and social welfare;

(b) *Large volumes*: Data-files handed in administration are normally quite large. Thousands of transactions take place every day in the treasuries of a State Government. City corporations maintain tax records of thousands of properties;

(c) *Intra-agency communication*: Most information has to come from numerous remote locations and to be processed quickly. Crime investigation and detection needs a central information system without sending the criminal physically from one police station to another;

(d) *Multiple files*: In most municipal offices, for example, information about a property is maintained by different sections in different contexts. This creates updating problems and causes delay;

(e) *Information problems*: This comprises lack of current

information, inability to quickly retrieve available information or to correlate information available in different departments, and inability to utilise existing data with the help of scientific management techniques; and

(f) *Improved service to public*: People not only demand more service but also an improved quality which is responsive to their needs.

Features of Computerisation

First, computerisation should be justifiable. In other words, there should be tangible benefits in the form of improved productivity of staff, quick collection of revenue and so on. The agricultural production plan, for instance, can use the data on land holdings, etc., to plan activities like supply of appropriate types of seed, fertilisers and insecticides to the farmer and arrangements for transport to collect and distribute harvest produce to the market without delay.

The second feature is privacy of information ensuring its integrity. Any access to data should be based on appropriate authorisation. Otherwise, the features endemic in the west of encroaching upon privacy of individuals would become visible in India too.

The third feature is the maximum use of existing administrative set-up. In other words, computerisation should be designed to suit the current skill levels of employees and, wherever necessary, the skills should be upgraded to provide suitable input and output control for computerisation. As things stand, the administrative bureaucracy is well-entrenched having its own ethos and internal dynamics. These points should be taken into account before introducing computing tools.

The fourth feature is the need for centralised processing supported by distributed availability of the computing power. Files with Government are normally of large size and can be accommodated in massive data bases. On the other hand, inputs to the applications often emanate from a large number of remote locations. For instance, Tamil Nadu Government has computerised crime-criminal information system which collects data from over 300 police stations in their State for all districts. Similarly, U.P. has introduced district level micro planning for 200 panchayats in the Almora district which is to be expanded to more districts in due course. Tamil Nadu has computerised accounting system receiving transactions from 300 documents by post. A similar effort by UP Government has to contend with 63 treasuries and 256 Sub-treasuries.

The fifth feature is processing. Quite often, quick response based on timeliness is the key factor for success in the case of crime detection. There is also immense potential available for personal computing power as personal computers can be given to even district level officers for computerisation of land-based records. With the help of query and response, graphics and electronic spread sheet, a district information system can be easily built on a personal computer which can use quick information and feed-back to take corrective actions and appropriate decisions.

The final feature is the existence of good back-up facilities and controls as audit trails. Due to the sheer size of Government information, the system has to be kept modular in design and open-ended to hold new additions to be made from time to time. There are many elements of computer-generated information which are used in processing along with basic data. These should be counter-checked through audit trails.

Implementation of Computerisation

Implementation of computerisation in Government departments has to be a coordinated effort which often needs major reorganisation of the current set-up of administration and practices. It has to be planned with a great deal of care and attention. The following factors have usually been found helpful to avoid costly errors, wasted efforts and public resentment:

(a) *Coordination Committee*

The planning machinery should be in the form of a steering committee made up of senior officials of various user departments. They should be able to look across current departmental boundaries and visualise their future requirements and demands that are likely to develop on their services.

(b) *Application Priorities*

The criteria for election may be any economic benefits, providing better service to public, better planning, or relieving pressure on administration.

(c) *Phased Implementation*

The applications should be implemented in a small area and other modules built on it over a period of time to ensure smooth progress. For instance, TN Government developed a job information system, for which the accounting phase was taken up first, the control phase next and finally job phase spanning a period of nearly five years. Similarly, UP State Electricity Board developed a computerised electricity billing system which was first introduced in Agra and Ghaziabad districts as a pilot project and thereafter in other districts of the western UP. A negation of such a pilot project idea created a lot of confusion in another state electricity undertaking creating questions in the parliament, the setting up of an enquiry committee and eventually redoing the whole project.

(d) *Review*

There should be a review of the progress of implementation and necessary corrective action to be taken in time. While introducing computerised electricity billing system, UP Government continued the financial ledgers earlier on manual basis. Only after they had reviewed the dependability of the computerised financial ledgers, the manual ledgers were discontinued. Again, another State undertaking averse to carrying out such a review had been in deep trouble, as computerised ledgers were not fully tested but meanwhile the manual ledgers have been discontinued.

(e) *Growth*

The Coordination Committee should periodically evaluate its performance in the light of changing environments or anticipated changes, and modify it to perform effectively in the light of these changes.

(f) *Flexibility*

The planning should be designed to be flexible so that it can be adapted easily to suit requirements of other similar governmental agencies. For example, a budget information system designed by one State Government should be capable of being adapted by other States with minimum effort.

(g) *User Education*

Education of staff at all levels who will be either furnishing input data to the new system or using it is of great importance. This can be handled with manuals containing detailed instructions with examples of coding, furnishing input documents, etc. and classroom sessions with actual practice in source document preparation. These methods were used extensively in Tamil Nadu Government, for instance, during implementation of police and budget information systems.

Bottlenecks of Computerisation

The prime bottlenecks in computerisation for public administration is in the field of data preparation. This is because quite often ill-trained and unmotivated people are used for data collection who have no commitment to the system. For instance, in computerising records of known criminals in different states, it has been observed that computer cells were at time used as dumping ground for inconvenient officials to whom no systematic training was given. When forms for filling up particulars for non-criminals were sent to police stations, the local staff often had no clue as to the purpose of these assorted forms and considered the extra work-load as an unfair and meaningless imposition. Another example is the Patwari. This village-level accountant has to do multiple jobs very often and must be suitably trained as well as motivated to make the administrative information systems a success.

The second important bottleneck is low utilisation of installed computers in Government. It is observed that equipment has been kept in crates for years in some police departments. Even when a trained and competent officer had been posted to a computer cell after years, he often found that the equipment had got damaged due to defective storage. Similar examples prevail in some State governments where large computers were known to be lying in crates for lack of air-conditioning and fungus developed on the processor chips, which delayed the eventual operation for a long period. Again, suitable prior planning is necessary to make computers useful from the day it has been installed. This can be done by way of designing as well as running computer applications on the neighbourhood computers so that the departments are in readiness for the ultimate in-house computerisation.

The third bottleneck is the emphasis placed on employment. Historically speaking, there was a stiff resistance against industrial revolution from the Luddites who were up against the early industrial machines and went hammer and tongs to destroy them. Obviously, the benefits of industrial technology have outweighed that resistance. Authorities like Professor Simon have assessed that all new technologies have thrown up the possibility of unemployment at the primitive technology level but have eventually generated a new kind of employment and provided for a higher quality of life. Computers in India are already generating large employment for educated manpower as computer managers, system analysts, programmers and operators. Even at a user level, people are needed to deal with inputs and outputs at a higher skill level. As banking applications help improve banking business, the number of branches go up to provide for more employment. In a State administration like AP, there are already concerted plans to generate and provide employment at district level for their massive computerisation programme. On the whole, the bugbear of unemployment is less a reality than a shadow, as is being proved in efficiency-increasing and performance-improving applications.

The fourth bottleneck is in making judicious selection and evaluation of computers. It is difficult to hold out against high-pressure sales tactics of most computer vendors and manufacturers who often promise panacea when there are not any! Fortunately, as micro-computers grow more in power and less in cost, the advantage lies with the new customer. Many public administrators can safely go for super-micro systems as a 32-bit device which are getting standardised in hardware around only 2 chips: Intel and Motorolla using MS/DOS and Unix operating systems respectively as basic software. With Unix providing compatibility with MS/DOS, problems of hooking up disparate intelligent terminals to the host-system are also getting diminished. In brief, the selection and evaluation problems are less apparent today, once user needs are assessed.

The fifth bottleneck is that of expandability. Since computer systems come from micro to the large main-frame range, a customer has to make sure, when he buys a computer at the lower end of the spectrum, that the system is capable of upgradation. This is a fact more often than not concealed at the time of purchase. Micros have their own inherent limitations in being upgraded, as not too much of peripherals (tapes and disks) can get added. At the larger end of the spectrum, addition of extra capability becomes relatively easy. Since computer usage tends to grow over time as more and more applications get loaded, it is a very good practice to look for upgradability in the systems while making one's initial purchase.

The sixth bottleneck is that of support services. There are a large number of computer vendors who are operating in India today purely based on screw-driver technology. This means that they import the latest system from overseas, change the name to an Indian one, give it an Indian packing and then sell it. At the low price of computers prevailing today, there is little incentive for computer vendors to provide customers a high-quality, on-going support which tends to be highly expensive as well. Moreover, when the vendors themselves have not much detailed knowledge of the system, their providing the support service can be even more elusive. This aspect, is worth examining closely by the public administrators before making purchase dialogue.

The seventh bottleneck is that of standardisation and portability. A lot of application packages are available today which are of standard nature and can be made useful on other computer systems. Even among different states and their administrative hierarchies, there is little exchange of what each one is doing. The dialogue is even less among public administrators on one end, and industrial managers and business executives at the other. Quite often, both may be engaged in developing the very same piece of computer software. The sooner such reinvention of the wheel is eliminated, the better. Expertise is available today to make computer software packages portable from one machine to another with minimal extra cost. Such expertise should be made use of, especially in public administration.

The eighth bottleneck is that of relative lack of user experience. Most pubic administrators are new-comers to the computer field and not much feed-back can be obtained by way of mutual dialogue when it comes to assessing the usefulness of a particular approach to computerisation. Moreover, as most applications have been at a routine accounting level, the management information systems that most administrators will prefer are seldom known. Computer is meant to be used of as a planning, monitoring, review and contro' ..ool. Such experience is a rare commodity to come by in India.

Finally the most significant bottleneck is that of lack of computer culture. The fact has to be squarely faced that Indian administrators and executives have not been brought up in a computer environment. Our schools and colleges are yet to teach computer programmes on a compulsory basis. Our administrators and managers are yet to pick up acquaintance with computerisation. In such an atmosphere, a high level commitment to computerisation is a rare experience. Thanks to the directives given by the Government, most public administrators are going through mandatory training programmes in which computer appreciation has been made an essential learning subject. But still there is many a gap between the cup and the lip, before today's administrators can demand appropriate computerisation, let alone what is best for them. It is of paramount importance to the country to imbibe and inculcate a computer culture in public administration so that such credibility gaps are quickly overcome.

Conclusion

To summarise, the country is in the throes of computerisation. There is a directive from the Ministry of Industry to all public sector enterprises that the Prime Minister's secretariat desires to have the figures on capacity, production target and production performance based on graphics produced by computers. While asking for such figures in the forms of graphs and charts is nothing new, what is novel is the explicit reliance being placed on computers. That is because there is less chance of anybody tampering with computerised data on a continuing basis and, therefore, more chance to get reliable indicators from time to time. Public sector undertakings like railways have gone for about Rs. 500 crore project for introducing on-line freight control and wagon movement system. A public sector undertaking like Bhilai Steel Plant was going for a 4-tier process control computerisation called INCOS at a cost of Rs. 204 crores. At the Central and State Government level, the phases of National Informatic Computer Networks are going to be quite cost-effective, using available satellite communication from Insat I-C.

All such expenditure would be worthwhile if the State administrators rise up to the need of using computer in a meaningful manner. Operational level accounting applications must yield to data banks of various sizes from which selective data, analysed data and integrated data can be gleaned. Only such processed data are of use to decision makers. An example is the decision support system being used in the UP where remote sensing data of soil erosion, land topography, under-ground water (by using infra-red photography) and forest canopy, etc., are being received at the Remote Sensing Centre at Lucknow. From there, the data is transmitted to the National Remote Sensing Agency computer at Hyderabad for processing. The processed data are thereafter placed on the terminals at the UPDESCO computer to be used on an inter-active basis. Such a usage leads to planning by public administrators through query and response from the data bank, on water reservoir structure and location of grass-lands. There is immense scope of using similar decision support systems in hilly states such as J & K, Himachal Pradesh, Assam, Meghalaya, Arunachal Pradesh, Nagaland and others to use remote sensing data and to arrive at rational public decisions. These are the new vistas of computerisation in pubic administration which are beckoning our executives of today.

28

LAW AND ORDER

Introduction

The innate conservatism of lawyers has been a serious problem in introducing computer in their practices. It has been observed that the profession is generally reluctant to deal with change. According to Westermier, a distinguished American attorney, lawyers do not deal well with matching immediate costs with long-term gains, nor are they good at strategic business planning, let alone strategic information planning.

Status in the West

The reason for the above is perhaps two-fold. First, lawyers are extra-cautious by nature. Secondly, most lawyers view their profit-making resources as the para-legal people at their command and not computer-based or manual information systems. But the situation in the West has been changing since the seventies. Until the sixties, while the other US business houses leaped into the twenty-first century, their law firms rested in the eighteenth. As business grew more complex, so did practising law. The spiralling costs of discovering, deposing and documenting made manual systems of billing and filing very costly. The trappings, entanglements and accompanying costs of litigation increased geometrically over years.

As a result, New York's prestigious Milbank Tweed, Hadley and McClay became the first to have a computerised data-bank. Washington's Wald, Harkrader and Ross were close to follow and developed more than in-house 200 programs on a Honeywell Level 62 computer to cover time-disbursement, general ledgers, billable hours, production analysis and a large litigation-support system (LSS). Another firm, Howrey and Simon, acquired a 16-turminal system for time-keeping and billing functions. It also developed a sophisticated LSS.

Computerisation in Law

The legal computerisation market in the world is today growing fast. It is a rule in the USA that in legal cases involving more than 50,000 pages of evidence material, both the contesting parties rely on an LSS. Full services are offered by Mead Data Control since 1973 through *Lexis* which is a private-file LSS for lawyers to do their own bibliographic coding and subjective analysis. More than 100,000 people have been trained on *Lexis* which reportedly controls 90 per cent of the legal market and more than 25,000 searches are performed daily. While a few other firms offer full services, limited services are divided between those who are on-line and those offering software packages for litigation support. Such packages are STAIRS from IBM; INQUIRE from Infodata Corporation; BASIC from Turnkey Systems; and so on.

In order to determine relevance of computer usage in law for India, it is interesting to observe how it has proceeded in the West. First to be put on compute are time and accounting billing, along with some amount of office automation. Next to follow is legal research and litigation handed by *Lexis* or *Westlaw* and available through the computer terminals of their proprietors: Mead Data Central or West Publishing Company. The third stage is case-handling (showing all cases currently handled, their status, responsibilities and detailed tracking) and management reporting (using information from accounting and billing to predict future economic potential). The last and most advanced stage uses calendar, library and substantive law systems. Calendar system tracks cases by attorney and data, organises schedule and coordinates appointment. Library system tracks books and periodicals which are either owned or ordered. Substantive law system uses the computer to help attorneys do their actual work.

Indian Situation

In India, computers are yet to make an inroad into the processes of law. It is being slowly realised that computers can be effectively used for speedy disposal of cases, thus reducing the cost of litigation. Further, facts relating to past cases and precedents can be made available in a case so that its outcome does not entirely depend on the skills of an attending counsel. Finally, computer-based retrieval of case-information can reduce the time spent by a counsel in preparing a case and hence reduce his charges, too.

Courts of Law

(a) Some Indian service-bureaus have developed the *justice information system*, maintaining data-bank on case-histories of current cases, orders pass on different hearing dates and court calendars. The system can be used for control and monitoring of pending cases, and provide such reports as statement of orders passed on given hearing dates; case-histories, statement of cases heard and not heard, statement of pending cases, statement of counsels and their parties, and so on.

(b) *The Act Data-Bank*: This can consist of acts, statutes, ordinances and amendments passed from time to time. The system can be useful to legislators judges and advocates for answering queries relating to the original acts, their amendments and current forms of the acts, in part or whole. Similarly, the case-law data-bank can maintain case-rulings on all decided cases. This can be useful both to judges (for giving precedent-based decisions) and to advocates (for preparing case-arguments). The system can list out all previously decided cases based on case-reference number, parties involved, deciding court, date of decision and ruling of the court.

Some Indian high courts have shown keen interest in computerisation of their own records. If found feasible, the computer can be installed at a central point and can process questions put it either in batches or through a number of terminals. Information on acts, statutes, ordinances and amendments can be collected from various legislatures and related bodies. The court can provide an information service to all lawyers or payment of a charge. It is possible to visualise a large system in Delhi (or elsewhere) connected to other courts, or a central computer in each State attached to the large central computer as well as to smaller computers installed in subsidiary courts in the State. The arrangement can serve locally for two-way traffic between all State computers and the central computer for exchange of legal material.

(c) *Computer-Based Case-Law Reference System*: This has been recommended to the Orissa high court. This system can be eminently useful to judges, on one side, for giving decisions based on points previously decided by the courts, and to advocates, on the other, for preparing case-arguments supported by the previous rulings. The system can answer from its date-bank logical queries, based on key-words, with such details as case-reference number, the act, sections and sub-sections, parties involved, data and court of judgement, and ruling of the court. The appropriate information on case-law can be collected from courts and legal digests prepared for storing in the computer.

Law and Order Situation

While the above activities are suited to the administering of justice through courts of law, there has been some good work done on computer to cater to law-and-order situation. The Tamil Nadu police have been operating independent computerised systems of *finger-print records* from 1974 and *crime-criminal records* from 1975, to serve the dual objectives of crime investigation and criminal identification. These systems, since elaborated by the National Crime Records Bureau (NCRB), are in various stages of implementation in different States on the indigenous TDC-316 computer in each state. Police computers are already installed and operational in Tamil Nadu, Andhra Pradesh, Maharashtra, Karnataka, Rajasthan, Gujarat, Madhya Pradesh and Delhi, while the installations are in final stages in Kerala and Punjab. Orissa police (with a data-bank of 6700 criminal cases and 130,000 finger-prints) and Uttar Pradesh police (with proposed terminals in 30 districts and records kept at 1302 police stations) are now poised to fully use for their forces.

In the *finger-print records system*, the enquiry generally relates to fetching information on a prior criminal record or arrest record for a person currently being held, on the basis of matching finger-prints. Match is sought on the ridge, whorl and loop counts in respect of the arrested person. Some States in the Western region are now extending the concept to the foot print records as well.

In the *crime-criminal records system*, the enquiry relates to fetching data on a criminals *modus operandi* in a given territory, along with retrieval of personal description and number of crimes committed earlier. It is interesting to observe that while the finger-print patterns are known to be unique universally, there is some thing unique also in sticking to a specific *modus operandi* or a given territory in the criminal world. Certain indices are also created such as crime-criminal index, criminal conviction index, etc., to help in the information retrieval process, apart from the routine data on date, time and place of occurrence, property lost and recovered special features, police and court disposals, etc., kept on the crime-enquiry file.

The move is currently finalised to link the police-computer wing in Tamil Nadu police with crime branch and police research centre of CID, finger-print bureau and microfilm-record section for use of voice, teleprinter and facsimile input/output on microwave and trunk-lines. Control rooms of Madras city and 20 police districts are, in turn, set to have voice input/output on VHF network with both static and mobile sets.

Computers in the States

Most State computers with police forces are having a three-phase plan for expansion. The first phase covers receipt of enquiries at the State computer centre from field-units by post or messenger and despatch of responses like-wise. The second phase visualises the provision of terminals in the district headquarters and their "on-line" linkage (through dedicated P & T line or microwave) in order to permit interrogations by field-units getting fast responses. The third phase would see the State police computer linked with the national police computer centre at Delhi in a network, so as to form part of a countrywide police computer grid. Such a plan, for instance, is visualised for the Uttar Pradesh police computer.

The crime-criminal records and finger-print records comprise information contained in police station registers, records and files, and do achieve the purpose of giving a scientific orientation to crime investigation and criminal identification. But much more information on crime incidence and behaviour can be fished out from the records of the law-courts, jails, correctional institutions, probation-offices and vigilance-homes. A cumulative inter-action of the personal, family, educational and environmental factors can give a social and psychological perspective helping not merely to understand the causes of the crime and criminal make-up, but also to reform and rehabilitate criminals by manipulating these factors. This is the matrix of a social defence information system which can elevate the earlier two objectives into those of crime prevention and criminal reformation. Many authorities urge that only such a system can help to defend the society from the deviants of its own making.

Conclusion

Both in law and in social justice, new developments have taken place. A number of Indian software developers are working on packages like JUDIPAC and LAWMAN both of which offer appointments, case-diary, billing, interesting points and sundry jottings by the individual lawyers. These efforts need be improved to reach the level of LSS.

In social justice, NCRB has been working single-mindedly to lead on to the district level computer-terminals and eventually to POLICENET with new computers installed at the State capitals and then networked. Their innovative use of teleprinter terminals from the districts to the States is working well for data-logging, considering that nearly 60 per cent crimes remain confined to the districts, another 20 per cent spread in the State and only the balance 20 per cent of an inter-State nature. Meanwhile, the CMC is testing for them a finger-print imaging systems (for all the 10 digits) which is certain to be a distinct improvement on the finger-print index-coding.

29

PUBLIC UTILITIES

Introduction

Public utilities are the main instruments through which the Government provides basic services such as health-care, transportation, housing etc. to the citizens. Such services not only constitute the welfare measures of the Govt. but serve as vehicles of all round socio-economic growth. Several Public Systems are turning to modern management techniques, including the use of computers, so that they may serve their objectives with increasing effectiveness. We present some of the major areas where computerised applications in Public utilities have substantially aided the administrative process, reiterating some of the grounds covered earlier.

Banking Organisations

It has been mentioned earlier that the use of computers in the banking industry has been fairly widespread. The RBI was one of he earliest users of computer in the country and the SBI, today, has powerful fourth-generation computers that enables the management to co-ordinate and control the operations of its 8000 and odd branches spread across the country. Several other leading banks are using computers, mainly for inter-branch reconciliation work.

To meet the ever-changing objectives being set for the banking industry, the banks can very gainfully use computerised information systems to (a) help in their planning process through a comprehensive data-base on community needs, economic conditions and policy guidelines of the Government and RBI, (b) set goals for branch offices and constantly monitor their performance, (c) analyse yearly returns from branches and prepare profit and loss statements at regional and all-India levels, (d) keep track of loans to various categories of clients to help conform to statutory requirements, and (e) optimise gains on investments.

Health Organisations

The health sector has been covered extensively earlier. In a country like ours, where the demand for health care fare outstrips the facilities available, the challenge for health administrators is indeed considerable. Planning for hospital services requires a vast amount of data on community, health needs, existing hospital services and their utilisation, population characteristics and environmental factors. Computers can greatly assist in building a data-base for hospital services planning.

Computers can be used to monitor utilisation of hospital resources—beds, medical and non-medical inventories, laboratory and operation theatre equipment, etc.—in each ward for specialised fields, so that planning for their optimal use is greatly aided. Policies on reallocation of beds or equipment and expansions of wards are also assisted by such an analysis. Monitoring the stocks of blood and life-saying drugs on computer can help prevent crisis situations. Records of all patients can he held on computer to help in studying seasonal variation of different diseases and in research activities undertaken by the hospitals.

Electricity Boards

Several of the State electricity boards are already using computers for consumer billing and financial accounting. This ensures regular generation of bills, timely collection of dues and ready identification of disconnection cases and defective meters. Data of all consumers on computers also helps in analysing consumption patterns among the domestic and industrial consumers, which aids in decisions pertaining to power-cut in times of short power supply.

Other major areas of computer-use can be: (a) planning for extension of power supply to new areas and monitoring the work on all such projects in terms of physical progress and expenditure; (b) materials management to minimise the capital tied up on inventories; (c) maintenance scheduling of power plants, as also power equipment like transformers, etc., to ensure uninterrupted power supply; and (d) network distribution analysis through OR techniques.

Water Boards

The need to plan and provide for sufficient water supply to all towns (in fact, all inhabited places) was never more dramatically realised than when Emperor Akbar had to abandon his capital city of Fatehpur Sikri! In more recent times, spurt in urban populations have put severe strain on the civic amenities available.

Several State water boards in the country are using computers to analysis the water needs of large towns and cities 20 years ahead, and are trying to look for sources of water supply and distribution network (pipelines) which would ensure sufficient water in remotest corners of the towns. Such long-term planning economises investment and prevents frequent alterations to existing pipelines.

Housing Boards

Housing boards undertake construction of houses for different income-groups of the society. These are offered on ownership basis with recoveries through instalments spread over 15 to 20 years. Computerised project management, based on network analysis, can substantially assist in monitoring the work on different housing schemes, both in terms of physical progress and financial status. Such constant monitoring aids in timely completion of projects and checks cost-escalations. Before launching of a new scheme, man-power planning and resource allocation can be done through the use of computers.

Financial accounting is another area where computers can significantly aid the administrative process. For instalment accounting, computers can hold details of all owners, monitor their payments and generate reminder notices in case of defaults.

Road Transport Corporations

Public transport facilities in most Indian towns and cities are far from satisfactory. Over-crowding in buses and serpentine queues at bus-stops are common sight everywhere. This is due to inadequate facilities in the one hand and mounting demand on the other. In the light of this, it is essential that the limited resources are most optimally utilised.

Computers have been widely used by road transport corporations across the country, particularly in the area of inventory and materials management. This not only ensures optimal inventory holdings but also the availability of vital spare parts in times of need. Minimal breakdown of buses can be achieved through computerised maintenance scheduling. Other areas where computers can assist are : financial accounting, vehicle scheduling, analysis of traffic on different routes and tariff fixation.

Telephone Organisations

Telephone administrations in metropolitan cities of India, such as, Mahanagar Telephone Nigams, have already computerised two vital areas of their operations : (a) consumer billing and accounting, and (b) printing of telephone directories at periodic intervals. For both of these, complete data pertaining to consumers are retained on the computer and constantly updated with changes to addresses, telephone numbers and new connections given. Computerise billing ensures accurate and timely generation of bills which in turn greatly facilities steady cash inflow. Identifying cases for disconnection and studying utilisation patterns are also rendered earlier. Printing of directory with the aid of computers eliminates the time-consuming task of manual updates to data for hundreds of thousands of consumers. Computer-generated paper-tapes are attached to photo-composing machines which automatically compose the matter to be printed in the directory. Videsh Sanchar Nigam (Overseas Communication Services) have been using computers for long to use optimally the line capacities and to "store and forward" calls both incoming and outgoing.

Civil Supplies Organisations

For effective distribution of civil supplies through fair-price shops, computers can assist the authorities by retaining data pertaining to all households on tape or disk files. Such a data-base can be used to study the demand requirement of various items in different zones and arrange for the supplies. The information can also serve in planning the location of fair-price shops, godowns, mills, etc., based on population densities. The annual task of preparing fresh ration could be easily one on computers, which would also ensure elimination of bogus cards. Similarly, information on temporary ration cards issued to floating population be used for planning purposes and to keep track of their expiry.

Computerised processing of cash-memos issued by fair-price shops would aid in the study of consumption patterns, reconciliation of dealer stocks and planning for fresh supplies. This would also enable trapping of cards which are not utilised over specific periods of time. The UP authorities are carrying out computer-based monitoring of supplies from the wholesale or ware-houses to the retail ration-shops for such essential commodities as sugar, kerosene and edible oil.

Dairy Development Corporations

Picking on the success of the Anand Project (which launched the "White Revolution" in the country), several States have set up Dairy Development Corporations to plan the growth of dairying. Perhaps, no other activity in recent times has contributed so much to the rapid socio-economic development of the rural areas as the dairy movement of "Operation Flood" in multiple phases.

Dairy development corporations effectively use computers in the following areas:

(a) demand analysis of various zones and planning for location of milk booths;
(b) financial accounting of daily collections at different milk distribution centres;
(c) optimisation of routes to be followed by vehicles between different depots and supply points;
(d) accounting and monitoring of loans disbursed among farmers; and
(e) statistical analysis of surveys conducted to study production and consumption patterns to help formulate growth policies.

Urban Development Authorities

Any process associated with urban planning must have accurate and reliable data, and, more important, must have the necessary tools and methodologies to analyse this data. Establishing inter-realtionships among a varied set of parameters affecting urban development-land use, housing and slum upgradation, public utilitics, environmental and ecological factors, etc.— can pose considerable technical challenge.

A comprehensive data-base can be built on the computers to store vital information on various aspects of urban life. Given the projections of population growth, the data-base can be used to help formulate policies on land-use, housing, transportation, roads, public services, schools, sanitation, law and order machinery, etc. The use of computer has numerous advantages over manual analysis of data in terms of scope, accuracy, effectiveness, versatility and computing power.

Conclusion

The public utilities form a premier source of public service in India. It can be observed with satisfaction how gradually they are using computer as a tool for rendering a better quality of service. Centre for Development of Telematics is a classic example of R&D-oriented public system which has developed several levels of digital switching for local, rural and main exchange (PAX, RAX and MAX) usage, which are now finding foreign buyers!

30

HELPING THE DISABLED

Introduction

1981, the International Year of the Disabled, ushered in a spate of fresh considerations a decade ago for the aid of the handicapped. It was at once evident that the falling price of the computer technology would lead to a new boon of opportunities for those persons whose developments had been retarded in one way or the other. From assistance to an independent living to flexible tools that can increase the variety and quality of job opportunities, the computer world today holds out immense possibilities.

Western Efforts

The progress in using the computer to help the disabled has been truely enormous in the West. This is in sharp contrast to the earlier fear that computer would make individuals obsolete, compete with them unfairly for jobs and curb down personal freedoms. The gains have, however, been really impressive for the computer age: space flights, productivity gains in many fields and immense gains in information handling and sharing.

The National Institute of Handicapped Research in the USA has now brought forth a sophisticated office environment in which the handicapped person can effectively use a computer-controlled system to handle the telephone, type-writer, tape-recorder and computer-terminal. This has been a logical development for a wide range of equipment which has adaptations for the disabled. For example, walking adoptors are available for the blind, while there are calculators which can help the handicapped individual tell time, perform basic useful functions and provide music for recreation. The above Institute has also developed a multi-purpose microcomputer system for use by the severely disabled. Such a system has a terminal with visual display and cassette recorder which can together help the individual with a rapid means of communication.

Quite often, the special education needs of thousands of handicapped children are anything but met. Inadequate or non-existing facilities in the schools, financial constraints, ignorance, feelings of guilt and embarrassment, lack of facilities, past discrimination and a host of other factors cause handicapped children to be hidden from public view. To rectify this situation, the Public Law in the USA now requires that the public education system should supply a free, appropriate education and related services to meet the unique needs of every handicapped child. The law emphasises that this educational service is to be provided in the least restrictive environment possible, an environment in which the handicapped child has optimum interaction with his non-handicapped peers. The law also provides for the use of instructional material including telecommunications, sensory, and other technical aids and devices.

Learning Devices

It is essential that handicapped children should achieve their potential and their maximum degree of mobility and independence, so that they can become self-sufficient and contributing members of the society. For this purpose, computer-aided *learning* devices are available in many Western schools and the technology can be applied to both physically and mentally handicapped students. A wide range of *communication* devices are available there, such as, readers for the blind, hearing and visual aids, voice synthesisers, etc., based on microcomputers.

Self-help devices are also available to assist children with such tasks as dressing, washing, eating, toileting, hand control and leg control. *Adaptive* devices assist in driving automobiles (including control), access aids to public transportation, and so on. *Warning* devices are required for many children with health problems, for alerting on an impending bowel or urinary accident. *Perceptual* devices are there for solving neurological problems and eye-hand coordination. The wide range of handicap conditions that are prevalent among school-age children make it necessary to have computer-based evaluation system and comprehensive data-banks.

Role of Communications and Microcomputers

The handicapped conditions occur whenever there is a *mismatch* between an individual and his environment. The environment is, of course, the individual's natural physical surroundings. Whether an individual is handicapped or not depends on his inherent capabilities, together with the availability of artificial aids and the individual's ability to use them. The handicap conditions can be corrected in two ways: either by enhancing an individual's capabilities or by modifying the environment. In order to improve an individual's capability for *communication.* One of the approaches is to augment or replace the damaged part. Computer-based communication devices are available today operated by switch, joystick or voice synthesisers. Some "personal" communication devices have also been developed which are owned by users, operated without help and not shared with other users.

Microcomputer-based devices mentioned above have often been disappointing in the light of production economics. They should not show tendencies towards excessive electrical and mechanical control which discourage general production and distribution. Microcomputer-based systems will not obviate the need for specially designed equipment particularly in areas dealing with severe or multiple handicaps. There are quite a few applications where microcomputer can provide low cost, easily available, easily maintainable and easily repeated solutions. These cover problems which were traditionally approachable only with specially designed aids. In addition, where specific aids are needed, they can often be made inexpensive and easily maintainable through the incorporation of standard microcomputer systems.

Basic Approaches

The above follows from three basic approaches for providing aids to the handicapped. First, there are commercially available aids which are generally designed to meet the needs of a whole class of individuals, but these may be inadequate to meet specific needs. Secondly, these are specially built aids designed and developed for specific individuals. These aids are no doubt tailor-made, but their production and maintenance costs may be quite high. Finally, there are modifications and adaptations of standard equipment suited either to one individual or a whole class of individuals. The use of microcomputers as aids for the handicapped falls in this category.

In the field of education particularly, microcomputers have come to provide a fairly *direct* aid. One area of difficulty involves the physically handicapped individuals slow rate of response, which lengthens the time for remedy or practice sessions. With microcomputer-based aids, an individual could work on lessions independently and at his own speed. Another problems involves manipulation necessary for experiments in chemistry, physics and other sciences. Here microcomputers and computer-aided instruction can allow physically handicapped individuals to carry out experiments and manipulations normally beyond their control. Furthermore, the need to see, to read and write, to take notes and to do independent work are all necessary capabilities for receiving education, but the physically handicapped people lacking such capabilities are at a disadvantage. Microcomputer-based systems can provide some of the basic capabilities for participating in education programmes. Finally, microcomputers can be used to teach basic programming skills which hold great promise for increasing employment potential.

In brief, microcomputers can be used as processors or controllers in helping — to some extent — any aspect of human activity that has been impaired. Common areas which have been or are being explored in the West include sensory enhancement or translation; manipulative controls; information amplification for the motion impaired; special control interfaces to other devices; recreation and development aids; educational aids and computer-aided learning; communication aids for telephone, writing and conversation; language assistance; and non-specialised general uses for work.

Indian Situation

While most of the above applications stem from the developed countries. India has taken up the use of microcomputer in the area of sensory enhancement or translation. This is to provide clarification of audio or visual information so that it can be easily understood, or translated from one medium to another. In theory, microcomputers can be used to expand visual displays; provide visual form for spoken words or spoken form for visual displays; translate printed text into speech or into Braille; and provide tactile displays and feedback to deaf and blind individuals.

In the Indian application at the Centre for Biomedical Engineering (located at IIT, Delhi), the primary problem tackled is the lack of direct access for the blind to the printed material of the sighted. Though Braille and recordings are useful for providing information to the blind, the requirement of intermediate translation is an inherently limiting factors. The system developed at the Centre is called "Blind Aid" which provides the blind with direct and independent access to the printed material. The concept of "Blind Aid" is generation on an array of vibratory pins a tactile image of a printed areas about the size of a book-page. The blind reader uses his finger-tips as a tactile retina with which he "reads" in the same way that a sighted person reads visually. In fact, the blind person feels the same shapes which are seen by the sighted. "Blind Aid" uses a microprocessor built by INTEL. The main aim of the microprocessor here is to allow for the information about the character to be processed and to give an output in the form of either Braille or true character-shape, apart from graphical forms being perceived at the fingertips.

Conclusion

Computer technology holds an enormous promise for the world's handicapped population. The task must be a partnership between government, industry and computer professionals with innovative ideas. The ultimate goal is improved quality of life for all handicapped persons and is attainable with creative leadership and technical effort. A most salutary effort has recently been sponsored by Computer Society of India with the aid of Department of Electronics, to provide computer data-entry and programming skills on the keyboard to blind persons so that they can join in the mainstream of computer profession with full dignity, with the cooperation of Tata Institute of Fundamental Research at Bombay.

31

AID TO THE ARTS

Introduction

Right from the time computer was built up in the East Coast universities in the USA, it was also realised that the computer could serve as a technical instrument for man's creative activity. What resulted as computer arts were the computer graphics, computer poetry, computer music and computer film. Even balletic choreography was attempted by Royal Ballet in Covent Garden—one of the very traditional places of dance—to the accompaniment of electronic music by Karlhinz Stockhausen. Along with the scientific pursuits as the original purpose for using a computer, such artistic efforts made strange bed-fellows indeed.

In the realm of arts, what originally started as examples of only conventional expressive forms have already developed new trends leading into exciting new territories. Franke describes this process as always the same. A programme is written which instructs the computer to execute certain logical or mathematical formalisms. By itself, such a programme assumes the ability to understand the formal and quantitative structure of the desired aesthetic creation, — be it graphic design, piano, piece of music or animation film. If this effort succeeds, the programming languages provide a kind of universal notation. The result of such an operation is stored in the magnetic media of tapes or discs. A more modern process enables direct control of the output devices by the computer — like television screen or more spectacular audio-visual phenomena to create computer arts.

Computer Graphics

Let us look at computer graphics first. In a recent study at the National Centre for Software Technology at the Tata Institute of Fundamental Research, now separated as NCST, Naresh Lalvani developed fascinating morphological patterns of Islamic kind on computer. According to him, geometric patterns were evolved by many cultures to serve varied purposes: functional, symbolic or just decorative. In architecture, these patterns are found in plans, sections, facades, ceilings, roofs, floors, walls, openings and caligraphy. Geometry found in Islamic architecture symbolises the fundamental principle of *unity* and are known as Islamic patterns: characterised by multiple centres of symmetry on a plane. Computer is used for coding and generating these Islamic patterns very successfully, — showing known and unknown patterns and suggesting their transformation from one to another. Such patterns beautifully correspond to the Mughal architecture of Delhi, Agra, Jaipur, Udaipur, Gwalior, Ahmedabad and the domestic architecture of Srinagar.

Graphic plotters and electronic displays resembling conventional television sets can be used for computer graphics. It takes anywhere from a few minutes to upto an hour to accomplish a drawing by *mechanical* means, but only a fraction of a second with the help of electronics. The speed of the reproduction suggests changing from single drawings to sequential pictures: successive changes during projection, computer-generated cartoon film, or play of graphic lines on a screen. The potential is enhanced by the nature of the programmes, — describing not a single configuration but a whole variety.

The above ideas has been usefully applied by Oil and Natural Gas Commission at their Dehradun Computer Centre. Complicated mass of data obtained from the offshore and on-land surveys come in the form of densely blocked records. After the necessary mathematical analysis, seismograms are prepared using graphic plotters, — to reveal pictorially the sections of the earth's crust at variable depths and to yield their secrets of holding oil or gas, or just being so may sterile layers. Judging by the thousands of line-kilometers surveyed in an ever-increasing tempo both offshore and on-land, the utility of computer graphics for arriving at a quick interpretation of the earth's surface cannot be overemphasised.

Public Participation

Some experiments enable the public at large to take part in the production of images on computer, — and thus break completely from the old accepted forms of presentation. This presupposes composition under visual control, which is quite possible with the aid of electronic screens. The easiest way to achieve this is having the participant push a button that selects those characteristic values left open by the program. At a later stage, the public could enter into a kind of dialogue with the aesthetic programme, playing a "graphics game" with it, as it were. As only future would show, every household may be connected to computer networks and databanks input and output equipment, and an entirely new form of intellectual, creative competition may develop.

There is another interesting possibility, — the continuous graphics memory originally constructed for use in medical scientillography. Its basic element is a paper tape whose characters appear on a colour video-display. The continuous graphics come from an "intelligent" terminal and offer the opportunity to change the images into connected colour-areas an colour-strips. The participant himself can conduct the program-routines and develop many different variations with fascinating design from a single basic pattern.

Poetry and Music

Use of computer in poetry has been anticipated earlier by the experimentation in verses in the middle of this century. Apolinnaire in France initiated some innovative ideas, giving rise to *concrete poetry.* The idea caught in the computer age and programmes were written using not merely abstruse linguistic and semantic rules, but also laying down guidelines in word-combination, imagery and symbolism within an aesthetic framework so as to satisfy certain standards. The outcome has been hailed more as gimmick than a serious aesthetic output. The outcome has been hailed more as gimmick than a serious aesthetic output. It is no doubt that experimentation stage is yet to be passed, apart from having to overcome misconceptions and emotional resistance. Along with machine-aided translation (MAT) and computer usage in linguistics, computer poetry will need a long time — probably decades — to reach the point where it can realise its full potential, It would thus be wrong to dismiss it — like computer graphics — as merely another ephemeral, modish trend.

Computer music literally took off with the use of modern electronics in the sound synthesisers. But before that, people like John Cage have been working on expansion of the sound-barriers. The restrictive expressions of vocal chords as well as musical instruments underwent a sea-change when electronics was pressed into service with filters, amplifiers, by-passes, modulators, picks-ups and selections. Even selective use of *noise* was appreciated and distinction was drawn between *white noise* with no preferred frequency or order, and *Brownian noise* known for its high degree of order. Devendra Lal of Physical Laboratory, Ahmedabad, has been working on *space music* which is an arbitrary combination and synthesis of musical composition. The absurdity in improvisation in space music is pleasant on the ear, as was evident in Jean, Michael Jarre's films *Oxygene* and *Equinox*, and Klaus Scheluze's films *Time Wind* and "X". Space music has no element or rhythm and has an element of surprise breaking off from the conventional rules for composition. Even in the all-time success film *Star Wars*, classical music was improvised upon to give the effect of being in space.

Musical Experiments

Moog's sound synthesiser and Karlhinz Stockhausen's tracks like *mixtur* and *telefunken* make a lot of use of specially generated sound from microprocessor-based musical equipment. Apart from *kuto* musical sound of Japan, *gamelan* music of Indonesia and temple-bells of India, — their works make very imaginative use of a large range of many special sound-effects with the use of computer. Another experiment has followed the lines of varying speeds and reversal of directions — just to name two features — in the placid classical notations of Bach or Beethoven, New-violin and piano concertos have thus been produced which the masters never conceived of, but which nevertheless emanate from their written music used with a difference.

The work of the musical team *Kraftwork* (literally meaning powerplant) at their Kling Klang Studio in Dusseldorf is worth a mention. While they have retained a heavy influence of John Cage and Xenakis — both pioneers in the field of electronics music — they have been using computers to play some very good music. Their performance in Bombay last year used a lot of electronic instruments, microcomputers, monitors and television-line screens, — but was marked by the singular absence of guitars and any other conventional musical equipment. The famous movie-maker Fassbinder picked on *Kraftwork* to score the sound-track for his film *Russian Roulette*. The music they produced ranged over mechanical and industrial sound (of the Dusseldorf industrial environment) with a metallic tinge, added on by the computer, — using their own program-routines. Their tracks include *Man Machine*, *Home Computer*, *Computer Love*, *Autobahn*, *Radio Activity*. Performances are accompanied by deep freeze sounds, neon signs and video effects. Their latest album *Computer World* had songs played on *electronic pads* used for percussion, and Texas and Casio calculators.

Films and Multi-Media

The fact that the same programme languages and the same computers can be used in so many different areas makes it easier to combine different forms of presentation. Music and image can be developed at the same time and multi-media shown in Germany offer spectacular examples of this, with controlling tapes, colour-slide projections, recitation of poetry and so on.

Computer film is a genre by itself. Animation techniques, started by the good old Walt Disney Studios, have long since entered into the electronic age. Computer makes the animation artists problems a lot simpler, with the use of electronic facilities and *chroma-key* kind of mixing. Fantasy films like *King Kong* have today graduated into *2002: A Space Odyssey*, *Jaws*, *Empire Strikes Back*, and the breath-taking visuals of *Close Encounters of the Third Kind.*

Indian Situation

National Informatics Centre (NIC) has played a key-role in assisting the Indira Gandhi National Centre for the Arts (IGNCA) to bring computers in the area of Indian art and culture. Apart from very substantial documentation and creation of databases on fundamental artistic terms, manuscripts and their repositories, Vedic chantings, invaluable art collections, the NIC is now poised to use the latest hypermedia technology (to combine the text with static visuals, kinetic visuals and sound, complete with their documentary descriptions) to create multi-media experiments on computer for use of scholars.

IGNCA has also used its Indian and foreign researches to create architectural graphics in computer for some of the cultural sites such as, Brahadisvara temple. Expert systems may soon be planned related to such diverse areas as rock art and anthropology.

Conclusion

It is not clear yet whether the computer-aided demonstrations of the artistic kind are themselves art of not. But technical developments go on, unconcerned about such theoretical questions. Whatever the results are, as long as it opens up new *visual, auditory* and *sensory* horizons — it enriches our otherwise so prosaic and so materialistic world of technology. India may soon be the gainer in some of its efforts, if the latest understanding between the IBM and the Apple Macintosh people come to full fruition, for multi-media fields will be of their principal areas of collaboration in the nineties decade.

32

COMPUTER-AIDED ENGINEERING

Introduction

Design and development of new products and projects in the engineering organisations usually involve three kinds of drawings: (i) Preliminary sketches – to record the initial idea on paper: (ii) Additional drawings – when modifications are needed prior to the approval of the design; and (iii) Production drawings – to do the detailed sketches as part of the production blue-print. Normally, the designer's time spent in the above preparatory work is quite substantial.

Computer-Aided Design (CAD)

In order to eliminate the difficulties and reduce the man-hours spent, CAD methodology has been developed using graphic display devices on the computer and special electronic pens in order to effect quick changes and modifications in the sketches of an engineer at two stages as follows:

(a) Once the initial drawings are finished and displayed to the engineer's satisfaction, the computer can be used to analyse the displayed design and report on certain characteristics;
(b) The interactive communication between the engineer and the computer may continue until a design is produced based on a desirable set of instructions.

CAD Tools and Building Blocks

The input to CAD can include: (i) technical knowledge of the engineer who enter design criteria, edit results and test the design; and (ii) information from libraries of technical standards of components, element sizes, etc. The latter can cover standard pipe-lengths for a fertiliser, factory, fittings for a hydraulic on piping system or standard integrated circuits (ICs) for a digital design system.

The tools required for CAD, as surveyed by *Computer Today* are: (i) the computer; (ii) the high-resolution graphics monitor; (iii) the magnetic disk storage; (iv) the digitizer for input; and (v) a light pen, mouse or some other device for cursor movement.

The output is displayed on the monitor screen (VDU) or recorded via a printer on a plotter. Images with a high degree of clarity can be plotted in colour to the finest detail.

CAD facilities include: (i) *erase* – without leaving any traces behind; (ii) *cut and paste* – to cut any part of the drawing and paste it where required; (iii) *search and replace* – to search where a particular shape has occurred in the design and to replace it with another specified command; (iv) *zoom* – to magnify a part of the drawing manyfold; (v) *pan* – to move over a drawing on the screen; (vi) *store* – to preserve symbols for repetitive use in the drawing. In the work or a design using the above tools, CAD can maintain an accuracy up to one inch over a sketch of several square kilometres!

Applications of CAD

A few cases of CAD are described here in the Indian setup for two large organisations: Engineers India Ltd. (EIL) and Bharat Heavy Electricals Ltd. (BHEL).

A. *The EIL Case*

EIL is a leading consultancy organisation in the South-East Asia in many areas of turn-key operations (from concept to commissioning) which include process design, detailed engineering, procurement, construction supervision, and so on. The areas of operation span over petroleum refining, petrochemicals, gas processing, pipelines, paper, power and cement, non-ferrous metallurgy, environmental engineering, and off-shore engineering.

The systems engineering and computer services use two powerful 32-bit computer systems, one ND-570 computer (with 8 MB main memory, 2000 MB disk drives, 20 terminals and 4-5 graphic terminals), and VAX 11/780 computer (with 4 MB main memory, 56 MB disk drives and 3-4 terminals) and have Robotron 1040 computer, besides other computers in the process, engineering procurement, personnel and word processing areas. EIL has a distributed processing environment to a large degree.

The structural CAD covers analysis, design and detailed drafting of 2-D and 3-D frames, trusses, grids, folded plates, cylindrical shells and RCC chimneys. The mechanical engineering CAD covers pipe analysis, pressure vessels design, design of storage tanks, silos, etc. The piping CAD covers pipeline optimisation, surge analysis and stress analysis, apart from 3-D isometrics (for the large-scale sites) and general layouts. The electrical CAd covers the following:

(a) *Basic engineering*: systems analysis (whether the whole system is valid); load-flow analysis; voltage and fault level calculations (on the accepted configuration);
(b) *Detailed engineering*: effect of a large-scale motor starter on the system; flexibility studies on operation and configuration (if hooked up to a captive generator), plotting for line-diagrams with graphics; and
(c) *Cable estimate and cable layout (for Rs. 1,400 crore project of IPCL)*: cable scheduling (sizing of requirement according to the load) and cable-layout drawing (on the plotter).

The instrumentation CAD covers process and instrumentation diagrams (updated locationwise and control-wise from the instrumentation angle), materials list, loop schematic diagram (master drawing for site-execution), and logic and control schematics (for plant operation). The process CAD is a vast area of design and drafting of the process and instrumentation of heat and mass transfer, exchanger and heater drawings (2-D graphics), Development and single-line diagrams play an important role in all the above.

B. *The BHEL Case*

BHEL is a very large engineering and manufacturing enterprise, ranking among the top 12 power plant equipment manufacturers in the world. Besides its turn-key capability in the power sector (from project feasibility studies up to after-sales services), it operates in the transportation, oil and gas, non-conventional energy sources and telecommunications sector. It offers a variety of electrical, electronic and mechanical equipment to industries such as fertilisers, petro-chemicals, refineries, paper, sugar, rubber, cement, coal, steel, aluminium and mining.

The organisation uses computers very extensively in engineering, manufacturing and information processing, covering such engineering fields as (a) design and analysis (with partly interactive graphics); (b) finite element methods (FEM) and finite element analysis (FEA) studies (using standard packages); (c) computer-aided drafting; and so on. Considering BHEL's vast need of transportability of information and design to various locations of widely spread computer centres, satellite communications is planned through micro earth-stations concept.

Examples of the computer-aided engineering areas of BHEL are as follows:

(a) *Design and analysis*: Design of steam generator for thermal and nuclear power plants; superheater material selection; fluid distribution network analysis; 2-D cutting plan; optimisation of boiler performance; heat-balance calculations and generation of heat-balance diagrams; plant drainage system design; sizing calculations for control valves, flow orifices, flow elements; relay coordination; transient studies during high-speed bus transfer; optimisation of AC ancillary system design, insulation design; electro-magnetic transient studies; transformer design; design optimisation calculations for water treatment plant, cooling tower, fresh water cooling system; generation and optimisation of valve body profiles.

(b) *FEM and FEA studies:* Structural analysis; space frame analysis with nuclear selection; creep analysis; design and analysis (static and dynamic) of chimney; design and analysis of foundations; design and analysis of pile configurations; force-time history for dynamic analysis; piping, flexibility study (using FEM); seismic qualification study (using FEM); hydroturbine blade design using a 3-D sculptured surface modeller; 3-D modelling and layout of fuel piping; optimisation of steam-piping routing and generation of isometric drawing; crack propagation studies in welds.

(c) *Computer-aided drafting*: Heat balance calculations and generation of heat-balance diagrams; generation of drawings and piping hanger assemblies; generation of logic diagrams; control-desk layout; generation of single-line diagrams; 3-D routing and optimisation of cables; optimisation of thermal power-plant piping, involving 3-D routing and generation of isometric drawings; generation of schematics for writing, electricals and piping and instrumentation diagrams; generation and optimisation of valve-body profiles.

Material databases are linked to the design diagrams as above, containing information regarding the planning procurement, storage and accounting of material used.

Model Visualisation for Designers

Modelling is similar to building a house with the bricks that can be viewed as solid primitives, assembled progressively to construct the required building. Similarly 2-D provides the designer with a range of solid primitives as building blocks for constructing a component or assembly. The technique employed resembles constructive solid geometry (CSG), used as a companion process to 2-D CAD which is mainly concerned with the efficient creation of correctly annotated drawings; and to surface modelling which is used for sculpturing complex surfaces.

Interactive screen menus including "icons" (pictures). Colour and on-line help are required for modelling the solids as follows:

(a) *Model Construction*: Wide range of geometrical building blocks using *box, cylinder, pyramid, snout,* etc., commands; ability to create swept or turned solids from 2-D shapes, ability to create sculptured solids; construction of model by combining simpler solids, using union, intersection, difference, assembly and sectioning operations;

(b) *Analysis*: Automatic calculations of volume, moments of inertia and surface area; interference checking; user-defined analysis operations; facilities for enquiring;

(c)*Database*: Hierarchy, construction and assembly; listing facilities of an objects structure, components parts and projects; *copy, rename* and *delete* facilities; facilities for creating commands and interactive;

(d) *Viewing and drawing*: Ability to create and save views of elevations, isometric directions, any angle of view, magnified to any scale; windowing and panning of views; hidden line removal; display of surface facets and object axes; ability to centre objects on the screen; and

(e) *Interfaces*: Ability to plot selected views; output of user-formatted reports; ability to select 2-D shapes, sculptured surfaces and snapshots.

Goals of Computer-Aided Engineering

In the developed countries, industries save considerable engineering costs by incorporating computer-aided design concepts and design optimisation. Design optimisation is even more relevant to developing countries who have to optimise their scarce resources and develop a self-reliant industrial base on appropriate technological designs. Automated design of engineering system can speed up design innovations and save several man-years of routine, stereotype engineering work. While such specialised time can thus be released for more productive work, efficiency can also increase by eliminating human errors likely in many design work.

As was seen earlier in the EIL and BHEL cases, the computer is becoming a powerful aid in the design of equipment and circuits, chemical and metallurgical processes, transmission and distribution lines, machine and automotive engine design, and so on. Computer application in the design of process systems, for instance, results in better utilisation of resources through optimisation of design, increased efficiency and improved reliability and quality. Last few years have seen increasing use of PCs and minicomputers to improve the production of plant and process.

UNDP-Aided CAD Centres

The UNDP assistance has been garnered today in a few centres of excellence for using computers in engineering design and control of plant and processes for the industrial development of India. These centres are listed below along with their fields of specialisation and the industries and organisations with whom they interact:

(a) *CAD Centre at the Jadavpur University, Calcutta*

It uses the ND-560 computer (2 MB main memory, 450 MB disk drive and 4 graphic terminals) for *heavy engineering and real-time control system applications.* The enterprises, having linkages in the CAD development work, are (i) EIL, (ii) Oil India Ltd., (iii) Coal India Ltd., (iv) Director General of Mines Safety, (v) Fertiliser Corporation of India, (vi) Steel Authority of India, (vii) Instrumentation Ltd., Kota, (viii) other agencies and institutions working in process control and instrumentation.

(b) *CAD Centre at the Indian Institute of Technology, Kanpur*

It uses similar computer as above and the OMEGA system for working in *mechanical and civil engineering* and also in *the development of fluid flow systems.* It has linkages with (i) BHEL, (ii) Structural Engineering Research Centre, Roorkee, (iii) Railway Designs and Standards Organisation, Lucknow, (iv) Triveni Structurals, (v) EIL, (vi) Heavy Engineering Corporation, Ranchi, (vii) Mazgaon Dock, Bombay, (viii) Kirloskar Oil Engines Ltd., Pune, (ix) other civil and mechanical engineering institutions and agencies.

(c) *CAD Centre at the Indian Institute of Science, Bangalore*

It uses a number of HP 9000 computers with graphic terminals to work on *electronic and semi-conductor circuit designs.* It interacts with (i) Bharat Electronics Ltd., (ii) Indian Telephone Industries Ltd., (iii) Semi-Conductor Corporation Ltd., Chandigarh, (iv) Electronic Corporation of India Ltd., Hyderabad, (v) KELTRON, (vi) other agencies and institutions in the electronics and semi-conductor area.

(d) *CAD Centre at the Indian Institute of Technology, Bombay*

It uses similar computer as at (c) for the CAD work in *chemical and metallurgical engineering.* It interacts with (i) Gujarat State Fertiliser Corporation Ltd., (ii) Fertiliser Corporation of India Ltd., (iii) Steel Authority of India, (iv) Bharat Aluminium Corporation Ltd., (v) EIL, (vi) National Organic and Chemicals India Ltd., (vi) Indian Drugs and Pharmaceuticals Ltd., (vii) other agencies and institutions in the chemical and metallurgical areas.

The aim of the above four UNDP-aided CAD Centres is to produce, inter alia, specialised consultants, training packages for user organisations and industries, CAD R&D work, and a library of software packages for engineering design.

Conclusion

CAD is today getting related to computer-assisted manufacturing (CAM). Such a CAD/CAM alliance has the computer prepare (i) detailed engineering blue-prints of the design, and (ii) control tapes that programme the automatic machine tools ((and robots) to produce precisely the component parts of new products according to the blue-print specifications. CAM implies the integration of all aspects of manufacturing systems within the factory. Thus, the computer is used not only for process control, but also for such aspects as automatic ordering of materials, predicting materials usage, factory, scheduling, inventory usage, predicting machine change over and even projecting manpower requirements. CAM, in a sense, naturally flows from CAD and it is only a matter of time before CAM becomes as widely prevalent in India as CAD is today. On the other hand, a flexible manufacturing system (FMS), which is quickly reprogrammed to handle design changes and produce new items, will perhaps take much longer to appear in the Indian scene compared to its Western counterparts due to the inherent technology and labour implications.

PART THREE

RELATED ISSUES

33

TRANSITION STRATEGY FROM MANUAL TO COMPUTER PROCESSING

Introduction

In a fast-changing scene for using computers, the large Indian organisations (who have gone partly or completely for computerisation) reveal a bewildering variety of situations. To give a few recent illustrations, Delhi Telecommunications – like Bombay and a few others – generated a billing system on computer where an outside computer service agency did the bulk of the job, using both manpower and computer time. UP State Electricity Board (UPSEB) – in common with APSEB, Delhi Electric Supply Undertaking (DESU) and others – used a number of computerised services such as billing, inventory management, etc., with the help of turnkey services from outside, but went for in-house computerisation in due course. Mother Dairy of Delhi had been using an outside agency to generate computer-based information reports for its milk distribution, inventory, payroll and financial accounting systems, but later acquired an in-house Galaxy system where some of the jobs were shifted. Two extreme examples in the Himalayan UP are Oil & Natural Gas Commission (ONGC) and the LBS National Academy of Administration (NAA). While ONGC uses a battery of large in-house modern computers in a star network to carry out seismic data-processing, it also shares computer-time of the National Informatics Centre (NIC) computer with an expanded system and with a French seismic software package for the same purpose. LBS, NAA has acquired a lot of computing power for its library and training jobs, having begun from scratch.

Transition Plans

There is often no clear-cut transition plan from manual data-processing to computerisation by most organisations, although such a plan would appear obviously desirable for adopting a rational outlook and getting best value for the money. Before suggesting a scientific strategy for such transitions, it is important to note the prevailing pattern which can be summarised as: complete outside dependence (users having total services from outside hardware and outside software team); partial outside dependence (users having in-house software team but outside hardware to provide computer-time); and complete self-sufficiency (users having in-house hardware and software teams). A variation on the theme of partial outside dependence can be users having in-house hardware and services from outside software team. But such a variation (say, for Scooter India which acquired an Uptron computer and hired an outside team to develop software) is relatively rare.

When an organisation desires to have a transition from manual data-processing to computerisation of any one of the three possibilities mentioned above, it is extremely useful to carry out a rough-and-ready diagnostic study as to whether the prevailing flow of information, linkage between different segments and the general workload pattern deserve computerisation or not. Many small to medium organisations are known to have been taken in by the highly aggressive publicity let loose by today's microcomputer vendors, – ending up in having highly redundant applications (like a computerised payroll system for 200 employees) or in generating new demands which cannot be met by the existing micro-computers due to not having any upward expandability.

Demand and Supply

If the above diagnostic study, by virtue of an outside expert's preliminary survey, establishes a prima-facie case for computerisation, – it is thereafter necessary to do a more detailed (and more expensive than preliminary survey) feasibility study. The latter should be approached from a *demand* as well as a *supply* side, and eventually there should be a demand-supply matching to arrive at the best method of computerisation in order to suit the organisation's specific needs. On the *demand* side, such a study (preferably carried out by a highly knowledgeable team) should assess from the potential users in every segment of activity their information needs and arrive at conceptual output reports to serve such needs. In the process, much of the physical flow of information is likely to become integrated and many insightful analytical reports are possible to be thrown up which cannot be made available without computer. The inputs are then to be assessed and procedures suggested to generate the requisite outputs. The detailed study in each workload area, with reference to the load factor and the possibility of computerisation would be in the form of a cost-benefit analysis: showing costs of introducing computerisation and the corresponding benefits (tangible and intangible) likely to accrue to the management.

Ultra-slim and Light-weight Computer

On the *supply* side, a feasibility study should first arrive at a probable configuration of the hardware best suited to meet the organisations requirements and then venture out to look at the available computer configurations and their prices in the market. Even after the needs have been matched with the availability, it is by no means essential to rush for buying and installing the appropriate computer system in-house. In fact, it is much more essential to inculcate "computer culture" first, under which the user managers are made accustomed to receiving computerised outputs and asking for more analytical (or integrated) reports and returns. Such a "culture" can be created by assigning the entire computerisation work to a competent service bureau in the neighbourhood and insisting on timely and accurate outputs from them based on the supply of quality input-data.

Many such service bureaus exist today, in the form of regional computer centres (in Calcutta, Varanasi, Roorkee, Chandigarh, Pune, etc.), centres in the public sector (like NIC and CMC, including the latter's INDONET centres); and centres in the private sector (like Tata Consultancy Service, Computronics India, International Data Management, etc., who all run chains of modern computer centres supported by software teams).

Laptop Computer

Service – Bureau Approach

The above suggestion has the merit of introducing the "culture" without creating immediately an elaborate infrastructure which will be costly to dismantle. On the other hand, the outside service bureaus can be forewarned of a transition process to, first, an in-house software team and, eventually, a compete self-sufficiency. The initial agreements should provide for these two sequential steps and the help of the outside service bureau made use of in the commensurate training programme. The software itself has to be modified in the latter stage to suit the new in-house computer, where again the outside service bureau should assist. Such a well-thoughtout strategy will have the advantage of reducing to the minimum the all-time dependency on an outside team and thus stopping a perpetual cash out-flow. The outside bureau, on its part, can plan to acquire new clients, once the existing clients switch on to their own teams and systems, in that order.

Having stated the above, it should be mentioned that some user organisations are hard put to get a suitable service bureau in their neighbourhood or, having found one, may find its service less than satisfactory. In some other cases, management may have been reasonably convinced that while introducing an in-house computer, they will be in a position to initiate simultaneously their own computer induction programmes (often with the help of the manufacturer) at both appreciation and application levels for the senior and junior levels respectively. In all such cases, the actual transition from the manual phase to the mechanised one may have to be carefully planned to make the change-over smooth rather than precipitate.

Actual Usage

No computer system can start delivering the goods from day one of installation, unless elaborate prior planning has been done to study the information systems, conceptualise computer-based flow-charts and integrations, and engage software teams (own or outside) to start designing the systems. System design and development has a long gestation period and needs suitable handling, in anticipation of introducing computerisation. It is an exciting process to visualise the structure of the computer-base information systems (for which the earlier feasibility study can be a great help) and the design and development work can be undertaken by the in-house team or the outside service bureau, in full collaboration with the line executives. Some managerial skills are imperative on the part of the systems team who act an "architects", in contrast to the more routine efforts to be put in for codification by the programmers who are in effect "brick-layers".

Implementation planning of the computerised activities should again go hand in hand with the line manager's involvement and should be preceded by a painstaking process of testing, de-bugging and parallel runs. Implementation of a computerised system cannot insist on instant discontinuance of the earlier manual processing. UPSEB, for instance, continued with its manual ledgers until it was certain of the fool-pro nature of the computer-generated ledgers. Another important aspect is the data input service to be streamlined, since the computer is invariably a hard task-master demanding "clean", consistent and complete data. Again, UPSEB's example of starting several "computer cells" to handle input data, headed by executive engineers, is worth noting.

Conclusion

An initial effort to introduce computerisation on a pilot-project basis, followed by a more comprehensive computerisation scheme (based on the lessons learnt from the pilot project), can pay handsome dividends. This has been the experience of UPSEB which has gone ahead for a phased transition from manual to computerised billing in its different divisions. The above notes of caution are highly deserved in any process of a massive transition, – as was proved in the case of DESU which appeared to gc through an initial traumatic phase due to the neglect of some of those factors, before settling down to a stable transition process.

34

MARKETING ASPECTS OF COMPUTER SERVICES

Introduction

With the development of computer usage in different sectors, it has become increasingly evident that the user organisations often need certain external services both before and after they decide to introduce computerisation. To start with, a counselling service is needed to ascertain whether a computer is needed at all and, if so, of what kind, and in which of the many application-areas. Often an outside expert opinion is a must, if the potential user organisation does not have the needed expertise in-house and if it does not want to be entirely influenced by the hard-selling computer vendors and manufacturers. Even after the initial decision has been in favour of computerisation, and after a feasibility study has been done on the nature and scope of computer usage, there still remains at least three options : the user may hire a computer service-bureau to avail of outside computer-time as well as outside manpower; or the user may build its own team of computer manpower but may still buy necessary computer-time from outside; or the user may go ahead to instal its own in-house computer supported by a full-fledged team of its own computer personnel. Except in the last case, the need for computer services from outside emerges as a clear necessity.

Computer Service Bureaus

It is the above user necessity that has given rise to the phenomenal growth of computer service-bureaus all over the world. India has been a late starter due to the earlier prevalence of second-generation machines, where the vendors themselves used to play the role of friend, philosopher and guide. The current situation is one of open-door policy in instilling a computer-culture in any organisation (with almost no government regulation to be faced if one wishes to buy an indigenous computer), and this has seen a mushrooming of computer service-bureaus in India, too.

The types of computer services marketed by an Indian service-bureau can fall into any of the ten categories of : (i) systems consultancy; (ii) hardware selection; (iii) hardware installation; (iv) hardware maintenance; (v) development of system software; (vi) development of application software; (vii) regular usage of application software; (viii) sale of computer-time; (ix) turnkey service; and (x) data preparation. A service-bureau may market some of all of the above computer services, and could follow a distinctive marketing pattern for each.

Variety of Services

(i) *System Consultancy* is quite similar to management consultancy services and can be offered for a preliminary survey, comprehensive feasibility study or detailed systems planning: all relating to computerisation in the client organisation. Preliminary survey deals with a rough and ready diagnosis whether computerisation is worth introducing and, if so, in which application-areas. Feasibility study is concerned with an in-depth analysis on costs of computerisation in each application-area with regard to the volume of work-load, needs for management reports and benefits arising out of a potentially integrated information system. Systems planning is an actual blue-print for a computer-based information system, taking into account the design aspects of systems output reports and corresponding input collection. All these kinds of systems consultancy can be marketed with the help of seasoned computer experts, for against a professional fee plus actual expenses.

(ii) *Hardware selection* is a tricky service in which a service-bureau has to match the need of a specific computer configuration for a client organisation (worked out on the basis of volume or data to be processed and types of reports to be generated, in a batch or on-line mode) and the availability of the proven computer systems which are most likely to meet those needs.

(iii) *Hardware installation* on the other hand, is a straight-forward process in comparison, involving civil (false flooring and ceiling, partitions, etc.) and electrical (power supply, air conditioning etc.) works. A client organisation, incidentally, should be cautious in not asking hardware selection to be done by any service-bureau which is vending or manufacturing large, medium, mini or micro computer systems.

Laptop Computer Showing Car Design

(iv) *Hardware maintenance* is a specialised computer service needing both knowledge of, and training in, computer machines sought to be maintained. Maintenance by the public-sector CMC, in-house team or the vendor are prevalent in India. Charges are either on prime-shift (and call service for non-price hours) or three-shift basis and an annual maintenance fee of around 10 per cent of the computer cost seems to be in order. Microcomputers are often maintained in-house or by vendor-recommended third parties.

(v) *Development of systems software* is one of the most sophisticated services and can only be marketed based on computer science knowledge of basic software like operating system, computer construction, etc. This service is usually marketed to the computer manufacturers who have to provide specifications of their requirements. Charges are usually quite high and only a handful of India service-bureaus have the needed expertise.

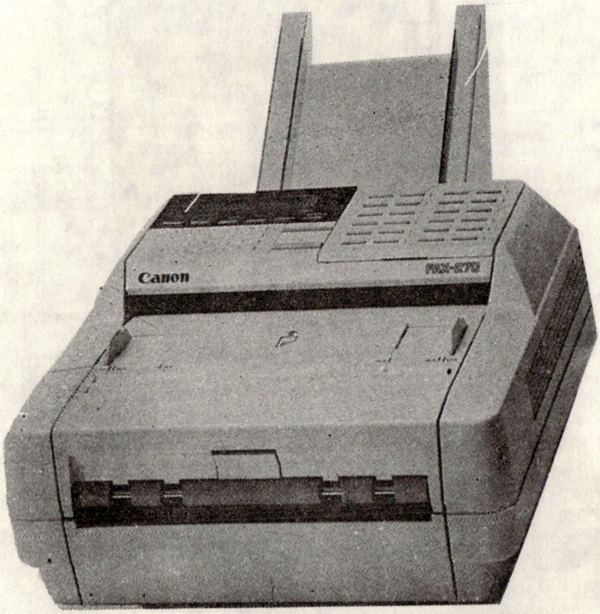

This Fax Machine goes with Computer

(vi) *Development of application software* is the most common computer service marketed today and employs the largest available computer manpower. Application software may be either general-purpose, ordered by the manufacturers themselves (to become their copy-right and to be marketed later along with the machine) or special-purpose, ordered by the user organisations (called "customised") for their tailor-made needs. Development charges include both manpower-time (in terms of months spent by systems analysis as well as programmers) and computer-time (for testing and parallel run, before implementation).

(vii) *Regular usage of application software* is a relatively rare service in India, where an available software package procured from overseas or other Indian software agency has to be suitably converted to the computer machine of the service-bureau and run for the benefit of the user organisation. Both one-time royalty as well as recurring commission charges may become payable for the used packages, apart from the running expenses.

(viii) *Sale of computer-time* is a common enough service where only time on computer is made available to the user organisation who runs their own application software (either developed in-house or procured as a package from the vendor) with the aid of its own operational staff. This is in sharp distinction with the *turnkey service* which involves development, regular usage and time-selling for application software : all rolled into one service and charged as a whole. While microcomputers charge for time based on clock-hours, mini and main frame computers have built in meters and often use computer-based job accounting system to log time for each device used in running a user-job.

(ix) *Data preparation* is a necessary but weak part of the computer service requiring low-skilled manpower to operate data-entry systems based on key-to-tape or key-to-floppy disc (and, later, to tape) operations. Some service-bureaus still operate the now obsolete key-punch and verifying machines whose maintenance has become a difficult job. A number of data-preparation bureaus have sprung up who only market this service, charged on the basis of records keyed and put on the floppies. Established service bureaus with a chain of fourth generation computer systems (like Tata Consultancy Service, Computronics India, etc.) quite often off-load their data preparation work to outside agencies after making sure of the proper performance of the agency-function.

Marketing of Computer Services

Marketing of computer services has become a very competitive activity, thanks to the proliferation of microcomputers and small groups of computer professionals offering limited services. The sheer pressure of competition makes for under-quotation and, in the absence of any standardisation of professional norms, the rates become quite often unremunerative. Most service-bureaus, having large or mini computers, find it uneconomic to offer competition to microcomputer bureaus except in large-volume jobs (e.g., examination result-processing, electricity billing, etc.) or for jobs calling for comprehensive specialisation (e.g., inter-branch reconciliation of banks, public issues through large issues houses, etc.). This is largely true in the western and northern parts of India with an already prevalent computer culture, although the competition is less fierce in the southern and eastern India.

Profitability of marketable computer services, therefore, varies widely today from job to job. A computerised share-issue system, for instance, can have substantial manual activities like coding and numbering, reconciliation with schedules, individual tallying and inserting share certificates (or refund orders) into envelopes, — comprising 20 to 25 per cent of the total work. Such a service will have cost-elements based on manual manpower, data preparation (in-house and outside) and stationery recoverable : all of which involve a drainage on liquid cash. If the above cost-elements are excluded from the amount billed as revenue, then the balance will represent contribution towards fixed expenses like salary of professional manpower (e.g., systems, programming, operation and marketing) and cost of computer-time. It is often the market experience that the latter is barely covered, let alone other overheads, except in really large-volume jobs.

Conclusion

The above is true for most service-bureaus in India, except perhaps those in the public sector where individual accountability may not be paramount and where the non-use ,or misuse of computer-time — although a drain or taxpayer's money — would seldom cost anybody his job. The need, nevertheless, is obvious today to achieve an industry-wide understanding of the computer services and the related expenses, so that the marketing efforts are not cut-throat, returns are viable and economic, and the users get the quality of service which they had paid for in the first place.

35

PUBLICITY PATTERN IN COMPUTER MARKETING

Introduction

High-Voltage publicity in computer marketing in India had reached a new peak, when the International Data Management (IDM) took prime space some time ago in a number of national newspapers and brought out the characteristics of their S-50 computer system, — along with a comparable space left just vacant alongside, which was purported to be reserved for any rival computer system having to talk about comparable (or better) features. Within days came an ad in *India Today* from the Zenith Computers which re-produced the IDM copy, circled a few salient features from there, and elaborated on the vacant space as to how their own ORION-3000 system would excel S-50 system in all respects. In a personal discussion with the author, the Managing Director of the IDM remarked good-humouredly how the Zenith had either missed out or ignored the main points of the earlier IDM ad which they had chosen to controvert. Whatever the viewpoint, such publicity pattern can only be confusing to the common man and needs to be properly analysed.

Aggressive Publicity

In the Western computer market, it is quite a usual practice to quote the characteristics of, say, IBM computer hardware or UNIX computer software by a rival firm who would then proceed systematically to demolish the IBM or UNIX superiority in order to argue in favour of its own product. This perhaps makes sense, if at all, in an environment where computer has invaded in all walks of life and every schoolboy has to learn today about computer usage. But in India, where computer is a relative newcomer, such aggressive advertisement and counter-advertisement — both couched in sophisticated language and vying for costly space in the popular press — would appear to make strange bed-fellows.

If one keeps the Indian target-audience in mind for the English-language national press or popular magazine, one would realise how an increasing sophistication (and corresponding aggressiveness) in computer advertising could only lead to an increasing bewilderment in the mind of the average reader. Two more illustrations will complete our case in point. Some time back, the PSI Systems of Bangalore came out with an eye-catching advertisement how it was time for all other advertisers of computer systems to stop talking now, so that they could listen to what the PSI had to say : in terms of excellence of their own products. In another brilliant series, the International Computers Indian Manufacture (ICIM) published pictures of men caught in action enquiring whether a computer could really help them in their mundane work-situations, and providing answers how ICIM-2904 computers could come to their rescue. A later copy for their ICIM-101 computer became comparatively gimmicky when it outlined some specific check-points which must be raised by every computer-buyer to be compulsorily answered by every computer-vendor in order to give full value for money. As the check-list was completed by extolling the virtues of ICIM-101 system, one then await a counter check-list which would sing paeans of praise for a competitive computer system.

Factors in Publicity Strategy

Three factors have influenced predominantly the computer marketing scene in India, and determined its publicity strategy. First and foremost, thanks to a liberal licensing policy, a large number of Indian manufacturers have been permitted to market microprocessor-based systems. Most of these micro-computers are configured around Intel chip which is a 16-bit or 32-bit device and can accept only a certain amount of peripherals, resulting in a somewhat comparable processing of throughput. They, however, vie with each other in proclaiming superiority over one another, based on the apparent belief that a publicity offensive is the best strategy for survival in a world of near-equals. Secondly, in terms of growth, they are all out to capture new users, who are often quite unsuspecting of the real computing power of the new generation of micro-computers. They are attempted to be lured by such statements that even a petite typist can handle the computer machine, such is the ease of operation! Finally, the prevalent lack of technology-cultrue in the wider body politic has kept the people generally unaware as to what the real economics is — in present as well as future terms — of any new technology. In consequence, even irresponsible publicity is undertaken promising many applications (without specifying the constraints) and ridiculously low down-payments along with instalment-terms, without any regard to the machine-limitations which will stop all future growth, once the computer-culture catches up.

Before trying to find out what would be more meaningful as well as ethical publicity strategy for computer marketing, let us look at the available options and their scope. Technical prevention and vendors' system-study are two options meant for *individual* enlightenment of a potential customer. Technical presentation can be done on hardware configuration, operating system, application software and special peripherals in response to customers query, with the aid of flip charts, slides and transparencies. For instance, a user organisation which might have issued tenders for a large computer system can allow such individual presentations from the computer vendors on various aspect so as to benefit from their on-the-spot clarifications and from the highlighting of special points which are not clear from the tender-documents. Also, a user organisation can have comparative bench-mark studies carried out for the offered system. Vendors' system-study is an assessment of the hardware and software needs of the customer as done by the vendor. IBM, for example, had earlier carried out quite a few such studies in the Indian steel sector to evaluate the latter's computer requirements.

Other Options

Collective enlightenment of a large body of potential customers can be attempted by other publicity options, such as, demonstration, display and advertising. A dynamic demonstration of functioning computer equipment (along with video-terminals, tapes, discs and printer) has become quite a popular feature at the foremost professional gathering at annual conventions of Computer Society of India, by a few hundred computer-vendors and manufacturers every year. Similar demonstrations and "road shows" are also arranged at hotels or meeting places in important towns by many vendors while announcing their new products. A display of computer equipment (based on static machinery or just pictures and posters) is arranged quite easily during national and international trade fairs, technical exhibitions organised by professional societies, – using publicity material, such as, colour-slides, film-strips and audio-visual facilities. Advertisement is the last publicity option, either through technical journals or through non-technical printed media such as, national and local press, and popular magazines.

A good publicity strategy for computer marketing can use any or all of the above options, giving regard to their relative costs and effectiveness. A satisfied user can provide the best publicity, as has been demonstrated time and again. An earlier bias against some EC computers was substantially dispelled when, for instance, a reputed educational and research institution in the eastern region found EC-1033 system quite satisfactory. Lease-hire publicity, based on loaned systems, has not gained much ground in India. "Show Window" publicity is based on service-bureaus running computer-based activities. Two such computers, located earlier at the Administrative Staff College of India, attracted enormous publicity for nearly 2,000 executive undergoing about 60 courses there every year and having exposure to the computer-based training or management games. "Goodwill" publicity is an interesting variation on the usually commercial theme, achieved for supporting a worthwhile cause. ITI of Naini, for example, announced in a recent computer conference at Allahabad that they would allow their powerful VAX-11 system to be used by computer professionals to organise education programmes and case-studies for using computer in law, and gained an instant gratitude of the professional community.

Conclusion

In the ultimate analysis, no publicity strategy can do better or worse than the actual track-record of the computer machine. Trouble-free system performance, continued reliability and fail-safe procedures are the *sine qua non* of today's usage of computers. Performance of central processing unit and the peripheral at the designed speeds for processing, transferring and printing of data — without any degradation — of data speaks volumes which no publicity gimmick can substitute. Vendors and manufacturers of computers in India are well advised to take heed of the above so that their publicity campaigns can

become more useful to the potential user. Among the factors which the latter would definitely treasure are : the attention to be given to the user training and education at both appreciation (for higher executives) and application (for supervisors) levels; the scope of augmenting the given hardware to a higher configuration to meet the tempo of future demands; the amount of software provided and its maintenance (in the face of modifications needed for change in management practice); and the quality of technical services to be rendered by a preferably widely-distributed office-network of the supplier of computer. A well-meaning time-frame for rendering all support functions and a scrupulous adherence of the same deserves to be heard of more in the Indian marketing scene, than has been usual so far.

36

COMPUTER, EMPLOYMENT AND AUTOMATION

Introduction

The role of computer in generating employment on being just a "labour killing" device has been debated for long. Since its massive advent in the last couple of decades, doubts have been voiced and eyebrows raised on the desirability or otherwise of introducing computerisation-often equating it with automation in a developing country like India where there is already a long queue of the unemployed.

Political Perception

In a major political statement in the Parliament in April 1983, the then Prime Minister Mrs. Indira Gandhi stated the following:

a. Wherever computerisation had been introduced abroad, to improve efficiency and quality of production, it had at the end generated more employment after some initial dislocation;
b. Computerisation would not affect employment potential;
c. In the high technology area, the country would be left behind if adequate steps were not taken on time.

In March 1986, the successor Prime Minister Rajiv Gandhi, always a strong votary of high technology, stated in the Parliament that:

a. Expenditure on computerisation would create more jobs and was crucial to the country's economy;
b. Computers could help to make the best use of available resources, both in terms of money and manpower and to reduce

hardships and harassment;

c. With computerisation, the employment had increased, with less menial work but more jobs for people.

With the cost of governance having gone up, the Prime Minister's secretariat had made it a point to monitor projects worth more than Rs. 200 crores, in order to ensure better performance of specific programmes and achieve better value for money, by using computers.

Earlier Studies

The impact of computerisation on employment has been studied in India since 1970. A report submitted that year by a works-study team under the Government of Maharashtra was the first of its kind in this country, which was inconclusive on the issue of linking computerisation with the current and potential employment situation.

The Dandekar Committee on Automation, appointed by the Government of India, submitted its report in 1972. Its conclusions revealed that computerisation of jobs had led to a slight decline in employment in the affected departments, but this was more than offset by an increase in the total employment. Unrestricted use of computers was recommended in educational, scientific and research institutions, while specific usage of computers was to be permitted in commercial and industrial establishments after prior consultation with existing workers.

A comprehensive study on impact of computers on employment was undertaken by two Professors from IIT, Kanpur and IIM, Ahmedabad in about 100 organisations and their findings published in 1975 showed that against a direct total employment of 8,850 and indirect employment of 12,670, only 8,000 persons were likely to have been displaced as a result of introducing computers.

A few cases can be examined here from the Indian environment to assess both direct and indirect impact of computers on the employment situation.

Experience at Clerical Level

a. For the private sector giant TISCO, computerisation was introduced early in the accounts department to convert the payroll and the entire employee services on a computer base for nearly 40,000 employees in the plant and another 20,000 or so in the mines and collieries. Scores of accounts assistants and superintendents engaged earlier in the manual effort were all retained, with fresh training given to handle computer inputs and outputs and to carry out their quality control. Nobody was found surplus. Efficiency also increased, as payment of arears of wages (after the wage negotiations with the management) could be done expeditiously, which would have otherwise needed protracted manual calculations.

b. Bihar Secondary Education Board and other State Government education councils which conduct school final (or 10th) and Intermediate (or 12th) examinations, found that computerised examination processing could ensure simultane- ously speed, accuracy and confidentiality of the results. All these factors could hardly be ensured for several lakhs of students, even if batteries of clerks were engaged for this purpose.

c. Northern Railways, in common with a few other Railways, have introduced on-line passenger reservation system where train tickets can be issued for any train, any class, any destination, any day and based on any criteria. A cost-benefit study, conducted under the aegis of the Department of Electronics, revealed that there was a large saving in the daily queuing hours for the intending passengers who could use that time for other productive proposes. At the same time, the booking clerks had savings of routine chores, like counting the ticket "cylinders" at the beginning and the end of the day, elaborate tallying of cash, etc.

d. Uttar Pradesh State Electricity Board (UPSEB) and many other state electricity authorities run computer-based electricity billing system. In the conversion process from the earlier manual system, an internal study of the UPSEB showed a gain of annual revenue, running into several crores, in the initial efforts for the Western UP districts, computerisation alone.

Experience at Managerial Level

a. Life Insurance Corporation of India (LIC) had initially a lot of reservation in introducing computerisation for premium notices, policy updating and settlement of claims. After these erstwhile manual jobs were put on computer, timely premium posting on policies and early settlement of claims for the needy widows and orphans earned LIC considerable goodwill. Simultaneously, time was relieved at managerial level from the routine trouble-shooting and fire-fighting activities, to plan and launch many new welfare insurance schemes for the population.

b. The Indian Police Organisation in around 16 states have introduced computerisation for the crime-criminal information system. Considering that about 20 per cent crimes are of inter-district kind and another 20 per cent are at inter-State level, a quick linkage and matching of the suspects with the extant records maintained by the human "collators" at each remote police station and centralised at the district headquarters can speedily bring the guilty to book.

c. Rourkela Steel Plant, along with other public sector and private sector steel plants, has been using process control computerisation for making quality steel from the hot metal comprising iron and its many impurities, by a timely and adequate oxygen-blow at an appropriate lancing angle several times during any single shift. These operations carried out manually earlier used to result in several off-heats, thus causing a loss of thousands of tonnes of steel as bad-quality products.

d. Centre for Railways Information System (CRIS) has been using state-of-the-art computers to develop freight informa- tion and operation system (FIOS) in order to ensure day-to- day monitoring of the Indian goods-train wagons and thereby enhancing their daily utilisation. With all other factors like locomotive engines, crew and yards held at the present level, this single effort of CRIS is likely to put into effective use the daily wagon-watch activities of the human "number-takers" and increase the goods traffic phenomenally, notching an additional revenue of several hundred crores of rupees.

New Job Creation

It will be interesting to note a few cases of new job creation as a result of the on-going computerisation endeavour in the country.

A. *Direct*

(i) National Informatics Centre (NIC) has launched a massive State and district level effort in creating a uniform information framework unparalleled in any other country at this gigantic scale Apart from the District Information Officers and Information Assistants for the 462 districts of India, this endeavour has generated a direct need of thousands of data-entry operators for every district and taluk. Andhra Pradesh (AP), for instance, has pressed into service all the Industrial Training Institutes (ITIs) to train up such operators, apart from the crash courses to produce trained programmers and systems analysis. This is an employment-scenario common in all other States, as many other computerisation efforts (including IRDP monitoring, land records, irrigation projects and labour exchanges, to name a few) are coming up in individual districts.

(ii) There is an urgent need of data-entry operators with a knowledge of word processing in the many industrial and commercial establishments in the country going in massively for computerisation. Their numbers would run into many thousands, if proper estimations are made.

B. *Indirect*

(i) Under the umbrella of National Natural Resource Management System (NNRMS) sponsored by the Department of Space, new knowledge is coming up every day with an enormous potential of creating employment. One example is the location of underground aquifers and other fresh-water sources so much needed to supply potable water to all our villages. Sinking of common as well as artesian wells, irrigation pumps, etc., need use of much unskilled and skilled manpower. Another example is the identification of schools of tuna and other fish (highly prized in the South and South-East Asian markets) in the shallow waters of our high seas. This knowledge has already generated immense enthusiasm in all the coastal districts of the country (running into a few scores) for setting up fishermen's cooperatives and running high-sea fishing trawlers to get the "catch" at the appropriate time and place.

(ii) State Bank of India (SBI) has been participating for long in the social banking scheme for providing loans and advances to the small-time operators, without tangible collateral support. This needs a close monitoring of the business activities of these operators so that their business does not run into bad debts for the SBI. Such computer based monitoring (including particularly bad debt monitoring in Bihar) has led to better disbursement and recovery of loans and advances, resulting in more banking business, by opening new branches and creating fresh employment.

Trade Union Perception

It needs undoubtedly an involvement and cooperation of the country's leading trade unions to appreciate that computers not merely cut down routine drudgery but also create higher efficiency and productivity which have the potential for a higher-level employment. This calls for a shift of attention from a mere guaranteeing of every primitive-level job to the imaginative creation of better-grade jobs using a modern tool of productivity and efficiency like computer. Such enlightenment is already coming to many organised unions in the corperate sector, who have come to a constructive understanding with the management on the use of computers. The banking and the steel sector are two cases in point.

An interesting variation on the theme is the use of computers by both management and the trade union in conducting a wage negotiation. Normally, trade unions tend to pitch their wage demands high and the management keep their commitment and concessions low, leading to a see-saw effort before leading to the eventual compromise. It has been the experience of both the AP State Road Transport Corporation (APSRTC) and the Indian Oxygen in the past to carry out such negotiations on the basis of both sides spelling out their position and using computer to work out the detailed monetary analysis so that both the sides stood wiser on the precise monetary implication of their respective stands.

Western Analysis

It would not be out of place to mention that new kinds of technology as are coming our way throw open new avenues of employment, but invariably at a higher standard of living. Every American home, for instance, today boasts of an available telephone connection. It was estimated that to sustain so many million lines, every adult American citizen would have to be at the telephone exchange as an operator, at the earlier manual exchange technology level with its attendant employment! Rajiv Gandhi used to talk about removing all the typewriters and "having a large number of scribes write down what was done in the government".

Professor Herbert Simon, the Nobel Laureate Computer Scientist, investigated into the phenomenon of every new technology making the employment redundant at the primitive technology level, but always helping to create a new quality of life with higher-level employment. He quoted from the experience of the late eighteenth and early-nineteenth century Industrial Revolution which saw the substitution of muscle power by prime movers like internal and external combustion engines. Many saw an imminent danger in this to "kill" all the coachmen and drivers of the horse-driven vehicles and bullock carts. Some of the die-hard, like the "Luddites", even went hammer and tong against the combustion engines in order to destroy them. Today we know that the Industrial Revolution was right and not the Luddites, in spite of the total substitution of that kind of employment.

Automation and Robotics

Nearly two centuries after Industrial Revolution, the Information Revolution has arrived, bringing revolutionary development by using computers and electronics to substitute human action in controlling many industrial processes and products. This has made possible industrial robots, computer-controlled machine-tools, automated guided-vehicle systems, etc., introducing flexibility in automated manufacturing systems.

Automation can be viewed as the highest form of mechanisation in which a manufacture-related process is carried out according to a previously set programme, wholly or partly, without human intervention. Its basic components are as follows:

a. *Feedback*, the basic mechanism underlying all self-regulating processes;
b. *Sensors and measurement systems*, acquiring information from the environment and the system components;
c. *Actuators*, converting information into actual motions or actions, working as "the muscle";

d. *Mechanisation,* generating, transforming and transferring complicated mechanical motions of different kinds;
e. *Computer* or *Controller,* processing all data and information, and generating command signals, working as "the brain";
f. *Display technology,* providing the interface with the outside world and the human operators who are the ultimate masters.

Landmarks of automation have been (i) simple production machines and mechanisation at the beginning of the Industrial Revolution, (ii) fixed automatic mechanisms and transfer lines for mass production in the early eighteenth century; (iii) machine-tools with simple automatic control (to perform a fixed sequence of operators) in the early twentieth century, (iv) numerical control (NC) in 1952 using automatic control through symbolically coded instructions, (v) computerised numerical control (CNC) in the early seventies with a microprocessor replacing the machine-control unit, (vi) industrial robots in 1960's and 70's and (vii) computer-aided design (CAD) and computer-aided manufacturing (CAM) techniques, often interfaced with a central computer in a flexible manufacturing system (FMS), in the 80's and 90's.

In the Indian situation, flexible automation in manufacturing can have justification only in the following circumstances:

a. *Safety,* to make the work safe and ensure the physical well-being of the human operator, say, in a poisonous mine, atomic reactor, hot-plate mill, etc;
b. *High degree of skill and accuracy,* to produce parts with the greatest consistency and stringent quality specifications, say, in a sophisticated machine-tool or watch factory;
c. *Increased Productivity,* for mass production system of high volume and a few part-varieties, with a very high adaptability for change over from one part-variety to another;
d. *Highly reduced manufacturing lead-time,* with fast turn-over and handling of parts, with respect to the processing times.

A careful consideration of the efficient utilisation of resources and reduced wastage and reduction of in-process inventory has often gone into considerations of automation in countries like Japan, but they are of limited relevance to India.

Conclusion

It has been said that we are witnessing a fundamental shift in business history today. Initially *entrepreneurial capitalism* held sway, which yielded to *managerial capitalism.* This is now giving way to what can be called *intellectual capitalism*, in a reversal of the Industrial Revolution. "Instead of dumbing down production, business is evolving a high-technology version of pre-industrial craftsmanship. This time the artisans are using their heads, not their hands". In this exciting process of computers ushering in the new intellectual capitalism, let human operators and workers do a new robe, never done in human history before.

37

USER EDUCATION FOR COMPUTERS – DISTRICT LEVEL

Introduction

It should be amply evident from the country's plan for computerisation that the civil services have to play a lead role here. If the non-technical services are taken alongside the civil service, their number can become very high. In the UP alone, it is estimated that some 14,000 members of the civil services, and non-technical services should be initiated into the mystique of computerisation, — to make the information revolution a success in public administration.

There can be hardly any doubt that no single training centre can perform this gigantic task. As things stand, not all of the 25 States have their own civil service training institutes, such as, the Administrative Training Institute, Nainital; Institute of Management in Government (IMG), Trivandrum; the Rajasthan Institute of Management in Public Administration; (RIMPA), Jaipur; and so on. Out of them, ATI and IMG are among the fortunate few to whom the Ministry of Personnel and Training has allocated large funds for computerisation so that they can undertake, in turn, massive training for public servants in information technology. Even them, only the surface can be scratched.

It is, therefore, suggested that district manpower training for computerisation should be planned in a systematic fashion in the following manner:

(a) Institutionali·ed training;
(b) Training through distance learning; and
(c) Training through self-learning.

An outline of such a scheme is indicated in the succeeding paragraphs.

Institutionalised Training

A specially designed institutionalised training programme can be used for heads and senior advisors, and officers of the district administration. At present, few of the programmes for the use of computers concentrate on the application areas which are of interest to district administration. Under the guidance of Mr. Rajiv Gandhi who had shown a desire to interact directly with district administration, the trend towards fully organised and comprehensive information systems had become unavoidable. Since the government has continued to take interest in developing administrative information systems with intensive computerisation, some of which are being implemented currently, it would be necessary to pave the way for smooth implementation through the use of specific training programmes.

The salient points of such a programme, termed computer-aided management for district administration (CAM-DA), can be as follows at all the State civil service training institutes:

(a) The participants should, on completion of the programmes, be able to effectively organise for the use of computers for the development and monitoring of the various district applications such as IRDP, NREP, NLREGP and also for various routine applications;

(b) Participants can be heads of district administration or senior officers (DCs, DMs, etc.) who are in a position to implement various computer applications. The programme can be of six-day duration and can comprise the following modules:

(i) *Decision Support System for Public Administration*

Presented herein can be software and methodology developed by administrative Training Institute at Nainital and others. The software and methodology can be made comprehensive and field-tested with the senior of IAS officers for integration into the programme.

(ii) *IRDP Module*

An effective monitoring and control approach can be developed using computerised project management for projects under IRDP. Some efforts in this direction have already been made by the Department of Rural Development, Government of India.

(iii) *Practical Sessions*

The effective use of the personal computer (PC) software and skills can be imparted through hands-on sessions. One PC per participant is visualised to provide training on a one-to-one basis and approximately 50 per cent of the course duration can be devoted to this aspect.

(iv) *Problems and Prospects of Computerisation in Public Administration*

An approach to identification and solving of problems in the area of public administration specifically linked with computerisation can be made with a social balance sheet on assets and liabilities. This module can be designed through interaction in depth with the State governments of Andhra Pradesh, Kerala, Uttar Pradesh, Punjab, etc. A similar module has already been successfully used in the programme for the senior IAS officers, including some Chief Secretaries of States at CMC and NIC.

(c) The number of participants can be restricted to 18 per batch. However, the ideal group would be between 13 to 15 officers;

(d) The same programme can be extended, in successive batches, to senior-level district administration officers below the rank of district collector.

Training through Distance Learning

Some management training organisations and National Informatics Centre (NIC) had earlier formulated ideas of a project for a post-graduate programme in management and informatics to meet the requirements of users of informatics through distance learning. Such a project can have a major thrust on informatics modules with a modicum of management knowledge considered useful for managers of informatics. The blended programme can be divided into three parts, with each part completed in a one-year period. The main emphasis of the programme can be kept at taking the knowledge of informatics to locations of user-managers who will enrol as students to this programme. The advantage of this approach of learning by distance education is that knowledge can be transported to the job locations of such self-motivated persons who somehow missed out on the formal courses of instructions at the universities but wish to make up for this deficiency by self-learning. Such a project can visualise that while the main academic work and the two-way communications with the student can be carried out by the organisers, the participating centres will provide local coordination like conduct of examination, providing computers facilities without straining their resources very much. Of course, the participating centres will have to provide the dynamic leadership in their respective states in overseeing the success of the entire programme. The unique benefit of this project can be to create a nucleus of competent and trained users of informatics with supportive knowledge of management, who will become assets in their respective locations in both consolidating and spreading the revolution of information technology surging through these locations.

The salient features of such a project can be visualised as follows:

(a) Practising public administrators with 25 years of age, with a graduate degree, with 2-3 years administrative executive experience plus current on potential users of information technology (preferably with some exposure to computers) should undertake such a programme;

(b) The project can be initially for a period of three years;

(c) Candidates meeting eligibility criteria should be screened and sponsored by the state governments. The candidates sponsored for the programme should complete the prescribed application form for registration in the programme; and

(d) The programme can consist of three parts, each part to be completed in one year. The depth and level of coverage can be moderate, providing adequate appreciation with sufficient practical orientation. Subjects covered can be as under :

PART I (Year I)

- Introduction to informatics;
- Programming concepts and data structure;

- Mathematics and statistics for informatics;
- Introduction to personal computers;
- Processes of management;
- Managerial economics; and
- Organisational structure and process.

PART II (Year 2)

- Operations research;
- Introduction to system analysis and design;
- Management information system and decision support system;
- Data communication and computer network;
- Data base management;
- Research methodology; and
- Human resource management.

PART III (Year 3)

- Corporate strategy for informatics;
- Systems software;
- Application software;
- Software engineering;
- Basics of CAD, CAM and CBL;
- Project work;
- Electives (Any one) : Artificial Intelligence and Expert Systems; Office Automation; and
- Special Application Areas : Agriculture, Transportation, Finance, District Administration, etc.

(e) The programme can be conducted through a distance learning package comprising both mailing system and two-way communication between the organisers and the enlisted students. This can cover the following:

- Text books;

- Programmed lesson-notes and activities;
- Periodic assignments to students and their evaluation with feedback;
- Postal tuition, including response to individual queries;
- Some students bulletin to students for academic guidance and providing quiz and objective tests;
- Some classroom teaching programme at a central location in the participating countries for short duration of one to three weeks spread over judiciously in the year; and
- Examinations and evaluation.

(f) Every six months examinations can be conducted at appropriate centres with the cooperation and collaboration of States. The answer sheets can be evaluated and the results informed to the students as well as to the State and district coordinators.

Training through Self-Learning

It is quite possible today to visualise taking computers to the doorsteps of the members of civil services and non-technical services, — by providing Personal Computers (PCs) on an appropriately distributed basis. The idea can be to have self-learning arrangement that can be called "PCs for Public administrators".

Depending on the levels of public administrators and the nature of usage, separate software package can be developed centrally and distributed at different locations covering the following aspects:

(i) *Spread-sheet*: to cover tabular calculations and their manipulations;
(ii) *Word-Processing* : to cover secretarial handling of texts, their storage and retrieval; and
(iii) *Data-base management* : to cover the raising of queries and retrieval of responses.

Such software packages can be kept extremely friendly to the users and can be made available on an inter-active basis between the user and the computer. The user administrator only need to be familiar with the basic commands which should be practised at his leisure. Such practice should be followed by exercises based on real-life situations in districts. The advantage is that the exercise can be furnished with solution-sets stored in the computer, for cross-checking purposes by the public administrator. Exercises can also be structured at the beginners level, advanced level and specialised level.

Such software packages can be accompanied by self-learning manuals, to provide a step-by-step approach. Such a work-book should be entirely user-oriented starting with basic commands, followed by handling of sub-routine (like sort, merge, etc.), file creation and live exercises. Administrative Training Institute at Nainital had been attempting to develop such packages accompanied by work-books. Their estimation was that the self-learning training could require approximately one week for the basic commands as follows:

(i) One day for spread-sheet commands;
(ii) Half-day for word-processing commands;
(iii) Two days for data-base management; and
(iv) One-and-a-half day for introduction to micro-computing and disk-based operating system (DOS) commands.

It is important to emphasise that work at home or in a homelike atmosphere with a PC would enable the public administrator to gain familiarity, practice and confidence. Conscious efforts will be needed to go from the beginner's level to advanced level, following the step-by-step approach.

Conclusion

To summarise, institutionalised training, training through distance learning and training through self-learning are all basically complimentary processes which can be judiciously used to achieve meaningful results. Concerted thinking is necessary to decide on the hierarchies of personnel, types of usages and the end-objectives so that the best possible value for money can be achieved by combining these three forms of training in public administration.

A very important aspect of training for computerisation is the role of organisation vis-a-vis information technology. First of all, organisations do fear dislocation of manual activities by the introduction of computerisation. Care has to be taken that such dislocations are avoided and emphasis is kept for increase in efficiency and not clerical labour-saving. Secondly, the factor of organisational learning (as distinct from individual learning) should not be minimised.

The organisation as a whole should learn to make best use of the information technology which should not be left merely to the few trained administrators. Otherwise, with the transfer of the trained administrators elsewhere, the entire benefit of computerisation would rapidly get lost.

Thirdly, a lot of emphasis is today shifting from the computer (or EDP) departments with large computers to administrators operating as end-users with individual terminals or PCs. In consequence, the earlier dependence on computer professionals for delivering the goods is getting replaced quite fast by "executive computing" where the user-administrator has a large say. This responsibility is to be clearly understood in the organisational thinking process.

Fourthly, quite often the middle-level perception for computer usage has turned out to be fairly different from the top-level perception. The learning process should ensure that too much hope should not be aroused at the top, which cannot be sustained by the hard labour of the middle level. Finally, introduction of computers in any organisation has always proved to be far easier than the institutionalisation of computers. Sadly, initial high hopes have been quickly dashed to ground, replaced by frustration, — because initial expectations after buying a computer could not be sustained by the results achieved. There is always a long and hard learning process in getting the best mileage out of computerisation. The earlier the public administrators realise this basic point, the better is it for the organisation, in order to nurture realistic expectations from computerisation.

38

USER EDUCATION FOR COMPUTERS – STATE LEVEL

Introduction

India has made strident progress in introducing computers in a wide variety of fields. A concerted plan is now required to orchestrate all the efforts in such a manner that obvious pitfalls (like wasteful experiments, duplicate efforts, inadequate manpower, etc.) can be methodically avoided well in advance.

In a federal structure, the State administration has a large say in the country's progress. It is imperative that plans for computerisation take their aspirations into account and let growth come in a planned way by avoiding two hazards of centralised planning : cooperation is not withheld from the States and rejection of a top-down approach does not take place.

The most significant plan for computerisation from the National Informatics Centre (NIC), which earlier acquired a large Cyber computer 1700/730 obtained with UNDP support. The NIC has enviable experience in working for nearly 100 Central Government ministries, departments, organisations and establishments where intelligent terminals are locally available from the main computer at Delhi. Based on this experience, a network structure has evolved already. The computer network, called NICNET, has four NEC S-1000 computers at Delhi, Bhubaneshwar, Pune and Hyderabad regional level. There are mini and super-micro computers in the 25 State and seven Union Territory capitals at the next level connected with the four large computers in the capital and elsewhere forming NICNET through INSAT 1-C satellite. At the third hierarchical level, NICNET reach out to all the 461 districts in India. It is an ambitious and exciting programme where the Centre-State linkage of NICNET has been ear-marked to cover sectors, such as, agriculture, health, education, etc., which are important national subject and for which sharing of information will be to everyone's advantage. NIC has already been assisting the States of Kerala, Madhya Pradesh, Gujarat, Karnataka, Tamil Nadu, Uttar Pradesh and Andhra Pradesh, in developing their governmental information systems, with all other states following up.

The policy-frame recognises the need for introducing computers at all levels of administration upto the district headquarters. The need for local capability for maintenance of computer systems and developing application software has been emphasised. Apart from carrying out studies on possible areas and potential users in government departments, some State Governments have started using computer facilities available outside government for specific purposes.

Computer Manpower for States

It is quite clear that availability of computer manpower is going to pose a problem in State computerization schemes. The current scene of computer manpower available is as follows:

(a) IITs	:	B Techs and M Techs in computer science;
(b) Regional Engineering Colleges	:	BEs in computer science; and
(c) Select Indian Universities	:	Master of Compute Application (MCA) and Diploma in Computer Applications (DCA) comprising three-year and one-year/eighteen month courses respectively at post-graduate level.

In the Seventh Plan, around Rs 3000 crores was visualised as the level of investment in computer hardware in the country over the Plan period. Computer manpower of around 100,000 would be required to service and utilise the computer systems. The requirement can be divided into the following categories:

(a) Computer science professionals	:	15 per cent – comprising computer hardware engineers and system software engineers to provide technical support;

(b) Systems analysts and programmers (including small systems managers) : 70 per cent – comprising the manpower providing : application development and maintenance support for all computer usages; and

(c) Computer maintenance : 15 per cent – providing hardware maintenance support.

It will be evident that unless schemes for local employment opportunities are created for the employable young people living in each district, it will not be possible to operate comprehensive computerisation schemes. This is because young people who are over-qualified at graduate and post-graduate levels are expected to have high aspirations and are unlikely to stay at district towns. The chances of providing them employment opportunity at State capitals are also limited and a severe turnover problem is bound to arise.

As regards computer maintenance, it is important to realise that graduate maintenance engineers are not required to maintain highly compact and rugged systems of today. Polytechnic-level technicians are enough to carry out such maintenance.

Data preparation is an important part of any computerisation scheme and there is a dearth of such personnel on a geographically widely distributed basis. Training of such personnel is not available on a sufficiently decentralised level where they can do justice to data entry systems made locally available. In order to provide inputs to the above levels, there has to be a general awareness among senior school students about computerisation. In spite of the computer-aided literacy and studies in schools (CLASS) Project, which is being carried on a limited scale, such widespread school-level computer literacy is almost totally absent in the States.

State Plan

Each State should appoint a Committee to estimate realistically the manpower needs at the programmer, systems analysts and computer centre manager levels, over the Five-Year plan period. Vocational institutes should then be planned in adequate numbers to provide this manpower.

Computer science professionals : The existing schemes of the

Department of Education, Government of India, and the University Grant Commission are adequate to cater for technical support needed on a selective basis.

Systems analysts and programmers : Vocational education should be seriously contemplated to meet the needs for these personnel. Those students, who have completed their Senior School Certificate Examination at (10+2) level and have come through science streams with high marks in mathematics, are ideal material for this purpose. Vocational training institutes should be set up to have the following education programmes after the (10+2) level:

(1) 1-Year Certificate Course : for computer programming;
(2) 2-Year Diploma Courses : for systems analysts;
(3) 3-Year Diploma Courses : for Information Centre Management.

The above courses should be at the under-graduate level and can be made "modular" so that each course can lead to the next higher course on a three-tier basis. Entry can also be permitted in these courses to graduate students. The candidates should come through an aptitude test specifically designed for the course.

Computer maintenance technicians : The State polytechnics should be geared up to graft computer maintenance courses in their existing teaching schedules. The number of years for such courses should be determined as continuation of the general-basis course provided at the polytechnics.

Data-entry operations : The vocational institutes can be utilised to run data-entry courses during week-ends. Data-entry operators should be the class 10 level and the training should be for 3-4 weeks.

Senior school students : School students upto class 10 should have exposure to computer literacy for a far greater number than is being attempted through the CLASS Project, which in any case has met with limited success. Vocational institutes are the ideal place to bring school children from the neighbourhood and give them the required exposure over week-ends and during vacation periods. No separate computer equipment is visualised at schools, which is a very difficult matter in terms of both computer resources and availability of computer-trained teachers. Vocational institutes should serve as the focal point for providing computer literacy to schools in the neighbourhood.

User Officers and Staff : There should be a computer appreciation and sensitation programme for State officials on a mandatory basis. This can be done at two levels : 2-3 days at the senior most level for computer appreciation and 12-15 days at the middle level for computer applications. At lower levels, there should be 10-15 days' exposure to the preparation of input data and quality control of the output reports. The psychological involvement of bureaucrats in the computerisation plan is an extremely important factor and should not be lost sight of.

Educational Curriculum

The educational curriculum can be planned as follows :

(i) *Certificate Course :* Computer programming should have elements of actual exposure to computer hardware (especially microcomputers and their terminals) and common programming language like BASIC, COBOL and 'C';

(ii) *Diploma Programme for Systems Analysts :* It should start from (i) and introduce elements of data processing, file management and several hands-on examples of actual software design, development and implementation. Management subjects can be offered as electives so that partial specialisation can be achieved; and

(iii) *Diploma Programme for Computer Centre Management :* It should again start from (ii) and add elements of computer centre planning, evaluation of performance, manning and job setting, cost management and relationship with users.

As regards educational curriculum for computer maintenance at the polytechnics, this should be decided by competent experts having knowledge of both polytechnic curriculum and computer maintenance subjects. Practical demonstration and hands-on experience should be built into the curriculum.

Data-entry requirements are fairly standardised. Vendors and manufacturers of data-entry systems can offer considerable help in this training and instructors can be initially trained by them, who can then take on data entry training on a distributed basis.

Teachers' training is a serious matter owing to the prevailing lack of qualified teachers. If vocational institutes have to be adequately manned, the only way to do it would be to draw science teachers from senior schools and junior colleges, and organise 3-month to 6-month crash programmes for them in computer programming and systems analysis. The curriculum for such crash programmes should be carefully designed by subject area specialists.

As regards computer centre management, the help of actual managers should be drawn to impart realistic support in training teachers.

It will be a good idea if courses offered by various organisations in the country can be studied so that some standard modules for curricula can be developed for all the above education programmes. It is also important that the various private organisations, which are running low-quality courses as "teaching shops" with scant regard to curriculum content, teaching qualification and actual exposure to computers, should be brought under serious review and some State certification should be adopted by a committee of subject area specialists. The Tamil Nadu experience is worth noting in this context, enhanced by the accreditation scheme for private sector training institutions, recently launched by the Department of Electronics under the aegis of All India Council of Technical Education.

Detailed Action-plan

The financial resources for organising such comprehensive schemes are going to be a major constraint. It can only be suggested that there can be a committee, preferably under the State Electronics Development Corporation, which can look into the scope for mobilising financial resources from various private and public sector organisations in the State who can provide assistance, in view of the fact that they would be gaining from the computer manpower coming out of the above scheme. The Committee can also look into the feasibility of obtaining computer hardware at reasonable price from the manufacturer and vendors for this purpose.

The State government needs approval of the entire plan as well as its financial commitment (after taking into account the financial contribution to be generated from user enterprises) at the highest level. Once the scheme is properly worked out as above and approved, the action plan can be implementation as follows :

– The Committees on manpower needs, curriculum design and financial resource mobilisation should be set up to operate simultaneously and to furnish their recommendations within one month;

– Thereafter, the crash programme on teachers' training should be initiated over six months at centres where computer resources are available. Simultaneously, the administrative action to set up vocational institutes should begin to identify sites, locate buildings, procure computer hardware, arrange furnitures and fixtures, and position the supporting staff. The idea is that by the time the trained teachers are available to the vocational institutes, their administrative infrastructure should be ready. For polytechnics, the existing teachers should also undergo a crash programme while the administrative support like computer equipment, etc., is put into position.

Conclusion

To summarise, there is an imperative need that the States get ready on a self-help basis to draw appropriate plans for computerisation. The above is an attempt to provide a conceptual framework which is both practical and relevant to such a plan. Central help can be drawn to the extent needed but a certain amount of self-reliance is essential to make such a widespread effort a success at the grass-root level of districts.

No specific suggestions have been made on the nature of actual applications. This is an area where the knowledge of the administrators as "users" should be utilised to the maximum extent. It is upto them to create a demand-side situation, whereas the above scheme is from the view point of the supply-side situation in terms of computer education and manpower. It is only to be hoped that we are alive to the situation and take action urgently to fulfil the needs of the new area.

39

COMPUTER EXPORT STRATEGY

It has been announced by the Department of Electronics that they would:

(a) hold regular dialogues with the professional associations like, Computer Society of India (CSI), Manufacturers' Association of Information Technology (MAIT) and National Association of Software and Service Companies (NASSCOM) and discuss the problems of the nascent computer industry of India;
(b) cease to view the private sector with a jaundiced eye and provide them with sub-contracts and R&D grants, apart form recognising private sector specialists and training institutions;
(c) encourage R&D by investing at least 2 per cent to 3 per cent in R&D in a shortened timeframe to remain at the forefront of technology. Major Government investment would be in computer-aided design (CAD), computer-aided manufacturing (CAM), knowledge-based computer systems (KBCS), telematics, industrial automation, Education and Research Network (ERNET), National Centre for Software Technology (NCST), Centre for Development of Advanced Computing (C-DAC), etc.;
(d) make export the key-issue with 10 per cent export target on hardware, earning 50 per cent foreign exchange for raw material and ensuring foreign exchange inflow in 5 years. Physical and monetary incentives would also be provided, with an emphasis on quality and on indigenous strong base.

Hardware Export Incentives

The hardware technology today is faster, cheaper and smaller than ever before, with an emerging dominance of reduced-instruction-set computing (RISC) technology, with high-powered work stations and massive parallel processing becoming a certainty with increased throughout, technologies like image processing, speech input-output and natural language interfaces are getting integrated. Knowledge-based computing are accompanied by parallel machines for symbolic procedures. Storage technologies have seen the advent of erasable optical discs and magneto-optic discs. While optical computing may increase speed manifold soon, networking has already made possible use of local-area networks (LANs) for office automation and wide-area networks (WANs) for cooperative computing. The collapsing time-frames of hardware technology in India are indicated in Table 39.1.

TABLE 39.1: Collapsing Time Frames

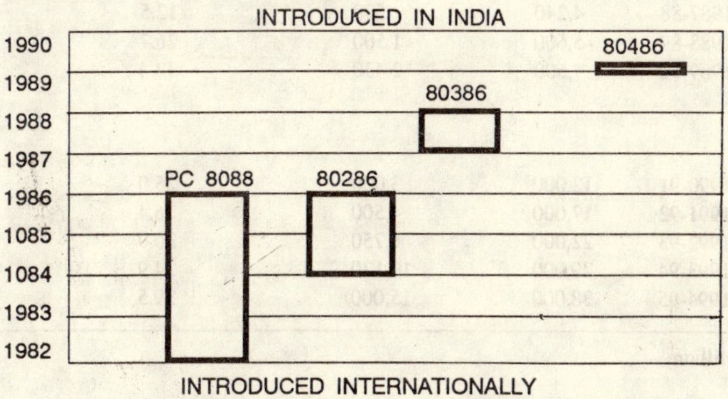

The proposed export incentives on hardware, as worked out by the Department of Electronics, include the following:

* Pass Book Scheme for established manufacturers;
* Blanket duty free advance licence up to:

  – 15 per cent of previous year production for new exporter,
  – 50 per cent of last year export for established,
  – 50 per cent of immediate preceeding FOB value of export;

* Replenishment on 50 per cent utilisation;
* 15 per cent net foreign exchange (FE) inflow;
* The net FE inflow to be monitored over a period of six months;
* Export obligation to be discharged with six months from date of corresponding import; and

* Under the advance licence, all items to be allowed for import, except the item of export.

In the above context, the computer hardware production and export – both actual and target – for half a decade each in India are reflected in Table 39.2.

TABLE 39.2: Computer Hardware Production and Exports

	Production*	Exports*	% of Exports
Actual			
1985-86	1,800	350	19.4
1986-87	3,200	390	12.2
1987-88	4,240	530	12.5
1988-89	5,600	1,500	26.7
1989-90	7,500	2,430	32.4
Target			
1990-91	12,000	3,000	25.0
1991-92	17,000	4,500	26.4
1992-93	22,000	6,750	30.0
1993-94	29,000	10,120	34.9
1994-95	38,000	15,000	39.5

* Rs. Million

Software Export

Software export possibilities have undergone a sea-change over the last few years. Technology parks for software export have started functioning in quite a few cities such as, Pune, Bangalore and Bhubaneswar, with foreign satellite links in some cities. No import licence is required ordinarily for import into the technology parks and the export commitments are based on such factors as cost of imported equipment, usage of satellite links, the type of software developed and cost of manpower.

Software export schemes include the following:

(a) The export obligation of 35 per cent of FE used, with the custom duty on import of equipment being 35 per cent;
(b) Use of imported computer system also for domestic activities;
(c) 30 per cent of excess software earning made over and above the

export obligation can be made use of by software exporter for import of new computer system etc.

Computer software export, actual from 1985 to 1990 and target from 1990 to 1995, is shown in Table 39.3.

TABLE 39.3: Computer Software Exports

	Exports*	Growth%
Actual		
1985-86	380	42.1
1986-87	540	48.1
1987-88	800	43.8
1988-89	1150	43.8
1989-90	1750	52.2
Target		
1990-91	3000	71.4
1991-92	5000	66.6
1992-93	8000	62.0
1993-94	13000	62.5
1994-95	20000	53.8

* Rs. Million

Current Software Trends

If software can be divided into two streams – system software and application software – changes can be said to have taken place in both of them.

System software is moving away from proprietory systems to open systems, with inter-operatibility and portability among different machines. The openness is with reference to operating system, networking, graphic interfaces and uses interfaces, expecting to occupy half the market share 1994. While cooperative computing is becoming common, Unix is recognised as the operating system for multi-user workstations, favouring open systems. Unix market share of the world is likely to go up to 35 per cent by 1994, although disc-based operating system (DOS) is likely to survive for micros serving as single-user workstations.

Application software today favours total solutions, including hardware and customised software. While application-specific software has increased, there is a high corporate priority on management information system (MIS) and decision support system (DSS). Many expert systems, based on artificial intelligence, are coming into being and on-line transaction processing (OLTP) is on the threshold of expansion. One major trend in computer-bound applications is towards parallelism and yet another trend is a shift of focus from machine-oriented computing to user-oriented computing.

World Software Opportunities

Apropos of the above trends, multi-billion dollar software opportunities in the developed world have been on the cards for long. These opportunities can be broadly divided into three areas as follows:

(i) *Technology*

This is the cutting edge of software comprising application-specific integrated circuits (ASIC), industry extended system architecture (IESA) and the rest. While there is a high potential of profit up to 250 per cent, there is also a grave risk of rejection.

(ii) *Labour*

This is "Body Shopping" involving labour work for conversion software. Profit potential can be about 40 per cent.

(iii) *Turnkey Project*

This is the major area of software export potential that exists today and can have three components, namely:

(a) Existing technology (involving 40% or so frequency): where existing technology has to be brought in, analysed and assessed for a modification, with a low profit potential of 50 per cent;
(b) Need for modification (involving 45% or so frequency): needing technical expertise and labour work with a very high profit potential of 200 per cent; and
(c) Implementation (involving 15% or so frequency): comprising

mainly labour work with about 40 per cent profit potential. It is thus obvious that the modification component of the turnkey project has the highest profit potential where world opportunities are knocking on the doors of Indian professionals.

World's Interest in India

A large number of Indians who have gone abroad for education have proven themselves as an excellent material in the world market. Many of them, often exposed to new technology, have brought new awareness in the country. This, coupled with the low cost of manpower in India, has turned the world's attention to India. It has also become increasingly evident that Indian technocrats can turn in a high cost-performance ratio if they have a basic structure. Left on their own, Indian technocrats are sometimes caught napping in showing chinks in their professional armour.

In the above framework, the world's interest in India is channelised through SDA and such other agencies by the foreign companies too provide them R&D support. In some cases, foreign companies have given sub-contracts to the Indian counterparts. In a few cases, Indian counterparts have put forth a consortium with the foreign companies involving sharing of the knowledge and data bank. Some large foreign companies have also used Indians as resource groups, for bidding together as resource groups, for bidding as resource centres in the world market.

Indian Growth

The following portents shall be taken into account:

(a) The software industry in India today has reached a take-off stage. Starting from Rs. 52 crores two years back, it has already touched over Rs. 150 crores at the turn of the decade, thus registering a three-fold growth rate. Contributions have come from Indian software-enterprises who have completed world-class projects in as many as 43 countries. During the next half decade, the software services are poised to grow twelve-fold;

(b) The national government has come forward to recognise the potential of software industries as a major force of the country for earning foreign exchange. Several concessions are available wedded to the new liberal policy so that the software development and export can turn out to be a highly profitable source of foreign exchange for the country;

(c) Young professionals are ready to quit well-paid jobs to branch out on their own, given the satisfaction and the opportunity to make it big. There is a spirit of entrepreneurship and they are confident of their abilities. This reflects a new phase in the growing up process of the country and is increasingly important in this region and the world; and

(d) The Indian middle class has matured along with the Indian State. In recent years, the Indian economy has performed well. The average growth in the last five years has been around 8 per cent and the country now exports not only traditional goods like tea and spices, but also the computer software. Major multi-nationals like Hewlett Packard, Texas Instruments and Unisys have set up software development concerns in India for exports.

Indian Bottlenecks

The following bottlenecks are often perceived:

(a) Government policies have often much to be desired. For instance, quite often 350 per cent export is laid down to be achieved in three years for imported machines. This often proves unrealistic as full knowledge of the machine is not available, to start with and such an ambitious target may not be fulfilled within a limited time-periods;

(b) Software technology parks are excellent investments by the government. But often only a shed is provided as a facility, with power and telecommunication system to be installed by the entrepreneurs;

(c) Technocrats have often proved unable to keep their promises on quality or dates of delivery. As a result, compromises are made to foreign customers which may not be acceptable to the world market. Hence, the "body shopping" seems to be the easier alternative;

(d) There is no protection available for software generated by Indian firms as patents and copyrights take 3 to 4 years to obtain. A stolen software package can be sold very cheap, although its original price can be quite high due to the development efforts involved; and

(e) Entry of a foreign company into the Indian market quite often upsets the Indian manpower employment situation. In the absence of an ethical code observed by everybody, such foreign companies may simply lift manpower from the Indian companies, leaving the latter in chaos.

Export Objectives

It is vital to evolve a software promotion strategy for export by the government in consultation with the software industries keeping in mind the following needs:

(a) Need of identification of niche areas in the world software market;
(b) Need for focussing energy on the niche areas; and
(c) Need to obtain marketing intelligence much before the software development efforts, followed up by market support to the product, much after the sale-deed has been struck and the delivery made. Such efforts help in obtaining marketing knowledge far in advance and customer's confidence even after the software sale is over.

The objectives of this framework should be to set up "software communes" keeping the above needs in view.

A. *Software Communes*

The "communes" should be set up with reference to products, keeping in consideration the niche areas. The communes should comprise firms and the groups with shared interest and values. There should be also adherence to constructive and ethical practices regarding manpower and documentation. The actual location of communes can be in single site or spread over a contiguous area and closely monitored on a regional and central basis. Further structuring of communes can be worked out by the government in consultation with the software industries.

B. *Market Demand*

The identification of the niche areas should come from a systematic survey of the developed as well as developing world by Trade Development Authority (TDA), Export Promotion Council and related agencies. Systematic help should be provided to the software communes through these agencies by the Commercial Advisors of the Indian High Commissions and Commercial Attaches of the Indian Embassies. The latter should also provide the channels of intelligence from the foreign software market.

C. *Leadership and Patronage*

Some of the top exporters in the software area and the top software developers should provide the necessary leadership. This should include TCS, WIPRO and others, under the guidelines and patronage of Department of Electronics. Cost-sharing criteria should be worked out on a pragmatic basis. The overall mandate under which the software communes will come into being as well as their operational terms and conditions should be helped to be evolved by the Department of Electronics in consultation with the software industry.

D. *Communication Channels*

There may be need to appoint brokers and agencies abroad, for obtaining intelligence. In terms of availability of telephones, fax and telex channels, these should be fully ensured to the software communes by the Videsh Sanchar Nigam. There should be also well-understood protocols for data communications and programme transmission. For the purpose of obtaining specifications from the customers, standard procedures should be followed. "Tele-conferencing" facility, if necessary, should be installed as is being done between Carnegie-Melon University in the USA and Keonics in Bangalore.

E. *Maintenance Support*

The software communes should have well-organised procedures for maintenance and for sales support for specific categories and levels of software work done for the foreign customers. These procedures should be well-publicised and can be channelised through Indian agencies abroad. The number and scope of Indian agencies for this purpose should be decided by the Department of Electronics in consultation with the Indian software industry.

F. *Computer as a National Resource*

The Department of Electronics may like to identify some large computers as 'national resource' for the limited purpose of use by the software communes. For this purpose, there may be a system of time available and use made particularly for government computers, such as, NICNET computers by the software communes devoted to promotion of export.

G. *Finance*

It was mentioned earlier that world opportunities comprise technology, turnkey projects and labour. The first two areas, out of the three above, need intellectual design and development unlike labour, which needs only 'body shopping'. Therefore, there is a need for venture capital for such intellectual design and development efforts. Basic valuation of the software is necessary, as quite often this cannot be valued based on the raw materials. For this purpose, the Department of Electronics may provide guidelines to the banks for valuation and commercial support. No collateral asset can be created in the software communes and, therefore, zero condition will have to be accepted in providing commercial back-up.

H. *Basic Education*

Proper guidelines are necessary to be laid down by the Department of Electronics to start software houses which can be affiliated to software communes. For this purpose, minimum qualifications have to be laid down for the software professionals, preferably with some exposure to finance. They should also be aware of the world standards of software, which can be widely circulated to all software communes and other agencies for general information.

Benefits of Software Export Promotion

It is envisaged that if such a software promotion strategy for export is evolved by the Department of Electronics in consultation with the Indian software industry, this will have many long-term benefits for the country, such as:

(a) capturing niche areas in the world market;
(b) doing full justice to the technology jobs and turnkey jobs besides 'body shopping';
(c) meeting time – targets and deadlines;
(d) ensuring quality during delivery and, later on, for after-sales support; and
(e) retaining satisfied customers in the world market with the Indian software industry.

All the above will ensure large foreign exchange earnings, for this very important industry emerging in today's world.

Conclusion

India, at this juncture, should look forward to an export thrust and an R&D base for mere existence and survival in the world computer industry. While manpower development has been extended to private sector, international competitiveness calls for quality, price and contemporariness. Foreign exchange balancing needs inflow through exporting. Open systems have literally opened up inter-operability, vendor independence, cooperative computing and emerging standards. Unix standardisation can lead to application portability and corporate LANs can, in turn, be hooked up to satellite-based application networks. Parallel processing technology in computing-bound applications definitely makes for speedy processing and use of Indian language interface is already a reality. Application-specific expert systems are unmistakably emerging in the government, medicine, industry inspection, education and service sectors, among others. All in all, it is a bright scenario and India must make the best of the given world order in the export field for computer hardware and software.

40

CONCLUSION AND OVERVIEW

Introduction

The spate of personal computers in the Indian scene has brought in a new revolution in the handling of information. In fact, the friendliness of the application packages, the indirect assistance available from the help-text and pull-down (and pop-up) menus, and the sheer flexibility of using the screen to deal with a myriad applications have unleashed an era of *executive computing* or simply *end-user computing.*

Much of what has been stated earlier in this book applies to the users of any computers: micro, mini or mainframe. But the sheer abundance of personal computers warrant some special attention to that genre, starting with selection of hardware, evaluation of software and the specific need of copy-protection security in today's piracy-ridden environment.

Selection of PCs

It is useful to reiterate and partly add to what was stated in Chapters 3 and 4 in the context of PCs using the following eight criteria:

(a) *Performance*

Even if a user starts from a short-listed serial of vendors (having regard to the latter's prices and availability), performance needs to be understood for any hardware device in relation to their competitors. While such performance evaluation is a difficult task, fortunately some comparative statements on *plus* and *minus* points appear in some useful way in a few journals like *Dataquest.* They are worth referring to.

(b) *User Experience*

A list of recent users is worth obtaining from the vendors in respect of their systems, who can then be informally approached to provide some feed-back on the systems. Surprisingly often, insightful remarks can throw light on the functioning of the devices.

(c) *Upgradability*

The PC-users are entitled to know if their main memory on hard discs can be enhanced keeping in view the increase in the computer load. If Xenix operating system is used in a PC/AT or super-AT (32-bit device), there is a chance of adding terminals: 4 to 16 in these two versions respectively. But the commensural response-time degradation is worth checking, in addition to the main-memory enhancement.

(d) *After-sales Service*

This is one single criterion where the computer vendors usually fail. What with the costliness of providing support-services all round and the relative unfamiliarity with the imported chips and operating systems, the levels of support often leave much to be desired. The points to ponder are: the spares back-up for the core-spares and non-core spares to be held by the vendor on behalf of the buyer; the possibility of vendor-help in the event of *bugs* in the system software with some computer-science training; and the possibility of vendor help if problem arises in the application software packages purchased.

(e) *Documentation*

The relevant manuals regarding the system or the operations on the application packages need all be available. These are costly documents and should be assured of supply by the vendor.

(f) *Training*

The vendor-given training to a broad base of the buyer's workforce is a must. Such training should cover usage of vendor's hardware, operating system and application packages. The more the people trained from the user organisation, the better is the assurance that turn-over in the trained manpower will not hit the user hard. Some negotiation to get the maximum number of people exposed to the vendor's training is quite in order.

(g) *Maintenance*

After the warranty period is over, there should be a decision, taken in advance regarding further maintenance. CMC maintenance, vendor maintenance, third-party maintenance or in-company maintenance are all possibilities in existence, whose merits should be weighed on pros and cons. An annual maintenance contract (AMC) is usually 10 per cent of the capital cost for prime-shift maintenance, but competitive terms can be negotiated.

(h) *Assured Power-up Time*

The buyer can ask for a high assurance of the computer's availability for his needs without any breakdown. But the more this assurance goes up from 85 or 95 per cent to 100 per cent, the more would be the price asked for by the vendor to give such a guarantee. This is because of his liability to provide free computer-time elsewhere, to the extent the actual power-up time falls short of the guarantee.

Availability of Software

Many application packages are available today for the PCs in the market, particularly for the PCs which are IBM-compatible. But most of these packages, if imported, have a large price-tag from the licensed vendors. Hence the universal tendency among the Indian users to get hold of pirated versions of these packages freely or at a nominal cost. There is everything to be said against such a piracy. For one thing, there is a software piracy prevention act of 1986 according to which such piracy is a punishable crime. For another, pirated software is most likely to be infected with a "virus" (a spurious programme which vitiates the parent programme if the former gets access to the latter and the damage is cumulative with more runs of the parent program).

Since the imported software (like LOTUS 1-2-3, WORDSTAR, AUTOCAD, etc.) tend to have a comparatively high cost, one way out is to go for good quality Indian software. The public sector undertaking ET&T has shown the way by introducing what it has named *peoples' computer* and associating them with low-priced Indian software which serve the purpose equally well. Ofcourse, the Indian software needs to be carefully evaluated for this purpose beforehand.

The points normally to be looked for evaluation of software are indicated below:

A. *Basic Information*:

1. Name of packages
2. Date and agency of evaluation
3. Name & address of the Vendor
4. Subject — category.

B. *Technical Information*:

1. Minimum hardware requirement
2. Hardware lock, if any
3. Operating system
4. Menu-driven or not
5. Help text
6. Option — sensitive help
7. Language in which programme is developed
8. Main options
9. Operating the options: satisfactory or not
   (a) Any addition required
   (b) Any deletion required
   (c) Messages adequate or not
   (d) Validation check
   (e) Scope of alteration (backtrack, etc.)
   (f) Frequency of bugs
   (g) Window help
10. R&D team
11. Enhancements/updations planned to be released
12. Enhancements/releases — schedule for new versions.

C. *Marketing Information*:

1. Similar software available or not
2. If yes, then

   (a) Name of competitor's software
   (b) Price of competitor's software
   (c) Quality/performance of competitor's software

(d) Corporate image of competitor's software

3. Comparative statement, if required

		Package A	Package B
Technical Feature	1	......	......
" "	2	......	......
" "	3	......	......
		......	......
		......	......

4. Customer list
5. Customer reaction, if any
6. Nature/special points, i.e., prospective clients/client segments
7. Export potential
8. After-sales support: network of offices and trained staff.

D. *Training Information*:

1. Availability of manual
2. Availability of tutor (containing terminologies, main feature, main menus, examples)
3. Availability of demonstration package
4. Expected training time (to provide full user instruction).

Copy-protection Security

Individual pieces of application packages are often made available by the developers in a copy-protected version. This prevents any copies to be made from the legally purchased product, by generating cautionary notes or junk messages whenever copying is attempted.

Copy-protection can be provided either through *software locks* or through *hardware locks*. *Software locks* are in the form of specific passwords or commands which need to be executed for opening up the lock. These locks are not very fool-proof and computer whizz-kids take special delight in breaking them. *Hardware locks*, on the other hand, are quite durable and not easy to break, although they are costly and their installation can be a tricky process for each run.

A recent via-media is use of a key diskette which must be run before the actual package is used. These diskettes are compiled from the package itself by generating deliberately a few bad sectors through laser burning. Although the process is software driven, it is not easy to replicate such software and prices of the key diskettes are reasonably low.

Incidence of 'Virus'

Computer *virus* is a software program, written by human programmes, which can run in a computer like the operating system or application program. The *virus* (e.g., 'Jerusalem', 'Happy Birthday', 'Trojan House', etc.) gets into computer memory usually through a corrupted floppy and can often sit unnoticed for a period of time before erupting (say, thirteenth day of a month which is a Friday). The virus normally has the ability to replicate itself and inject different sectors of the memory, affecting other programs and data.

While the virus is a damaging program created by malevolent individuals without any benefit to themselves, computer *hacking* was resorted to earlier by some individuals either simply playfully or with an ultimate benefit to themselves. Playful innocence was illustrated in the chilling science-fiction film *War Game* where a few whizz-kids broke into inadvertently the secret software code for letting loose a nuclear was between the two superpowers. Selfish benefit came to light when some computer hackers gained entry to the New York Stock Exchange transactions and tried to build up a personal account from the fractions of dollars normally ignored while rounding off to the nearest integrals.

Anti-virus measures can be *preventive* kind (disallowing any new virus to appear) or *curative* (removing an existing virus) or both. These can be either software devices or hardware devices. Scanning unknown disks before loading is essential to ensure that they are without virus. Regular backup data is highly desirable to prevent sudden losses of medical records, air-traffic systems data and so on, where the damage can be far-reaching.

Piracy of Software and Data

Use of unauthorised software without payment of licence fee to the developer and vendor is known as *software piracy* quite rampant in India. In spite of stern warnings and stringent provisions of software piracy act of 1986, the pirated software is used by a very large number of computer installations. The high licence fee and the ease of obtaining copies on the floppies are both responsible for the existing state of affairs.

Purchase of licensed software is important in order not to face punitive measures from the authorities. Many vendors issue their products in copy-protected versions, although many programmers are not averse from breaking these codes. Recently the government has planned to make bulk purchase of popular operating system (like MS-DOS for PCs) and application packages (like LOTUS 1-2-3), and allow cheaper copies to be made within the country.

National and international piracy of critical or sensitive data has also been noticed. Security of trans-border data flow, when multiple companies are involved in satellite-based transmissions as well as receptions, can compromise a country's defence interest or affect vital financial deals. Encryption procedures and various locks are used to prevent these *malafides*, not always with total success.

The Finale

The computer revolution has literally taken the common man by storm. The hardware prices are coming down every day with phenomenal increase in computing power, thanks to the micro- electronics technology of producing cost-effective processors and storage devices. The design-standardisation has enormously contributed to the ease of availability, upgradability, reliability and maintainability.

The software development is not as yet an easy process, although identifying objects (physical or conceptual) and their attributes can show the way to future approach to standardisation. Many tools are developing to handle logic and create data-bases, though creation and maintenance of very large data-bases still have their problems.

On the whole, the situation has never been more exciting. Both hardware and software seem to become enticing to the common users with many supportive facilities made available like the tutorials, on-line help of every kind, use of menus and icons. Conversation with the computer in the perfectly natural language of the common man does not appear to be all that distant a dream and India is well-poised not to miss out on the fascinating sojourn of putting computer in the service of common man.

APPENDICES

APPENDIX A

CURRENT STATUS OF OPERATIONS RESEARCH

Introduction

Operations Research (OR) has been understood over the years to mean the application of the methods of science, particularly those of mathematics and statistics, to solve the problems of management and to help in decision-making. Having originated in the time of World War II, its practice has spread from the UK and USA to other countries including India, with an increasing use of computers.

In one of the recent annual conventions of the OR Society of India, there were 55 OR papers presented. Assuming the annual convention as the foremost gathering of the OR professionals of all shades, the papers could be taken to represent a fair sample of the current interest-areas. Looking into the cross-section of the papers, only 14 papers could broadly satisfy the criterion of practice papers, 3 were survey papers, and the remaining 38 could be termed academic and scientific papers whose concern was somewhat remote from the fields.

If 25 per cent papers above related to the grass-root applications of various types, it would only mean that the interest of the OR community at large in a developing country is still predominantly centred around methodology. This is not surprising, considering the excellence in formal sciences (such as mathematics and statistics) that this country is known to produce, and the encouragement given by our academic institutions to pure research. If, however, one accepts the premise that the *raison d'etre* of good OR lies in its real-life problem-solving capability, the situation is worth analysing further.

OR Methodology

Two factors are central to our observation. First, the status of OR methodology has progressed far from being purely *classical* (applying analytical and statistical methods to decision-making) and *technical* (applying highly developed techniques of optimisation, networking and simulation) to being largely *contextual* (applying knowledge of theory and practice of the context in which OR is sought to be used). In other words, OR methods have grown sufficiently diverse so as to keep up with the distribution of the functions of data gathering, information processing and control of a modern complex organisation. Secondly, the computational power of today's computers has grown even faster so as to provide a tremendous boost to the OR calculations in any mode: centralised or decentralised; at any level of hierarchy; and with any combination or networking of the two.

Technical literature for OR abounds in recording methodological development. The evolution of macro-models has been particularly evident in the work carried out in the scientific and academic institutions. A striking feature is what Ackoff described as "systemic" modelling, where there is a systematic amalgamation of divergent models, such as, goal programming with statistical forecasting, or, input-output analysis with linear and mixed-integer programming. While such an approach has widened the horizon of the capability of OR models, it has also helped the genre of micro-models for probing problems in depth. In particular, a lot of attention has been paid to diversity coverage, sensitivity tests, parametric ranging, variational analysis and consistency checks.

Macro and Micro Models

The main disadvantage perceived in the evolution of both macro-and micro-models within their academic constraints has been that basically any such model reflects a *snapshot* of reality at a given instance. It lacks the flexibility of an *open loop* system, under which the model-builder can handle a continuously changing environment and can still remain in control all the time by suggesting optimal solutions to satisfy constantly shifting requirements. Also, such a model lacks the capacity of a "see-saw" adjustment, where any one variable can be changed at a time, introducing oscillations in the model until a balance is finally reached and optimal controls can be fully imposed.

Operational Research in practice, on the other hand, has followed a phenomenological approach which has been intimately connected with decision-making. At the operational control level, specific tasks are carried out effectively and efficiently. OR has been an invaluable aid at this level, making use of optimal decision parameters based on Linear Programming (LP), queuing and inventory control techniques. At the management control level, the managers have to ensure that resources are obtained and used judiciously in the accomplishment of the organisation's objectives. This is the design phase of functional relationships (e.g., rates of output, cost coefficients, market demands, etc.), objective functions (to maximise profit minimise cost, etc.) and prediction of outcomes for the best policy. OR methods help to define and determine the optimal policy. At the higher management level, all choices and values (with regard to objectives or goals) may not be very clear. While mathematical optimisation loses ground (unless based on unrealistic assumptions), the decision-maker may "simulate" the behaviour of the system under alternative courses of action and determine responses to "what if?" questions, in place of having a clear "What is best?" choice. At the corporate level of strategic planning, there is the process of deciding on objectives of the organisation, changes in these objectives, resources used to attain these objectives, and the policies that are to govern the acquisition, use and disposition of these resources. OR, in a technical sense, has been of little use here, although some trends exist in simple contextual modelling, such as, setting parameters, finding objectives, checking consistency, separating guess work from forecasts, and structuring combinatorial sets of scenarios.

Information System Links

Since decision-making is firmly linked with handling of information, it is necessary to understand the role of this linkage. At the operational control level, the physical source of information, the observational data, the inferential logic and the choice-parameters are all palpably obvious and action taken is virtually automatic. At the management control level, choices (and even inferences) are not so clear and hence the need of evaluating the best course of action and getting responses to "what if?" questions. At the corporate level, the decision-maker reserves the inferences, choices and actions, and uses only the physical source and the observational data. The need, therefore, of a good data-bank and a timely updating of its data is supreme for the corporate decision-maker.

It is evident from the above that a decision-taking information system, to help initiating automatically a purchase order when the inventory has dropped below the reorder point, will be fairly simple in nature at the operational control level. On the other hand, a data-bank information system to support corporate planning by top management will be highly complex. Furthermore, if OR methods have to make a transition from the trivial operational level to the top corporate level, two factors can be of immense help : a timely capture of data from the source and an understanding of the deep structure of the decision problem.

An interesting example of the above transition is the computer-based decision-support system, developed at the TELCO, which uses forecasting techniques (adaptive filtering, double exponential smoothing and moving averages) as an aid to decision-making. In a fairly dynamic industrial environment, the system captures data from the source of application, viz., manufacturing of automobiles; analyses the data on consumption of small tools; makes suitable inventory modelling; and generates the desired decision parameters, viz., determination of order level, buffer level, order quantity, etc. What is more important, the recommendations and the computed decision parameters are, along with other relevant information, fed back to the source of application for the entire materials planning.

Diverse OR Modelling

State-of-the-art OR modelling is, in practice, largely evident today at the managerial control levels. This can be illustrated along with the diverse nature of modelling in the following cases:

(a) *Economic modelling* : A computation facility, needed for econometric model-building, was built up for the national planning exercise and given the endearing name VIDHATA. Developed in the form of a software package, VIDHATA used a number of sub-programmes and was linked with a data-base which contained all the information needed exogenously. The data-base could be updated and a new one created through a series of matrix manipulations (including addition, substraction, multiplication, division, inversion, transposition and creation of identity matrix). VIDHATA worked as an admirable interface between the complexity of the data-base and the easy-to-use language of the user;

(b) *Environmental modelling :* Mathematical models applicable in hydrological problems have expanded creditably over the last two decades. These models are either deterministic with a definite linking between rainfall and river flood, or, stochastic when the chances of occurrence of the variables are taken into consideration. The SACRAMENTO model successfully applied the watershed concept to the upper Yamuna catchment and Tungabhadra river for the run-off simulation. The model, used on IBM 360/44 computer, calculated recursively the six-hourly values of water transfer (interception, evaporation and percolation) for the different phases of water cycle and the flow at the area outlet (direct run-off, surface run-off, interflow and baseflow);

(c) *Exploratory modelling :* Mathematical models for various oilfields of ONGC was applied for the study and development of reservoir simulation, particularly for the three-dimensional three-phase black oil, radial coming and multi-component analysis. The models used IBM 370/145 studied the general behaviour of a complete reservoir or part of it. The radial coming model studied specific wells which may develop water or gas coning. The multicomponent model studied gas condensate, highly volatile fluids and retrograde phenomenon;

(d) *Industrial modelling :* This area, after defence, has the highest incidence of OR models of impressive quality. In order to illustrate a grassroot application (which can often be a very high dividend-earner, as is the case here) the LP model used repetitively in AGRICO product on planning can be considered. Several agricultural implements like spades, pick-axes and shovels were produced there tailored to demands which fluctuated widely based on seasonal factors. The production capacity varied according to the capacity available (against break-downs) of forges, presses and other machines. The labour, too, had a diversity of skills which had to be taken into account. The LP model was run every month and quarter within the upper and lower bounds of predicted market demands, on computer. The fine tuning of the production plan concentrated upon contribution to profits, and provided a highly effective and dependable document to management; and

(e) *Health modelling :* A significant use of OR model in health application has been for the disease forecasting and control in the malaria eradication scheme. Taking an Andhra taluk of malaria-prone villages, both epidemiological factors (incidence of disease, rainfall, soil condition, drainage, etc.) and entomological factors (breeding of malaria germ) were studied to build a statistical model based or Markov process, where the probability of the spread of the disease to nearby villages could be forecast. This was an eminently useful model, helping the Andhra health authorities rush their medical and paramedical personnel to those villages, and spread them in advance with DDT.

Conclusion

The above, in a nutshell, recapitulates the current status of OR applications in India. While industrial and business applications are certainly gaining ground, the same cannot be said for economic and social science applications where much more acceptance has still to find its place for OR modelling.

APPENDIX B

ROLE OF COMPUTER-AIDED OPTIMISATION

Introduction

The solution procedures in the Operational Research (OR) modelling efforts have also evolved from the pioneering days of static solutions arrived at without the use of computers. All OR applications based on earlier generation computers, working in a batch mode, were able to yield dynamic solutions. An example is the optimization model for slit combination of jumbo coils in Geep Industrial Syndicate, which ran on an early Reyad computer. The number and type of torches, to mention just one product, varied over a broad range. Each torch was made of a large number of components each of which, in turn, could be derived by cutting jumbo coils of varying dimensions. The OR model aimed at minimising the number of coils to be cut per slit. Dynamic batch solutions were derived by running the model every month to give production schedules to the factory, with a highly reduced wastage of coils.

Real-time Solutions

Real-time solutions are a further step ahead and are obtained on-line. There are two types of real time solutions: dedicated and time-sharing. Dedicated usage is based on a microprocessor chip which has the solution procedure as part of the built-in memory. For instance, the medium and light structural mill of any Indian steel unit has the need of cutting billets and yet reducing wastage. The OR model can be built into the microprocessor memory and thyristor control exercised to sense the dimensions of the incoming billets and to shear them according to pre-set calculations. Dedicated solutions are even faster when the micro-processor has the solution procedure built in as part of the hardware. Such 'firmware' has already become prevalent in India.

Time-sharing solutions, on the other hand, are obtained from terminals linked to mini or mainframe systems. Examples abound in industry where such terminals are made to operate on a real-time basis. For instance, the maintenance of thermal and chemical stability of a blast furnace can be achieved by letting the computer calculate the balanced burden-mix in order to satisfy all the requirements and assisting the operator to change the burden optimally. The inputs to the system are the chemical analysis of material desired level of wind-rate, hot blast temperature, blast moisture and fuel injection to be used, — apart from the feed-back information about the previous cast, the actual raw material, and the actual hot metal and slag analysis. The printed output a provided at the terminal on the furnace, giving the quantities of each type of material to be charged into the furnace and the excepted analysis of the slag and hot metal, all on a real-time basis.

Computing Power

In order to match the needs of the increasing higher level of management functions and allow the task to be amenable to OR methods, the state-of-the-art computing power can be examined from both centralised and decentralized points of view. A mainframe computer can handle many diverse tasks in running a complex modern organization. Alongside, a comprehensive data bank can be built up in different application areas and facilities provided for instant data updating. With such a centralised facility, every processing loop can have access to the data related to every other loop, and the task of supervision and maintenance becomes easy. On the other hand, such a facility is likely to have initial high cost independent of the size of applications, poor field expandability, unsuitability for certain fast processing loops and perhaps poor security and reliability problems (in the absence of a duplicate or stand-by centralized computer which may be economically unjustified).

An alternative to the above is the use of two or more low-powered central processing units (CPUs) in parallel to perform the trial task. The CPUs may be structured to operate *either* with shared memory and input/output (I/O) devices in a 'tightly coupled' manner *or* with own memory and I/O devices, but interconnected to other CPUs through communication interfaces in a 'loosely coupled' manner. The total task can then be split into clearly defined and related sub-tasks : each handled by multiple loosely coupled CPUs chosen for efficient handling of the specified task. This approach is based on the concept of decentralized control, distributed data acquisition and distributed information processing

Hierarchical Functions of Control

In keeping with the hierarchical functions of operational control, management control and corporate control, a serial distribution of computing power can be attempted. At the operation control level, dynamic optimisation can be done by functional computers — with a very high degree of reliability and with the task of monitoring performance with mutual back-up support in the event of failures. In the TISCO set-up, more than 100 interactive terminals are already operational which serve this function by being hooked up to 4 minicomputers of Unisys 1955 kind located at the Stores, Rolling Mill-2, General Superintendent's Office and the main computer centre. Such intelligent terminals are able to read or alter any data in the host Unisys 6806 computer to achieve *overall* optimisation, if needed. It is possible to build in control functions which would allow for local optimisation, on-line diagnostics and provision for switch-over to other terminals in emergencies. The mini-computers can be linked with each other through data communication links, for a local area network.

At the management control level, the mini-computers should have the capability to detect and react to any changes in the control variables, and then to optimise the performance of the unit under the constraints imposed by the host computers. The 'managerial' computer should handle a simple conversational language, have on-line programmable features and possess a powerful display capability. According to some authorities, the 'managerial' computer should react to individual operational exigencies and optimise over-all operations at any instance. In process industry, it should manage the tasks of energy management, maintenance schedules of plant and machinery, process yield, quality control information, raw material input, inventory control, sales management and so on, most of which functions are susceptible to OR approach. Since the expectations made and jobs entrusted are so widely varied, the CPUs should be modular and should have features to maximise throughout by choosing appropriate configurations of CPUs, memory and I/O devices.

At the corporate control level, a strong management information system (MIS) capability can come through a host mainframe computer. There should be, from software viewpoint, a multi-user environment with a high degree of data security. Facility for multiple storage of information coming from field, alongwith storage in the host computer, is useful in any distribution processing with an assured quality of inter-CPU communication.

Computer-Aided Optimisation

The above kind of computing power available today, can be made use of, along with the robust and contextual OR techniques, in real-life environment to achieve computer-aided optimisation (CAO) at all levels. We have seen how sources of physical activities and recording of data have to be linked with inference logic and rules for choice in order to facilitate decision-making. The more the logic and the rules made integral to the same computing device which also handles captured data, the better are the chances that unstructured decision will become structured by the appropriate MIS.

To the above extent, the state of the technology available simply demand use of CAO at all decision-making hierarchy. If we combine the types of usage with their tasks to be performed (under single or multiple criteria, as the case may be), there would emerge four classes of combination, viz., single-user single-task; multiple-user single-task; single-user multiple-task; and multiple-user multiple-task.

(a) *Single-user single-task applications* are among the most commonly occurred ones. In a refinery, industry, for instance, such operational level applications can comprise optimisation of shutdown scheduling of various HDS units and platformer unit; optimisation of crude-heat exchange train; blending of fuel oil and motor spirit; simulation of process, unit and equipment; and crude planning and tanker scheduling.

(b) *Multiple-user single-task applications* have the objective of optimal cost reduction at managerial level that can be achieved through minimisation of demurrage in computer-aided material handling and rail-traffic control system for watching over availability, movement and handling of rail-wagons through communication terminals for any major wagon-using organisation. The same objective can be viewed as optimal resource allocation, in which case the Indian Railways computerisation plan for an on-line freight control and wagon movement system, discussed earlier, may be cited for different zones.

(c) *Single-user multiple-task applications* can be commonly seen again in a process industry where various kinds of OR models for optimal resource allocation are tried out. For optimal allocation of energy (steam, power and fuel), the data communication facilities can be utilised to operate a real-time energy allocation model. Product-mix studies are found quite useful to achieve optimal use of resources in keeping with the market demand of steel product. Simulation studies, too, are a common practice to achieve the highest utilisation of resources and carryout in a steel industry, the optimum scheduling of open hearth furnaces; the optimum scheduling of soaking pits; the improved utilisation of loco-power and captive rolling-stock; and determination of optimum number of iron-ladles, slag pots and ingot cars.

(d) *Multiple-user multiple-task applications* can be exemplified in two cases. The first case was that of the quantitative model for the Sixth Plan (1980-85) which could simultaneously treat both supply and demand, and their interaction between sectors and time. Its core-model had seven inter-dependent blocks, e.g., input-output, investment, private consumption, financial resources, import, employment and perspective planning. Its major sub-models were agriculture exports, demography, autonomous investment and public consumption. The model comprised a set of supply and demand equations, a set of inequality relations with given *upper* bounds (to ensure that demand did not exceed the market supply of commodities, services, capital, labour, foreign exchange and non-renewable resources) as well as *lower* bounds (to ensure that the community attained minimum welfare target). The model, although of a non-linear programming kind, had to cater for a multi-stage decision process and hence it was solved by iteration with the input of alternative values, for achieving a maximum growth rate.

The other case pertained to the copper mining industry in Zambia of Africa. Nchanga open pit there covered a vast expanse and had 14 shivols at different depths upto 1000 feet where the debris was transported by 75 gigantic trucks of 150 to 200 tonnes each. Given constraints were those resources, the travel-time from ore-dumps and overburdens to shovels and back, the breakdown pattern of shovels the production priorities and the pit-manpower. The computer-based

OPTIMA model used a dynamic allocation pattern for trucks to shovels, where parameters could be added and deleted on-line. Service call-ups were also generated for maintenance manpower to carry out an efficient maintenance management. Communication was not through terminals but shovel-radio, truck-radio, dump-location radio and route-monitoring radio. The output was flashed on signboards at strategic points.

Conclusion

The above is necessarily a birds-eye view of current status of OR methodology, its linkages with information system, and its interaction with latest available computing power. There is an unmistakable emergence of computer-aided optimisation (CAO) not feasible at any time earlier. The cases of single/multiple user, combined with single/multiple tasks, are further strengthened by the emergence of all India computer networks, such as, INDONET for 5 computer centres under CMC, NICNET for the Central Government and the State Government computer centres; ERNET for NCST, and IITS and other academic centres of excellence; and the proposed TRANSPORTNET for the Railways, the Air in India and the Indian Airlines. The availability of the first and second generation INSAT satellites will, if anything, raise expectations for more public (and even private) networks. The sharing of OR models, as already done in the ARPANET of the USA, for their pan-Indian usage is certainly not a distant dream anymore.

COMPUTER BIBLIOGRAPHY

SELECT BIBLIOGRAPHY OF INDIAN BOOKS

General/Introductory

Bitter, *Basic for Beginners*, Tata Mc-Graw Hill.

Chasen/Cohen, *Basic-Computing-Book D*, BPB Publications, New Delhi.

Chasen/Cohen, *Basic-Computing-Book E*, BPB Publications, New Delhi.

Chasen/Cohen, *Basic-Computing-Book F*, BPB Publications, New Delhi.

Craddock, *An Introduction to Computer-Studies*, Tata Mc-Graw Hill.

ECC, *Computer Tutor – An Introduction*, BPB Publications, New Delhi.

Hanavan, P., *Basic-Computing-Book A*, BPB Publications, New Delhi.

Hanavan, P., *Basic-Computing-Book B*, BPB Publications, New Delhi.

Hanavan/Chasen, *Basic-Computing-Book C*, BPB Publications, New Delhi.

Jain, S., *Introduction to Computer-Science (CBSE-XI)*, BPB Publications, New Delhi.

Margolis, A., *Trouble Shooting and Repairing PC's*, BPB Publications, New Delhi.

Margotis, A., *Troubleshooting and Repairing PC's*, BPB Publications, New Delhi.

Mehta, S., *Introducing Computers Part I*, BPB Publications, New Delhi.

Mehta, S., *Introducing Computers Part II*, BPB Publications, New Delhi.

Mehta, S., *Introducing Computers Part III*, BPB Publications, New Delhi.

Mehta, S., *Let us learn Computers*, BPB Publications, New Delhi.

Pale & Orshalick, *Introduction to Pascal and Structured Design*, Tata Mc-Graw Hill.

Sharma, M., *Computer Ek Purana Parichay*, BPB Publications, New Delhi.

Sinha, P., *Computers Fundamentals,* BPB Publications, New Delhi.

Verma R., *A Guide to Successful Computerisation,* BPB Publications, New Delhi.

Verma, R., *A Guide to Successful Computerisation*, BPB Publications, New Delhi.

Walker, R., *Understanding Computer Science Applications*, BPB Publications, New Delhi.

Walker, R., *Understanding Computer Science Applications*, BPB Publications, New Delhi.

Willis/Miller, *Computers for Everybody*, BPB Publications, New Delhi.

Programming

A.S.S., *dBase III Plus (Students & Instructor WKBK)*, BPB Publications, New Delhi.

Ashton Tate, *dBase Programmes Utilities*, BPB Publications, New Delhi.

Ashton Tate, *dBase Programming Utilities*, BPB Publications, New Delhi.

Ashton Tate, *Introduction to dBase III Plus Programming*, BPB Publications, New Delhi.

Ashton Tate, *Using dBase III Plus*, BPB Publications, New Delhi.

Awate, *8085A Assembly Language and Applications*, Tata Mc-Graw Hill.

Awate, *8085A Assembly Languages, Programming and Applications*, Tata Mc-Graw Hill.

Balagurusamy, E. and Sushila, *Computer Systems and Application: Recent Trends*, Tata Mc-Graw Hill.

Balagurusamy, E., *Fortran For Beginners: Including Fortran 77*, Tata Mc-Graw Hill.

Balagurusamy, E., *Programming in "C"*, Tata Mc-Graw Hill.

Batis/Fortino, *dBase III Plus Local Area Networks*, BPB Publications, New Delhi.

Beam, J., *Illustrated C Programming*, BPB Publications, New Delhi.

Bharucha, D., *dBase II A Comprehensive Users Manual*, BPB Publications, New Delhi.

Bharucha, K., *dBase III Plus: A Comprehensive Users Manual*, BPB Publications, New Delhi.

Bitter, *Basic for Beginners*, Tata Mc-Graw Hill.

Breem, G., *Clipper dBase Computer Applications*, BPB Publications, New Delhi.

Brown, *C for Basic Programmes*, Tata Mc-Graw Hill.

Brown, *C for Basic Programmers*, Tata Mc-Graw Hill.

Carlton, T., *dBase III Plus Applications Library*, BPB Publications, New Delhi.

Castro/Hanson, *Advanced Programmes Guide for dBase III*, BPB Publications, New Delhi.

Cowart, R., *ABC's of dBase III Plus*, BPB Publications, New Delhi.

Dale and Lilly, *Pascal Plus Data Structures, Algorithms and advanced Programming*, Tata Mc-Graw Hill.

Desai, *Fortran Programming and Numerical Methods*, Tata Mc-Graw Hill.

Freedman, A., *dBase II for the first time User*, BPB Publications, New Delhi.

Gramillo, R., *Illustrated Foxpro*, BPB Publications, New Delhi.

Kapoor, *Computer Assisted Decision Models in Fortran*, Tata Mc-Graw Hill.

Krishnamoorthy, *Finite Element Analysis: Theory and Programming*, Tata Mc-Graw Hill.

Krishnamoorthy, *Programme for Analysis of Structural Systems by Finite Element Method*, Tata Mc-Graw Hill.

Marton, J., Basic: *Step by Step Programming*, BPB Publications, New Delhi.

Mathur, *Introduction to Pascal*, Tata Mc-Graw Hill.

Mueller, J., *Illustrated Clipper 5.0*, BPB Publications, New Delhi.

Pugh, K., *C language for Programmes*, BPB Publications, New Delhi.

Ramkumar, *Programming with Fortran 77*, Tata Mc-Graw Hill.

Rao, *Computer Programming: Including MS-COBOL and COBOL-85*, Tata Mc-Graw Hill.

Roy and Distidar, *Cobol Programming: Problems and Solutions*, Tata Mc-Graw Hill.

Rugg, *More than 32 Basic Programmes – IBM PC*, BPB Publications, New Delhi.

Seigal, C, *Mastering Foxpro*, BPB Publications, New Delhi.

Sence, R., *Clipper-5 Programming Guide (2nd edition)*, BPB Publications, New Delhi.

Simpson, A., *Advanced Techniques in dBase III Plus*, BPB Publications, New Delhi.

Simpson, A., *dBase III Plus Programmes Reference Guide*, BPB Publications, New Delhi.

Simpson, A., *Understanding dBase II*, BPB Publications, New Delhi.

Stevens, A., *C-Data Base Development*, BPB Publications, New Delhi.

Thro, E., *The Database Dictionary*, BPB Publications, New Delhi.

Townsend, C., *Mastering dBase IV Programming*, BPB Publications, New Delhi.

Zaks, R., *Your First Basic Programme*, BPB Publications, New Delhi.

Application Software

Ahson, *Microprocessors with Applications in Process Control*, Tata Mc-Graw Hill.

Balagurusamy, E., *Office Automation and World Processing*, Tata Mc-Graw Hill.

Balagurusamy, E., *Selecting and Managing a Small Computer*, Tata Mc-Graw Hill.

Jain, *Basic Programming with Applications*, Tata Mc-Graw Hill.

Juneja et.al, *CAD/CAM Robotics and Factories of the Future*, Vol. I, Tata Mc-Graw Hill.

Juneja et.al, *CAD/CAM Robotics and Factories of the Future*, Vol. II, Tata Mc-Graw Hill.

Juneja et.al, *CAD/CAM Robotics and Factories of the Future*, Vol. III, Tata Mc-Graw Hill.

Operating Systems

Ashely, *Teach Yourself – Unix*, BPB Publications, New Delhi.

Cuthbertson, T., *The ABC's of SCO Unix*, BPB Publications, New Delhi.

Deikman, A., *Unix Programming on the 80286/80386*, BPB Publications, New Delhi.

Dunean, R., *Advanced MS-DOS Programming*, BPB Publications, New Delhi.

Gofton, P., *Mastering Unix Serial Communications*, BPB Publications, New Delhi.

Harvey/Nelson, *DOS Instant Reference*, BPB Publications, New Delhi.

Hyman, M., *Advanced DOS (Version-4)*, BPB Publications, New Delhi.

Kelly/Bootle, *Mastering Unix*, BPB Publications, New Delhi.

Kings, R., *IBM-PC DOS Handbook*, BPB Publications, New Delhi.

Kings, R., *MS-DOS Handbook*, BPB Publications, New Delhi.

Morgam, C., *Inside Unix*, BPB Publications, New Delhi.

Muster/Birms, *Unix Power Utilities*, BPB Publications, New Delhi.

Prata, S., *Advance Unix: A Programmers's Guide*, BPB Publications, New Delhi.

Robbins, J., *Mastering DOS*, BPB Publications, New Delhi.

Shultz, R., *Illustrated MC/PC-DOS*, BPB Publications, New Delhi.

Winberg/Groff, *Understanding Unix*, BPB Publications, New Delhi.

PCs

Bremmer, R., *IBM PC Troubleshooting & Repairs Guide*, BPB Publications, New Delhi.

Hann, H., *Mastering XENIX on the IBM PC AT*, BPB Publications, New Delhi.

Held, G., *IBM PC AT User's Reference*, BPB Publications, New Delhi.

Lasselle/Ramsay, *ABC's of IBM PC & Compatible*, BPB Publications, New Delhi.

Meieller, S., *Upgrading & Repairing PC's*, BPB Publications, New Delhi.

Neibaur, A., *The Hand-me-down PC Handbook*, BPB Publications, New Delhi.

Norton, P., *Best of the Peter Norton Chronicles - IBM PC*, BPB Publications, New Delhi.

Norton/Wildon, *New Peter Norton Programmes Guide to PC/PS-2*, BPB Publications, New Delhi.

PC World, *The Fully Powered PC (with 2-Disks)*, BPB Publications, New Delhi.

Rosenthal, E., *Absolutely Essential Utilities-IBM PC's*, BPB Publications, New Delhi.

Sandler, C., *Insiders Guide to IBM PC's (Hardware & Software)*, BPB Publications, New Delhi.

Sawusch/Summers, *1001 Things to do with Your IBM PC*, BPB Publications, New Delhi.

Teja/Johnson, *IBM PC & PS/2 Graphics Handbook*, BPB Publications, New Delhi.

WSI, *IBM PC XT User's Handbook*, BPB Publications, New Delhi.

INDEX